As signed by
President George W. Bush on July 30, 2002

Sarbanes-Oxley Act of 2002

Law and Explanation

James Hamilton, J.D., LL.M.
Ted Trautmann, J.D.

CCH INCORPORATED
Chicago

EDITORIAL STAFF

James Hamilton, J.D., LL.M

Ted Trautmann J.D.

ISBN: 0-8080-0840-4

4025 W. Peterson Ave.
Chicago, IL 60645-6085
1-800-248-3248
http://business.cch.com

Foreword

The Sarbanes-Oxley Act of 2002 was signed into law by President George W. Bush on July 30, 2002. The Act is a landmark and comprehensive piece of legislation that will fundamentally change the way public companies do business and how the accounting profession performs its statutorily required audit function. The Act makes structural changes in the auditing of financial statements and the corporate disclosure regime. It establishes a comprehensive framework to modernize and reform the oversight of public company auditing, improve the quality and transparency of corporate financial reporting, and strengthen the independence of auditors and audit committees alike. As a corollary, it enhances investor decisionmaking throughout the capital markets and seeks to correct shortcomings that have threatened the reputation of those markets for integrity.

The Act creates a strong and independent accounting oversight board to oversee the conduct of the auditors of public companies and strengthens auditor independence from corporate management by limiting the scope of non-audit services that auditors can offer their audit clients.

The Act also requires steps to enhance the direct responsibility of senior corporate management for financial reporting and for the quality of financial disclosures made by public companies. The Act clearly establishes that CEOs and CFOs are responsible for the presentation of material in their company's financial reports.

Sarbanes-Oxley establishes clear statutory rules to limit, and expose to public view, possible conflict of interests affecting securities analysts. The Act also authorizes substantially higher funding for the SEC.

Under the Act, company audit committees would be responsible for the appointment, compensation, and oversight of the work of their auditors. The independence of audit committees is enhanced by barring committee members from accepting consulting fees or being affiliated persons of the company other than in their capacity as board members.

The Act prohibits insider trades during pension fund blackout periods. It also requires prompt disclosure of insider transactions in company stock, which must be reported by the second day following the transaction. Finally, Sarbanes-Oxley establishes a new federal crime of securities fraud, with a tough 25-year prison sentence.

In addition to a detailed explanation of the Sarbanes-Oxley Act provisions, the book includes the full text of the Act, selected portions of the legislative history, a table of statutes added and amended, and a topical index.

July 2002

Table of Contents

PART I. EXPLANATION

Chapter 1—Overview

Chapter 2—Accounting Oversight Board

PART II. SARBANES-OXLEY ACT OF 2002

Title VIII—Corporate and Criminal Fraud Accountability

Title IX—White Collar Crime Penalty Enhancements

Title X—Corporate Tax Returns

Title XI—Corporate Fraud Accountability

PART III. LEGISLATIVE HISTORY

PART I EXPLANATION

CHAPTER 1

OVERVIEW

¶ 101 Introduction

Congress intended the Sarbanes-Oxley Act of 2002 to address systemic and structural weaknesses affecting the capital markets that have been revealed in recent months and that show failures of audit effectiveness and a breakdown in corporate financial and broker-dealer responsibility. The legislation will fundamentally change the way public companies do business and how the accounting profession performs its statutorily required audit function.

The Act establishes a comprehensive framework to modernize and reform the oversight of public company auditing, improve quality and transparency in financial reporting by those companies, and strengthen the independence of auditors. It promotes competition among service providers, enhances accurate investor decision-making throughout the capital markets, and seeks to correct shortcomings that have threatened the reputation of those markets for integrity.

As discussed briefly in this overview chapter, the Act's principal reforms include: (1) the creation of an independent accounting oversight board (see ¶ 102); (2) auditor independence provisions that restrict the non-audit services that accontants may provide to their audit clients (see ¶ 103); (3) a range of corporate governance and responsibility measures (see ¶ 104); (4) expanded disclosure requirements, including accelerated Section 16(a) reporting by insiders (see ¶ 105); (5) mandatory disclosure by analysts of potential conflicts of interest (see ¶ 106); and (6) a range of tough new penalties for fraud and other violations (see ¶ 107). Other provisions in the Act increase the SEC's funding and enforcement powers (see Chapter 7), and require various studies and reports (see Chapter 8).

¶ 102 Accounting Oversight Board

Title I (discussed fully in Chapter 2) creates a public company accounting oversight board. The board is empowered to set auditing, quality control, and ethics standards, to inspect registered accounting firms, to conduct investigations, and to take disciplinary actions. As a check on the board's power, its decisions are subject to SEC oversight and review.

This body will be a strong, independent, and full-time oversight board with broad authority to regulate auditors of public companies, set auditing standards, and investigate violations. The board is subject to SEC review and will establish auditing, quality control, ethics, and independence standards for public company auditors and will inspect accounting firms that conduct those audits. It will investigate potential violations of applicable rules and impose sanctions if those violations are established.

Until now, there has been reliance on self-policing of the audit process, private auditing and accounting standards setting, and, for the most part, private disciplinary measures. But questionable accounting practices and corporate failures have raised serious questions about this private oversight system.

For the first time, the Act creates a truly independent accounting oversight board, staffed with objective, unbiased overseers, who can enforce rules and prosecute violators without having to vet their decisions elsewhere. Unlike the former Public Oversight Board, which depended on fees from the very auditors it was meant to regulate, this new board will be funded by mandatory fees paid by all public companies. These are fees that cannot be withheld at the whim of those who have the greatest interest in undermining the work of the board. (See remarks of Sen. Diane Feinstein, Cong. Rec., July 15, 2002, p. S.6762.)

In the view of Sen. Mike Enzi, the legislation is federalization of the accounting industry. The Act places a federal government bureaucracy at the helm of accounting regulation. While the Act does not prevent state accountancy boards from continuing to regulate accountants registered in their states, it does establish an overlord regulator to oversee the firms, which audit publicly traded companies. (See Cong. Rec., July 8, 2002, p. S6338.) But according to Sen. Patty Murray, the Act does not attempt to federalize accounting oversight. Instead, it strengthens the federal government's historic role of regulating publicly traded companies and their auditors. The state boards of accountancy will continue their important role of regulating accountants who audit private companies. (See Cong. Rec., July 15, 2002, p. S6758.)

The Act also improves the Financial Accounting Standards Board, giving it for the first time full financial independence from the accounting industry. (See ¶ 207.)

¶ 103 Auditor Independence

Title II (discussed fully in Chapter 3) strengthens auditor independence from corporate management by limiting the scope of consulting services that auditors can offer their public company audit clients. This works to prevent auditors from controlling the entire financial reporting system at an individual company by both designing the internal audit system, and then purporting to offer an unbiased external audit. (See remarks of Sen. Diane Feinstein, Cong. Rec., July 15, 2001, p. S6762.)

The Act applies only to public companies that are required to report to the SEC. It says plainly that state regulatory authorities should make independent determinations of the proper standards and should not presume that the Act's standards apply to small- and medium-sized accounting firms that do not audit public companies.

¶ 104 Corporate Governance and Responsibility

Titles III and IV (discussed fully in Chapter 4) heighten the responsibility of public company directors and senior managers for the quality of the financial reporting and disclosure made by their companies. For example, the Act provides for a strong public company audit committee that will be directly responsible for the appointment, compensation, and oversight of the work of the public company auditors, which makes it clear that the primary duty of the auditors is to the public company's board of directors and the investing public, and not to the managers. Audit committee members must be independent from company management. (See ¶ 401.)

The Act will stiffen the resolve and oversight of audit committees by requiring, among other provisions, that all committee members be independent and that they be given free reign to question auditors without executive officers present. (See remarks of Sen. Diane Feinstein, Cong. Rec., July 15, 2002, p. S6762.)

The Act requires that the audit committee develop procedures for addressing complaints concerning auditing issues and also that they put in place procedures for employee whistleblowers to submit their concerns regarding accounting. There is also a provision prohibiting the coercion of auditors.

As to corporate misconduct, the Act presents a number of new provisions to deter wrongdoing. For the first time, CEOs and CFOs will have to certify that company financial statements fairly present the company's financial condition. (See ¶ 402.) If a misleading financial statement later resulted in a restatement, the CEO and CFO must forfeit and return to the company any bonus, stock, or stock option compensation received in the twelve months following the misleading financial report.

The Act also prohibits any company officer or director from attempting to mislead or coerce an auditor. (See ¶ 403.) In addition, the Act requires auditors to discuss specific accounting issues with the company's audit committee. The statute also enables the SEC to remove unfit officers and directors from office and bar them from holding any future position at a public company. (See ¶ 405.)

Among other reforms, the Act: empowers the SEC to bar certain persons from serving as officers or directors of a public company (see ¶ 405); prohibits insider trades during pension fund blackout periods (see ¶ 407); directs the SEC to adopt rules requiring attorneys to report securities law violations (see ¶ 408); and requires that civil penalties imposed by the SEC go into a disgorgement fund to benefit harmed investors (see ¶ 409).

¶ 105 Issuer and Management Disclosure

The Act imposes a range of new corporate disclosure requirements, discussed more fully in Chapter 5. As to financial disclosures, the law requires public companies to report all off-balance-sheet transactions and conflicts. Also, companies must present any pro forma disclosures in a way that is not misleading and must reconcile them with a presentation based on generally accepted accounting principles. (See ¶ 501.) More companies are releasing these pro forma disclosures, and Congress expressed concern that this information does not accurately reflect the company's financial conditions.

The Act also accelerated the required reporting of insider transactions. Amendments to Section 16(a) require officers, directors, and ten-percent shareholders to report their purchases and sales by the end of the second day following a covered transaction. (See ¶ 503.)

In addition, the Act requires new disclosures concerning a company's internal controls. Annual reports filed with the SEC must include a statement by management asserting that it is responsible for creating and maintaining adequate internal controls, and assessing the effectiveness of those controls. (See ¶ 504.)

Among other reforms, the Act requires companies to disclose whether or not they have adopted an ethics code for senior financial officers, and, if not, why not (see ¶ 506), and whether the audit committee includes at least one financial expert (see ¶ 507). The Act also requires the SEC, based on certain enumerated factors, to regularly and systematically review corporate filings. (See ¶ 508.)

¶ 106 Analyst Conflicts of Interest

The Act also addresses analyst conflicts of interest, discussed in Chapter 6. Title V seeks to limit and expose to public view possible conflicts of interest affecting securities analysts. For example, it prevents investment banking staff from supervising research analysts or clearing their reports and prohibits analysts from distributing research reports about a company they are underwriting. (See ¶ 601.) The Act requires analysts to disclose potential conflicts of interest, for example, the extent to which the analyst holds securities in the company subject to a research report. (See ¶ 602.) Moreover, the law protects analysts from retaliation for making unfavorable stock recommendations. (See ¶ 603.)

¶ 107 Fraud and Criminal Penalties

The Act imposes a range of tough new criminal penalties for fraud and other wrongful acts, discussed in Chapter 9. For example, the Act establishes a new federal crime of securities fraud, with a 25-year maximum jail sentence. (See ¶ 901.) The Act also, for the first time, creates federal protection for corporate whistleblowers who report fraud to the authorities or testify at trial. (See ¶ 908.) In addition, the law closes loopholes and increases penalties for shredding documents. It requires audit documents to be preserved for five years and provides tough criminal penalties for their destruction. (See ¶ 902.) The Act provides victims the right to recoup their losses by preventing fraud artists from hiding in bankruptcy. (See ¶ 904.) Also, the Act extends the statute of limitations for securities fraud. (See ¶ 903.)

The Act increases the penalties for mail and wire fraud from the current 5 years to 20 years. (See ¶ 906.) The law also increases the penalty for those who file false statements with the SEC to a maximum penalty of $5 million and 20 years in prison, and, if a corporation files a false statement, then the fines increase up to a maximum of $25 million. (See ¶ 909.)

The legislation punishes top corporate executives that certify the financial statements of the company knowing they are false by subjecting them to fines of up to $5 million and 20 years in prison, or both. (See ¶ 402.) Rep. Sensenbrenner also pointed out that the restitution laws for all criminal activity are in place for these crimes as well, so the court can order restitution for those shareholders and employees who have been defrauded. (See remarks of Rep. F. James Sensenbrenner, Cong. Rec., July 25, 2002, p. H5464.)

CHAPTER 2

ACCOUNTING OVERSIGHT BOARD

Overview

¶ 201 In General

Title I of the Sarbanes-Oxley Act (Sections 101–109) contains the legislation's most fundamental reforms. That title establishes the Public Company Accounting Oversight Board, a regulatory body subject to SEC supervision that is independent of the accounting industry. The board, funded through fees imposed on public companies, has broad powers to set auditing, quality control, and ethics standards for accounting firms that audit those companies. The board also has authority to inspect, investigate, and bring disciplinary proceedings against such firms.

Background and Purpose

Congress intended the new oversight board to bring together various issues and responsibilities that previously have been subject to "a bewildering array of monitoring groups," under the auspices of the accounting profession. (S. Rep. 107-205 (July 3, 2002), pp. 4-5.) Testifying before the Senate Banking Committee, Shaun O'Malley, Chairman of the 2000 Panel on Audit Effectiveness (and former Chairman of Price Waterhouse LLP), remarked:

> The profession's combination of public oversight and voluntary self-regulation is extensive, Byzantine, and insufficient. The Panel found that the current system of governance lacks sufficient public representation, suffers from divergent views among its members as to the profession's priorities, implements a disciplinary system that is slow and ineffective, lacks efficient communication among its various entities and with the SEC, and lacks unified leadership and oversight. (S. Rep. 107-205 (July 3, 2002), p. 5.)

Thus, the Act creates an oversight board with broad standard-setting and enforcement powers, and funded in a manner that assures its independence.

Nature of Board

Section 101 establishes the accounting oversight board. The board's fundamental purpose is to oversee the audit of public companies subject to federal securities law to help ensure the accuracy and independence of financial reporting on which the investing public depends. (Section 101(a).)

The oversight board is a corporate entity, operating as a nonprofit corporation, that will exist indefinitely until Congress dissolves it. The board is not an agency or establishment of the federal government and, except as the Act otherwise provides, is subject to—and has all the powers conferred upon a nonprofit corporation by—the District of Columbia Nonprofit Corporation Act. Thus, the board's members, employees, and agents will not be deemed a federal government official, employee, or agent because of their service with the board. (Sec. 101(a), (b).)

¶ 202 Membership

The accounting oversight board must have five members that meet certain standards of competence and independence, as discussed below. In addition, the Act establishes standards and procedures for the appointment, term of service, and removal of board members, as discussed further below.

Competence

The board's members must be "prominent individuals of integrity and reputation" who have a demonstrated commitment to investors and the public. The board's members must understand: (1) the responsibilities for, and nature of, the financial disclosures required under federal securities law; and (2) the obligations of accountants in preparing and issuing audit reports concerning those disclosures. (Sec. 101(e)(1).)

Independence

As to independence, the Act restricts the board's ties to the accounting industry. The Act states that two—and only two—members must be or have been certified public accountants. Moreover, if one of those two members is the chair, he or she cannot have been a practicing CPA for at least five years prior to his or her appointment. Each member must serve on a full-time basis and cannot, during their service, be employed by any other person or engage in any other professional or business activity. Finally, members cannot share in any of the profits of, or receive payments from, a public accounting firm (or any other person, as determined by SEC rule), other than fixed continuing payments under standard arrangements for the retirement of accounting firm members. (Sec. 101(e)(2), (3).)

Appointment, Term and Removal

The Act provides for the appointment of board members. The SEC, in consultation with the Chairman of the Federal Reserve Board and the Treasury Secretary, must appoint the accounting oversight board's chairperson and other initial members and designate a term of service for each. The Commission must complete this within 90 days after the law's enactment. A vacancy will not affect the board's powers, but must be filled in the same manner as applies to appointments. (Sec. 101(e)(4).)

Special provisions govern the terms of service. In general, each board member will serve a five-year term. There are two exceptions: (1) terms of the initial members (other than the chairperson) must expire in annual increments, one on each of the first four anniversaries of the initial appointment date; and (2) members appointed to fill a vacancy that occurs before the departed member's term expires may serve only for the remainder of that term. The Act also imposes term limits: no person may serve for more than two terms, whether or not those terms are consecutive. (Sec. 101(e)(5).)

In addition, the Act establishes procedures for a member's removal. Specifically, it authorizes the SEC to remove a board member, in accordance with Section 107(d)(3) (discussed at ¶ 253), "for good cause shown" before his or her term expires. (Sec. 101(e)(6).)

¶ 203 Powers and Duties

The accounting oversight board has a broad range of powers and duties, discussed briefly below and in more detail elsewhere. The board's actions are subject, however, to SEC oversight. (See Sec. 107.) Moreover, the board cannot carry out its statutory mandate until the Commission first determines, no later than 270 days after the Act takes effect, that the board is so organized and has the capacity to fulfill its duties and enforce the Act. (Sec. 101(d).)

General Duties

Section 101(c) specifies the board's general duties. Subject to the SEC oversight, and once the Commission determines that the board can fulfill its responsibilities, the board must:

- Register public accounting firms that prepare audit reports for companies (see ¶ 205);
- Establish auditing, quality control, ethics, and independence standards relating to the preparation of audit reports (see ¶ 220 et seq.);
- Inspect accounting firms (see ¶ 230 et seq.);
- Conduct investigations and disciplinary proceedings concerning, and impose appropriate sanctions where justified against, accounting firms and their associated persons (see ¶ 240 et seq.);
- Perform any other duties that it deems necessary or appropriate in the public interest: (1) to promote high professional standards of registered accounting firms and associated persons; (2) to improve the quality of their audit services; or (3) otherwise to carry out the Act;

- Enforce compliance with the Act, the board's rules, professional standards, and the securities laws relating to preparing and issuing audit reports and to accountants' duties and liabilities concerning those reports; and

- Set its budget and manage its operations and staff. (Sec. 101(c).)

General Powers

Section 101(f) delineates the board's general powers. The statute provides that—in addition to any powers otherwise granted under the Act, and subject to SEC oversight—the board may:

- Sue and be sued, complain and defend, in its own name and through its own counsel, with SEC approval, in any federal, state, or other court;

- Conduct its operations and maintain offices in any state without regard to any qualification, licensing, or other statute in that state;

- Lease, purchase, or otherwise acquire, improve, use, sell, exchange, or convey any property wherever situated;

- Hire employees, accountants, attorneys, and other agents as necessary or appropriate, and determine their qualifications, define their duties, and fix their compensation (at a level comparable to similar private sector positions);

- Allocate, assess, and collect accounting support fees established under Section 109, for the board, and other fees or charges imposed by the Act;

- Enter into contracts, execute instruments, incur liabilities, and take any other actions necessary, appropriate, or incidental to the conduct of its operations and the exercise of its duties, rights, and powers. (Sec. 101(f).)

¶ 204 Rulemaking

The accounting oversight board may adopt rules subject to SEC approval. These include rules governing the board's operation and administration, the exercise of its authority, and the performance of its statutory duties. (Sec. 101(g)(1).) They also include rules permitting the delegation of any board functions to particular members, employees, or divisions, as discussed below. In addition, the board may establish ethics rules and standards of conduct for board members and staff, including a bar against practice before the board (and the SEC with respect to board matters) of one year for former board members, and appropriate lesser or equal periods for former staff. (Sec.

101(g)(3).) Finally, the board may implement rules the provide as otherwise required by the Act. (Sec. 101(g)(4).)

Delegation of Functions

As mentioned, the board may adopt rules governing its delegation of any functions to an individual member or employee, or to a board division, including functions with respect to hearing, determining, ordering, certifying, reporting, or otherwise acting as to any matter. (Sec. 101(g)(2).)

Action pursuant to any such delegation is, however, subject to review. Specifically, the board retains a discretionary right to review any action pursuant to a delegated function. In addition, a person is entitled to board review of any matter so delegated, and the board's decision on review will constitute the action of the board for all purposes (including appeal or review of that decision). If the board declines to exercise its right to review, or if no other person seeks a timely review, then the delegated action in question will constitute the action of the board for all purposes. (Sec. 101(g)(2).)

¶ 205 Registration

Public accounting firms that prepare audit reports must register with the accounting oversight body. Beginning 180 days after the SEC determines that the board is capable of fulfilling its statutory duties (see ¶ 203), only public accounting firms that register with the board may prepare or issue, or participate in the preparation or issuance of, any audit report concerning any issuer. (Sec. 102(a).) The Act imposes requirements on various aspects of the registration process, including such matters as applications, periodic reports, and fees, discussed below.

Applications

Section 102(b) governs applications for registration. Under the statute, an accounting firm must use whatever form the board prescribes, by rule, to apply for registration. (Sec. 102(b)(1).) The firm must, as part of its application, submit in such detail as the board may specify:

- The names of all companies for which the firm prepared or issued audit reports during the preceding calendar year, and for which the firm expects to prepare or issue audit reports during the current calendar year;

- The annual fees that the accounting firm received from each such company for audit services, other accounting services, and non-audit services, respectively;

- Any other current financial information for the firm's most recently completed fiscal year as the board may reasonably request;

- A description of the firm's quality control policies for its accounting and auditing practices;

- A list of all accountants associated with the firm who participate in the preparation of audit reports, stating the license or certification number of each such person, as well as the firm's own state license numbers;

- Information relating to criminal, civil, or administrative actions or disciplinary proceedings pending against the firm or an associated person in connection with any audit report;

- Copies of any periodic or annual disclosure filed by an with the SEC during the preceding calendar year that discloses accounting disagreements between the issuer and the firm in connection with an audit report by the firm; and

- Any other information that the board or SEC specifies, by rule, as necessary or appropriate. (Sec. 102(b)(2).)

Consents

The accounting firm must also agree to cooperate with any investigative measures taken by the board. Specifically, each registration application must include a consent executed by the accounting firm to cooperation in and compliance with any board request for testimony or production of documents. The firm must also agree to secure and enforce similar consents from each of its associated persons as a condition of their continued employment by or association with the firm. (Sec. 102(b)(3)(A).) Finally, the application must include in its application a statement that the firm understands and agrees that its cooperation and compliance, as described in the consent, and the securing and enforcement of those consents from its associated persons, is a condition to the continuing effectiveness of the firm's registration. (Sec. 102(b)(3)(B).)

Approval or denial

The board must approve a completed registration application within 45 days after receiving it, in accordance with board rules, unless the board, prior to that date, issues a written notice of disapproval to, or requests more information from, the applicant. (Sec. 102(c)(1).) A written notice of disapproval of a completed application will constitute a disciplinary sanction for purposes of Section 105(d) and 107(c) (discussed at ¶ 252). (Sec. 102(c)(2).)

Annual Reports

Once registered, accounting firms must file periodic reports with the board. Specifically, each registered accounting firm must submit an annual report to the board, and may be required to file more frequently, as necessary to update the information in the firm's registration application and to provide the board with any additional information that the board or SEC specifies. (Sec. 102(d).)

Public Availability

An accounting firm's registration application and subsequent annual reports are subject to public inspection. Under Section 102(e), registration applications and annual reports, or such portions of these documents as designated under board rules, must be available for public inspection, subject to rules of the board or the SEC and to applicable laws protecting the confidentiality of proprietary, personal, or other information. The statute further provides that the board must protect from public disclosure information reasonably identified by the subject accounting firm as proprietary information. (Sec. 102(e).)

Fees

The Act also imposes registration and annual fees. Under Section 102(f), the board must assess and collect a registration fee and an annual fee from each registered public accounting firm in amounts sufficient to recover the costs of processing and reviewing applications and annual reports.

¶ 206 Foreign Accounting Firms

The Act treats foreign accounting firms essentially the same as it treats domestic accounting firms. This helps to eliminate an incentive for companies to favor foreign accounting firms as a means to circumvent the Act's objectives. As the Senate Committee noted:

> Companies that sell shares to U.S. investors, and are subject to the federal securities laws, can be organized and operate in any part of the world. Their financial statements are not necessarily audited by U.S. accounting firms, and the Committee believes that there should be no difference in treatment of a public company's auditors under the bill simply because of a particular auditor's place of operation. Otherwise, a significant loophole in the protection offered U.S. investors would be built into the statutory system. (S. Rep. 107-205 (July 3, 2002), p. 11.)

Covered Firms

Thus, the Act covers foreign accounting firms that prepare audit reports for public companies subject to federal securities law as it does domestic accounting firms. Under Section 106(a)(1), any foreign public accounting firm that prepares or furnishes an audit report concerning an issuer is subject to the Act and related SEC and board rules "in the same manner and to the same extent" as a U.S. accounting firm. The statute clarifies, however, that registration with the board will not by itself subject a foreign accounting firm to federal or state court jurisdiction, other than with respect to controversies between those firms and the board. (Sec. 106(a)(1).)

The board may expand the Act's coverage to include certain firms, as well as exempt other firms from that coverage. Under Section 106(a)(2), the board may, by rule, determine that a foreign accounting firm (or class of such firms) that does not issue audit reports nonetheless plays such a substantial role in the preparation and furnishing of those reports for particular issuers that they should be treated as covered firms. Conversely, the SEC and the board (subject to SEC approval) may, by rule or order, exempt any foreign accounting firm from any provisions of the Act, the SEC rules, or the board's rules, as necessary or appropriate in the public interest. (Sec. 106(c).)

Production of Audit Work Papers

The Act deems certain foreign firms to have consented to produce their audit work papers. If a foreign accounting firm issues an opinion or otherwise performs material services on which a registered firm relies in issuing all or part of any audit (or opinion in an audit), the Act deems the foreign firm to have consented:

- To produce its audit work papers for the board or SEC in connection with any investigation by either body; and
- To be subject to federal court jurisdiction for enforcement of any request to produce those papers.

Domestic accounting firms that rely on a foreign firm's work receive corresponding treatment. The statute deems a registered accounting firm that relies on the opinion of a foreign accounting firm to have consented to supplying the foreign firm's audit work papers in response to a board or SEC request for production. Moreover, the domestic firm is deemed to have secured the foreign firm's agreement to such production as a condition of its reliance on the foreign firm's opinion. (Sec. 106(b)(2).)

¶ 207 Funding

The Act also provides for guaranteed funding of both the accounting oversight board and the Financial Accounting Standards Board (FASB). Congress concluded that guaranteed sources of funding is essential to protect the independence of those bodies. The Senate Committee noted that several witnesses testified to the problems various attempts at auditor oversight had encountered when voluntary funding was withheld. Discussing the FASB, former SEC Chief Accountant Michael Sutton testified that:

> To restore confidence in our standards setters, we should take immediate steps to secure independent funding for the FASB—funding that does not

depend on contributions from constituents that have a stake in the outcome of the process. (S. Rep. 107-205 (July 3, 2002), p. 13.)

Thus, under Section 109, public companies must pay "accounting support fees" to fund the annual budgets of the board and the FASB. Amounts payable by public companies to either body will generally be allocated among those companies based on relative average annual monthly market capitalization for the 12 months preceding the year in which the support fee relates. Both the board and the FASB may distinguish between various classes of companies in allocating the fees. (S. Rep. 107-205 (July 3, 2002), p. 13.)

Sources and Uses

Section 109(c) describes the various sources and permitted uses of funds. Under the statute, the board's budget (reduced by any registration or annual fees received under Section 102(e) for the preceding year) and the FASB's budget will, for each fiscal year, be payable from annual accounting support fees in accordance with Section 109(d) and (e) (discussed below). Accounting support fees will not constitute public money of the federal government. (Sec. 109(c)(1).)

The statute also prescribes the use of funds from the collection of money penalties. In general, the board must use all funds that it collects resulting from the assessment of monetary penalties to fund a merit scholarship for undergraduate and graduate students enrolled in accredited accounting degree programs. Such a program must be administered either by the board or an entity or agent identified by the board. (Sec. 109(c)(2).)

Accounting Support Fees

Section 109(d)–(g) describes the accounting support fee. In general, the fee must cover the budget and expenses of the board and the FASB. The fees collected cannot exceed the recoverable budget expenses of either body, respectively (which may include operating, capital, and accrued items). (Sec. 109(f).) Slightly different requirements apply to the support fee assessed by the board and that assessed by the FASB. Discussion of the respective requirements appears separately below.

Board's fee

The accounting oversight board must establish a reasonable support fee to sustain its operations. Under Section 109(d)(1), the board must establish, with the SEC's approval, a reasonable annual accounting support fee (or a formula for computing the fee) as necessary or appropriate to establish and maintain the board. The fee may also cover costs incurred in the board's first fiscal year (which may be a short fiscal year), or may be levied separately for that short fiscal year. (Sec. 109(d)(1).)

The board must adopt rules for allocating, assessing, and collecting the fee. Specifically, the board's rules must provide for the fee's equitable allocation, assessment, and collection, among companies, in accordance with Section 109(g) (discussed below), which allows for differentiation among classes of companies as appropriate.

FASB's fee

Similar requirements apply to the support fee for the FASB. Under Section 109(e)(1), the FASB must allocate the fee in accordance with Section 109(g), and assess and collect it against each company, as may be necessary or appropriate to pay for the budget, cover its expenses, and provide for an independent and stable source of funding, subject to SEC review. The FASB, like the board, may differentiate among different classes of companies. (Sec. 109(e)(2).)

Allocation

Section 109(g) governs the allocation of support fees among companies. Under the statute, the total fee amount due from issuers (or a particular class of issuers) must be allocated among and payable by each issuer (or each issuer in a particular class, as applicable) in an amount equal to the total amount multiplied by a fraction:

- The numerator of which is the particular issuer's average monthly equity market capitalization for the 12-month period immediately preceding the fiscal year to which the budget relates; and

- The demoninator of which is the average monthly equity market capitalization of all such issuers for the same 12-month period. (Sec. 109(g).)

Standard-Setting Role

¶ 220 In General

The Act gives the accounting oversight board broad authority to set standards for the accounting industry. Under Section 103, the board must adopt rules that establish auditing, quality control, and ethics standards for accountants. These powers are significant in that they enable the board to adopt or amend standards issued or recommended by private accounting industry groups, or to adopt its own standards independent of such private industry standards or recommendations. As the Senate Committee concluded, "the Board's plenary authority in this area is essential for the Board's effective operation . . . ." (S. Rep. 107-205 (July 3, 2002), p. 8.)

Section 103(a)(1) describes the board's general standard-setting power. Under that provision, the board must adopt rules, as required by the Act or SEC rules or as necessary or appropriate in the public interest, establishing auditing (and related attestation) standards, quality control standards, and ethics standards governing registered public accounting firms in the preparation and issuance of audit reports.

This authority does not, however, exclude practicing accountants from participation in the standard-setting process. The statute permits the board, to the extent it determines appropriate, to adopt standards proposed by one or more qualifying professional accountants' or advisory groups that meet certain conditions. (Sec. 103(a)(1).) Moreover, the board must cooperate with such groups on an ongoing basis. (Sec. 103(c).) More detailed discussion of these requirements appears at ¶ 222.

The Act, while granting the board general and expansive standard-setting powers, identifies various particular standards that it must establish. Under Section 103(a)(2), the board must include among the auditing standards that it adopts certain requirements as to supporting documentation, concurring or second partner review, and testing of internal controls. The board must also adopt specified quality control standards. These particular auditing and quality control standards are discussed at ¶ 221.

The Act also requires the board to adopt independence standards for auditors. Under Section 103(b), the board must, as necessary or appropriate in the public interest, establish standards for auditor independence pursuant to Title II of the Act. These standards are in addition to the auditing, quality control, and ethics standards authorized by Title I. More detailed discussion of auditor independence standards appears elsewhere (see Chapter 3).

¶ 221 Particular Mandated Standards

The Act requires the accounting oversight board, pursuant to its broad standard-setting authority, to establish certain particular standards. Under Section 103(a)(2), discussed below, the board must adopt as part of its auditing standards specified requirements relating to supporting documentation, concurring or second partner review, and testing of internal controls. In addition, the board must include among its quality control standards various particular requirements in areas such as supervision of audit work, acceptance and continuation of engagements, and internal inspections, as discussed further below.

Auditing Standards

The board must adopt, as part of its auditing standards, three particular requirements. First, the board must establish a requirement that each public accounting firm prepare and maintain supporting documentation relating to its audit reports. Specifically, the each such firm must prepare and maintain for at least seven years audit work papers, and other information relating to any audit report, in sufficient detail to support the conclusions reached in that report. (Sec. 103(a)(2)(A)(i).)

Second, the board must require accounting firms to provide a concurring or second partner review of each audit report. In particular, the board must require firms to provide a concurring or second partner review and approval of each audit report, and a concurring approval in its issuance, by a qualified person associated with the firm who is not in charge of the audit, or by an independent reviewer. The board will prescribe the qualifications of associated and independent persons who may conduct such a review. (Sec. 103(a)(2)(A)(ii).)

Finally, the board must require accounting firms to describe their testing of the client issuer's internal accounting controls. Specifically, the accounting firm must describe the scope of testing by the auditor of the company's internal accounting controls required by Section 404(b) (discussed at ¶ 504). In addition, the firm must present:

- The auditor's findings from the testing;
- An evaluation of whether the company's internal accounting controls: (1) include maintenance of records that in reasonable detail accurately reflect the company's transactions and dispositions of assets; (2) reasonably ensure that the company's records will enable the preparation of GAAP-compliant financial statements; and (3) reasonably ensure that the company's receipts and expenditures received the proper authorization from its management and directors; and
- A description of any material weaknesses in those internal controls, and of any material noncompliance found based on such testing. (Sec. 103(a)(2)(A)(iii).)

Quality Control Standards

The board also must adopt the quality control requirements listed in Section 103(a)(2)(B). That provision requires the board to adopt, as part of the quality control standards it establishes, specific requirements for every registered public accounting firm relating to:

- Monitoring of professional ethics and independence from companies that the firm audits;
- Consultation within the firm on accounting and auditing questions;
- Supervision of audit work;
- Hiring, professional development, and advancement of personnel;
- Acceptance and continuation of engagements; and
- Internal inspection. (Sec. 103(a)(2)(B).)

¶ 222 Professional and Advisory Groups

The Act authorizes the accounting oversight board to adopt standards proposed by professional accountants' groups and advisory groups. As discussed below, Section 103(a)(3) permits the board to adopt certain auditing or other professional standards proposed by a professional group of accountants. Section 103(a)(4), discussed further below, allows the board to convene an advisory group to make recommendations as to auditing, quality control, ethics, and independence standards.

Accountants' Groups

The board, in carrying out its standard-setting function, may adopt as its own certain standards developed by a professional group of accountants. Under Section 103(a)(1) and (3)(A), the board may adopt as its rules, subject to SEC approval, any portion of any statement of auditing or other professional standards governing accounting firms in preparing and issuing audit reports that: (1) the board determines are required by the Act or SEC rules, or are necessary or appropriate in the public interest; and (2) were proposed by one or more professional groups of accountants designated or recognized by the board for this purpose (or by one or more advisory groups convened pursuant to Section 103(a)(4), discussed below).

Modification

This power to adopt other standards includes the power to modify or even repeal them. Under Section 103(a)(3)(A)(ii), the board retains "full authority to modify, supplement, revise, or subsequently amend, modify, or repeal, in whole or in part, any portion of any statement described [above]."

Initial or transitional standards

The Act also provides for the adoption of initial or transitional standards on an accelerated basis. Specifically, the board must adopt standards proposed by a professional accountants' group as initial or transitional standards, to the extent that the board deems necessary, prior to the SEC's determination under Section 101(d) that the board is capable of executing its statutory duties. The Commission will separately approve any such standards at the time of that determination, without regard to the Section 107 procedures (discussed at ¶ 251) that would otherwise govern SEC approval of the board's rules. (Sec. 103(a)(3)(B).)

Advisory Groups

The board also must convene an expert advisory group as appropriate to help it set auditing and other professional standards. Specifically, the Act requires the board to convene such expert advisory groups as are appropriate to make recommendations concerning the content (including proposed drafts) of auditing, quality control, ethics, independence, or other standards. These advisory groups may include practicing accountants and other experts, as well as representatives of other interested groups, subject to the board's rules against conflicts of interest. (Sec. 103(a)(4).)

Cooperation with Groups

The board must cooperate with these groups on an ongoing basis. Under Section 103(c), the board must cooperate on an ongoing basis with professional accountants' groups and advisory groups (as described above) in examining the need for changes in any standards subject to the board's standard-setting authority. In addition, the board must recommend issues for inclusion on the agendas of these groups, and take any other steps that it deems appropriate to improve the standard-setting process. (Sec. 103(c)(1).)

Finally, the board must be responsive to requests from these groups. Under Section 103(c)(2), the board must respond in a timely fashion to requests from any professional accountants' groups or advisory groups described above for any changes in standards that the board has authority over.

Inspections

¶ 230 In General

The accounting oversight board has broad powers to inspect accounting firms. Stressing the importance of a regular and comprehensive review of each firm's compliance, the Senate Committee Report noted:

> A program of inspections is essential to identify problems in firm procedures, training, and "culture" before those problems can produce audit failures that trigger large investor losses and threaten confidence in the capital markets. (S. Rep. 107-205 (July 3, 2002), p. 9.)

Thus, under Section 104(a), the board must "conduct a continuing program of inspections to assess the degree of compliance of each registered public accounting firm and associated persons . . ." with the Act, the board's rules, SEC rules, or professional standards, in connection with the firm's audit work.

Frequency

The frequency of board inspections depends on the extent of a firm's auditing activity. For registered accounting firms that regularly provide audit reports for more than 100 companies, the board will conduct inspections annually. For firms that provide audit reports for 100 or fewer companies, the board will conduct inspections at least once every three years. (Sec. 104(b)(1).)

The board may, however, adjust these inspection schedules if it finds that different schedules are consistent with the Act's purpose, the public interest, and investor protection. Moreover, the board may conduct special inspections at the SEC's request or on its own motion. (Sec. 104(b)(2).)

¶ 231 Scope and Procedure

The Act delineates the scope and procedure for board inspections. The board must, in each inspection and in accordance with its rules for inspections, identify any act, practice, or omission by the accounting firm (or any associated person) revealed by the inspection that may violate the Act, the board's rules, SEC rules, the firm's own quality control policies, or professional standards. (Sec. 104(c)(1).) The board must then report any such act, practice, or omission, if appropriate, to the SEC and the proper state regulatory authorities. (Sec. 104(c)(2).) In addition, the board must begin a formal investigation or take disciplinary action, if appropriate, as to any such violation in accordance with the Act and the board's rules. (Sec. 104(c)(3); see ¶ 240)

Conduct of Inspection

In conducting the inspection, the board must inspect and review selected audit and review engagements of the firm, performed at various offices and by various associated persons, as selected by the board. (Sec. 104(d)(1).) The board also must evaluate the sufficiency of the firm's quality control systems, and the manner of the system's documentation and communication by the firm. (Sec. 104(d)(2).) Finally, the board must perform any other testing of the firm's audit, supervisory, and quality control procedures that are necessary or appropriate. (Sec. 104(d)(3).)

Record Retention

The board may impose special record-retention rules for inspection purposes. Under Section 104(e), the board has authority to require registered accounting firms to retain for inspection records that Section 103 or the related board rules do not otherwise require.

Firm's Response

The board must allow a firm to review and respond to an inspection report. Under Section 104(f), the board must adopt rules establishing a procedure for the review of and response to a draft inspection report by the accounting firm under inspection. The board must take whatever action in connection with such a response that it deems appropriate, including revising the draft report or continuing or supplementing its inspection activities before issuing a final report. The board also must attach to the final inspection report the text of the firm's response, appropriately redacted to protect confidential information. (Sec. 104(f).)

¶ 232 Report

Section 104(g) governs the transmittal and public availability of the board's final report following an inspection. Under the statute, the board must transmit to the SEC and each appropriate state regulatory authority a written report of its findings in each inspection. The board must attach to the report any letter or comments by the board or the inspector, and any letter of response from the accounting firm in question. (Sec. 104(g)(1).) The report is subject to review by the Commission, as discussed at ¶ 233.

The board must make the report publicly available in appropriate detail (subject to applicable confidentiality requirements). The statute, however, specifically prohibits the board from making public portions of the report dealing with criticisms of or potential defects in the firm's quality control systems if the firm addressed those criticisms or defects to the board's satisfaction within 12 months after the report date. (Sec. 104(g)(2).) In other words, the firm has one year to correct defects in its quality control systems, to the board's satisfaction, before the board may add portions of the report concerning those defects to the public record. (S. Rep. 107-205 (July 3, 2002), p. 10.)

¶ 233 Interim SEC Review

The Act provides for interim SEC review of the inspection report. Under Section 104(h), an accounting firm may seek review by the Commission of the report, pursuant to SEC rules, in two circumstances. First, the firm may seek SEC review if it provided the board with a response under Section 104(f) (discussed at ¶ 231) to particular items in a draft report, and disagrees with the assessments in the final report following the firm's response. (Sec. 104(h)(1)(A).) Second, the firm may seek review if it disagrees with the board's determination that the firm failed to address criticisms or defects identified in an inspection report within 12 months after the report. (Sec. 104(h)(1)(B).)

The firm has 30 days to seek SEC review. Specifically, the statute permits a firm to seek review during the 30-day period following the event giving rise to review under Section 104(h)(1)(A) or (B). (Sec. 104(h)(3).)

The SEC's decisions regarding its review of a report are not themselves reviewable. The Act declares that any decision of the SEC concerning a review of an inspection report is not reviewable under Exchange Act Section 25, nor is deemed a "final agency action" for purposes of 5 U.S.C. 704. (Sec. 104(h)(2).)

Investigations and Disciplinary Actions

¶ 240 In General

Section 105 governs investigations and disciplinary actions. The statute empowers the board to investigate registered accounting firms and their partners and employees and to conduct disciplinary proceedings if it discovers violations of the Act, the board's rules, professional accounting standards, or the federal securities laws relating to auditing. The statute further provides that the board must adopt rules establishing fair procedures for these investigations and disciplinary proceedings. (Sec. 105(a).)

Investigatory and disciplinary powers are critical to the board's oversight role. Testifying before the Senate Committee, former SEC Chairman Arthur Levitt stated:

> We need a truly independent oversight body that has the power not only to set the standards by which audits are performed, but also to conduct timely investigations that cannot be deferred for any reason and to discipline accountants. (S. Rep. 107-205 (July 3, 2002), p. 10.)

Similarly, Robert Glauber, Chairman and CEO of the National Association of Securities Dealers, testified that:

> Any form of private-sector regulation must be empowered to effectively enforce the rules: [it must have] the ability to levy meaningful fines, place conditions on continued participation in the industry, suspend, and where appropriate, banish those who misbehave from the industry. (S. Rep. 107-205 (July 3, 2002), p. 10.)

The Act therefore gives the board expansive investigatory and disciplinary powers, as discussed separately below (see ¶ ¶ 241 and 242).

¶ 241 Investigations

Section 105(b)(1) prescribes the board's authority to investigate accounting firms. It permits the board, in accordance with its rules, to conduct an investigation of any act, practice, or omission by a registered accounting firm and/or its associated persons that may violate the Act, the board's rules, the federal securities laws and SEC rules relating to preparing and issuing audit reports, and professional standards. The board may launch such an investigation regardless of how the act, practice, or omission came to the board's attention. (Sec. 105(b)(1).)

Testimony and Document Production

The board may, during its investigation, compel testimony and the production of documents. Under Section 105(b)(2), among other necessary or appropriate actions, the board may adopt rules allowing it to:

- Require testimony from the accounting firm or its associated persons on any matter that the board deems relevant to an investigation;

- Require the production of audit work papers and any other document or information possessed by the firm or any associated person (wherever domiciled) that the board deems relevant, and to inspect the books and records of the firm or associated person to verify the accuracy of any documents or information supplied;

- Request testimony and the production of documents from any other person, including the accounting firm's clients, that the board deems relevant, with appropriate notice;

- Establish procedures to seek a subpoena issued by the SEC to compel testimony and the production of documents as described above. (Sec. 105(b)(2).)

Sanctions for Noncooperation

The board may impose sanctions for failing to cooperate with an investigation. If a registered accounting firm or any associated person refuses to testify, produce documents, or otherwise cooperate with the board's investigation, the board may: (1) suspend or bar the person from his or her association with a registered accounting firm, or require the firm to end the association; (2) suspend or revoke the firm's registration; and (3) invoke any other lesser sanctions that the board deems appropriate, as specified by its rules. (Sec. 105(b)(3)(A).) Any such sanctions are, however, subject to SEC review under Section 107(c) (discussed at ¶ 252). (Sec. 105(b)(3)(B).)

Coordination/Referral of Investigations

The board must coordinate its investigations with the SEC's enforcement activities, and may refer the investigation to the Commission or other appropriate body. Under Section 105(b)(4)(A), the board must notify the SEC of any pending board investigation involving a potential violation of the securities laws, and thereafter coordinate its work with the Commission's Enforcement Division, as necessary to protect an ongoing SEC investigation.

Section 105(b)(4)(B) governs the referral of investigations. Under that statute, the board may refer an investigation:

- To the SEC;
- To any other "federal functional regulator" (as defined in Gramm-Leach-Bliley Act Section 509), in the case of investigations of an institution subject to such a regulator's jurisdiction; and
- At the SEC's direction, to the U.S. Attorney General, any state attorney general, and any appropriate state regulatory authority. (Sec. 105(b)(4)(B).)

Confidentiality

Documents and information obtained during an investigation are, with limited exceptions, confidential and privileged. Under Section 105(b)(5)(A), all documents and information prepared or received by the board, and deliberations of the board and its employees and agents, in connection with an inspection under Section 104 or an investigation under Section 105 are confidential and privileged as an evidentiary matter (and not subject to discovery) in any federal or state court or administrative agency. Moreover, all such documents, information, or deliberations are exempt from disclosure by the federal government under the Freedom of Information Act or otherwise unless and until presented in connection with a public proceeding or released in accordance with Section 105(c), discussed below. (Sec. 105(b)(5)(A).)

The statute creates certain exceptions, however. The board may disclose the documents, information, and deliberations described above to the SEC and—if necessary to accomplish the Act's purposes or to protect investors—to the U.S. Attorney General, an appropriate federal functional regulator, a state attorney general, and any appropriate state regulatory authority. Each such recipient must maintain the information as confidential and privileged. (Sec. 105(b)(5)(B).)

Immunity

Board employees have immunity from civil liability stemming from an investigation. Specifically, any board employee engaged in carrying out an investigation is immune from any civil liability arising out of the investigation to the same extent as a federal investigator in similar circumstances. (Sec. 105(b)(6); see also S. Rep. 107-205 (July 3, 2002), p. 48.)

¶ 242 Disciplinary Proceedings

The accounting oversight board may impose a full range of sanctions against accounting firms and their partners and employees for violations. Potential sanctions include revocation or suspension of the firm's registration, or of the association of particular individuals with that firm or any other registered accounting firm, civil money penalties, mandated professional education or training, and censure. Certain sanctions are available only for intentional, reckless, or repeated negligent conduct. Other sanctions are available for failure to supervise reasonably a partner or employee. (S. Rep. 107-205 (July 3, 2002), p. 48-49.) Discussion of these and other matters governing disciplinary proceedings appears below.

Preliminary Considerations

Section 105(c)(1) requires the board to give notice and keep a record of each disciplinary proceeding. Specifically, the board must adopt rules providing that in any disciplinary proceeding the board will: (1) bring specific charges as to the firm or associated person; (2) notify the firm or associated person of those charges and provide an opportunity to defend against them; and (3) keep a record of the proceeding.

Disciplinary proceedings typically are not open to the public. The Act states that hearings will not be public "unless otherwise ordered by the Board for good cause shown, with the consent of the parties to such hearing." (Sec. 105(c)(2).)

Sanctions

The board may impose a range of sanctions for specified violations. If the board finds that an accounting firm or associated person engaged in an act or practice (or failed to act) in violation of the Act, the board's rules, the securities laws and SEC rules concerning the preparation of audit reports, or professional standards, the board may impose any disciplinary or remedial sanctions that it deems appropriate, subject to specified limitations. The available sanctions may include:

(1) Temporary suspension or permanent revocation of the firm's registration;

(2) Temporary or permanent bar of a person from further association with any registered accounting firm;

(3) Temporary or permanent limitation on the activities, functions, or operations of the firm or person;

(4) A civil money penalty for each violation of up to $100,000 for individuals and $2 million for firms, except that, for violations involving

intentional, reckless, or repeated negligent conduct, the limit is $750,000 for individuals and $15 million for firms;

(5) Censure;

(6) Required professional education or training; and

(7) Any other appropriate sanction that the board's rules permit. (Sec. 105(c)(4).)

Some sanctions, however, are available only for intentional or similarly culpable conduct. Specifically, the temporary or permanent injunctive remedies listed above (items 1–3) and the larger of the two civil penalties described above (item 4) apply only to: (1) intentional or reckless conduct that results in a violation of applicable statutory, regulatory, or professional standards; or (2) repeated instances of negligent conduct, each resulting in a violation of applicable statutory, regulatory, or professional standards. (Sec. 105(c)(5).)

The board must support any determination to impose sanctions with a prescribed statement. That statement must set forth: (1) each act, practice, or omission by the accounting firm or associated person that forms a basis for the sanction; (2) the specific provision of the Act, the securities laws, the board's rules, or professional standards that the board determined was violated; and (3) the sanction imposed, including a justification for that sanction. (Sec. 105(c)(3).)

Failure to Supervise

The board may impose sanctions for failure to supervise. Under Section 105(c)(6), the board may impose sanctions on a registered accounting firm or on its supervisory personnel if the board finds that: (1) the firm failed reasonably to supervise an associated person; and (2) that person violated the Act, the board's rules, the federal securities laws relating to auditing, or professional standards.

The Act, however, provides a limited safe harbor. It precludes a finding that the firm "failed reasonably to supervise" if two conditions are met. First, the firm must have established procedures complying with applicable board rules that would reasonably be expected to prevent and detect any such violation by the associated person. Second, that person's supervisor must have reasonably discharged his or her duties by reason of those procedures, and had no reasonable cause to believe that the procedures were not being complied with. (Sec. 105(c)(6)(B).) This provision resembles language in Exchange Act Section 15(b)(4)(E), governing broker-dealers. (S. Rep. 107-205 (July 3, 2002), p. 49.)

Effect of Review

Review of a disciplinary proceeding will operate as a stay of any sanctions. Under Section 105(e)(1), application to the SEC for review, or the SEC's own institution of review, of any disciplinary action by the board will operate as a stay of that action, unless and until the SEC orders the stay's termination. The Commission must establish for appropriate cases an expedited procedure for considering and determining the stay's duration pending review of any disciplinary action. (Sec. 105(e)(2).)

SEC Oversight of Board

¶ 250 In General

The accounting oversight board is subject to SEC supervision and review. This ensures that the board's policies are consistent with the administration of federal securities laws, and protects the rights of accounting firms and individuals subject to the board's jurisdiction. SEC oversight also allows the public an important forum for commenting on board rules relating to auditing, quality control, and ethics standards. (S. Rep. 107-205 (July 3, 2002), p. 12.)

The board is generally subject to the same degree of SEC control as the National Association of Securities Dealers. Thus, the board must file its proposed rules with the Commission, which in turn must publish them for public comment. The board's rules in most cases will not take effect without SEC approval, and the Commission may reject or amend them. Disciplinary sanctions imposed by the board are subject to SEC review, and the Commission may cancel, modify, or enhance them. In addition, the SEC may relieve the board of any enforcement responsibility, censure or limit its operations, or remove a board member for cause. Finally, the Act clarifies that any violation of its terms constitutes a violation of the Exchange Act for purposes of the SEC's enforcement authority under that law, thus enabling the Commission to proceed directly if appropriate. (S. Rep. 107-205 (July 3, 2002), p. 12.)

Section 107 prescribes the contours of this SEC oversight function. Discussion of particular aspects of this function follows below.

¶ 251 Board Rules

The board's rules are, as mentioned, subject to SEC review and approval. In general, no board rule will become effective without the Commission's prior approval in accordance with the procedures under Section 107. An exception applies to the board's initial and transitional standards (discussed at ¶ 222), which the SEC must approve separately when it determines that the board is ready to begin operating. (Sec. 107(b)(2).) The Commission must approve a board rule if it finds that the rule is consistent with the requirements of the

Act and the securities laws, or is necessary or appropriate in the public interest. (Sec. 107(b)(3).)

Approval Procedure

The procedure for SEC approval of board rules is essentially that which governs rulemaking of the National Association of Securities Dealers (NASD) under Exchange Act Section 19(b). The Sarbanes-Oxley Act states that Exchange Act Section 19(b)(1)–(3) will govern the board's proposed rules as fully as if the board were a "registered securities association" for purposes of that Section 19(b). (Sec. 107(b)(4).)

Thus, the board must file its proposed rules with the Commission, which in turn must publish them for public comment. Under Exchange Act Section 19(b)(1), the NASD (and, hence, the board) must file with the SEC copies of any proposed rule or any proposed amendment to or repeal of its rules accompanied by a concise general statement of the basis and purpose for that change. The Commission must then publish notice of that proposed change and give interested persons a chance to comment. No proposed rule change will take effect unless approved by the SEC or otherwise permitted under Section 19(b). (Exchange Act Section 19(b)(1).)

The Commission must approve a proposed rule change if it finds that the change is consistent with Title I of the Sarbanes-Oxley Act and the related rules, or as necessary or appropriate in the public interest. The SEC must disapprove the proposed change if it does not make such a finding. (Exchange Act Section 19(b)(2); Sarbanes-Oxley Act Section 107(b)(4)(A).)

Abrogation or Amendment of Rules

The SEC has broad authority to abrogate or modify the board's rules. Section 107(b)(5) states that Exchange Act Section 19(c) will govern the abrogation, deletion, or modification of board rules by the SEC as if the board were a "registered securities association" (i.e., the NASD) for purposes of that statute. Thus, under Section 19(c), the Commission may adopt rules that abrogate, add to, or delete from the board's rules as the SEC deems necessary or appropriate. The Commission must first notify the board and publish notice of the proposed rulemaking in the Federal Register, and then allow interested persons the opportunity to make oral presentations and submit written comments. (Exchange Act Section 19(c)(1) and (2).)

¶ 252 Board-imposed Sanctions

Sanctions imposed by the board, as mentioned, are likewise subject to SEC review. The procedure for SEC review of board sanctions is essentially that which governs disciplinary actions of the NASD under the Exchange Act.

The Sarbanes-Oxley Act states that Exchange Act Section 19(d)(2) and (e)(1) will govern review of the board's final disciplinary sanctions as fully as if the board were a "registered securities association" (i.e., the NASD) for purposes of that statute. (Sec. 107(c)(2).) Thus, under Section 19(d)(2), board-imposed sanctions are subject to SEC review on the accounting firm's own motion, or upon application of any aggrieved person.

Moreover, under Section 19(e)(1), if the SEC finds that the accounting firm or associated person committed the violation found by the board, the Commission must affirm the sanction imposed, modify it as the statute permits, or remand to the board for further proceedings. If the SEC does not make such a finding, it must set aside the sanction and, if appropriate, remand to the board for further proceedings. (Exchange Act Section 19(e)(1).) The Sarbanes-Oxley Act clarifies that the SEC may enhance, modify, cancel, reduce, or require the remission of a board-imposed sanction against an accounting firm or associated person if the Commission finds, after a proceeding required by the statute, that the sanction:

- Is not necessary or appropriate in furtherance of the Act or the securities laws; or

- Is excessive, oppressive, inadequate, or otherwise not appropriate to the finding or the basis for the sanction. (Sec. 107(c)(3).)

To facilitate the review process, the board must give the SEC notice of any sanctions that it imposes. Under Section 107(c)(1), the board must promptly file notice with the Commission of any final sanction on an accounting firm or associated person, in such form and containing such information as the SEC may prescribe.

¶ 253 Sanctions Against Board

The SEC may impose various limitations or sanctions on the board for specified reasons. Those measures include rescission of the board's authority, censure of the board, and censure of individual board members. For example, the SEC may—consistent with the public interest and the purposes of the Act and the securities laws—adopt a rule rescinding the board's powers to enforce compliance with any provision of the Act, the securities laws, the board rules, or professional standards. (Sec. 107(d)(1).)

The Commission may also censure the board or restrict its activities for certain reasons. Under Section 107(d)(2), the SEC may, as necessary or appropriate in the public interest or otherwise in furtherance of the Act or the securities laws, issue an order censuring the board or imposing limitations on its activities, functions, and operations. The SEC must, however, first find (after notice and opportunity for a hearing) that the board:

- Has violated or cannot comply with any provision of the Act, the board's rules, or the securities laws; or

- Without reasonable justification, has failed to enforce compliance with any such provision or rule, or any professional standard, by an accounting firm or associated person. (Sec. 107(d)(2).)

Finally, the SEC may impose sanctions against board members. Under Section 107(d)(3), the Commission may, as necessary or appropriate in the public interest or otherwise in furtherance of the Act or the securities laws, remove from office or censure any board member. The SEC must, however, first find (after notice and opportunity for a hearing) that the member:

- Has willfully violated any provision of the Act, the board's rules, or the securities laws;

- Has willfully abused his or her authority; or

- Without reasonable justification, has failed to enforce compliance with any such provision or rule, or any professional standard, by an accounting firm or associated person. (Sec. 107(d)(3).)

Accounting Standards

¶ 260 In General

Since 1973, the SEC has generally required public companies operating in the United States to prepare their financial statements in accordance with principles, standards, and practices promulgated by the Financial Accounting Standards Board (FASB) in the absence of specific SEC pronouncements on particular accounting questions. (See Accounting Series Release No. 150). The Act seeks to formalize the SEC's reliance on FASB and strengthen the independence of FASB by assuring its funding and eliminating any need for it to seek contributions from accounting firms or companies whose financial statements must conform to FASB's rules.

Section 108 amends Securities Act Section 19 specifically to allow the Commission to recognize as generally accepted (for securities law purposes) accounting principles established by a standard-setting body that meets certain criteria. To qualify, the standard-setting body must:

- Be a private entity and be funded by public companies in the same manner as the newly established accounting oversight board;

- Have adopted procedures, including acting by majority vote, to ensure prompt consideration of necessary changes to the body of accounting principles;

- Have a board of trustees the majority of whom are not currently, and within the past two years have not been, associated persons of any registered public accounting firm; and

- In adopting accounting principles, consider the need to keep standards current to reflect changes in the business environment and consider the extent to which international convergence on high quality accounting standards is necessary for investor protection.

Any such standard-setting body must submit an annual report to the SEC and the public, containing audited financial statements.

Thus, the Act effectively grants statutory recognition to FASB and sets outs its obligation to act in the public interest to ensure the accuracy and effectiveness of financial reporting; states that the trustees who elect FASB's members must represent investors and the public, not just the accounting industry or corporate interests; and streamlines FASB's operations by requiring it to act by majority vote instead of through a supermajority.

According to Sen. Carl Levin. the Act sets up a system that provides FASB with an independent stable source of funding through fees assessed on public companies. Once this new system is set up, it will no longer be the case that FASB will have to go "hat in hand" for funds from the very companies and accounting firms that want to affect its decisionmaking. Sen. Levin believes that this conflict of interest has contributed to some of the distortions and weaknesses in current accounting standards. (See remarks of Sen. Carl Levin, Cong. Rec., July 10, 2002, p. S6565.)

Section 108 clarifies that FASB's funding cannot be affected by the congressional appropriations process and the political pressures that can be exerted through it. The statute's purpose is to set up an independent, stable source of funding that is insulated from political pressure and funding threats so that FASB can do its work free of such influences.

Once the new funding system is in place, Sen. Levin urged FASB to begin to reassess U.S. accounting standards and to begin resolving some of the problems that have allowed so many companies to engage in dishonest accounting while claiming to be in compliance with GAAP. (See remarks of Sen. Carl Levin, Cong. Rec., July 10, 2002, p. S6565.)

¶ 261 Principles-based Accounting Study

An important issue addressed by the Senate Banking Committee was the potential difference between an accounting regime that contains detailed rules for the treatment of particular items, and a regime that simply outlines general concepts or principles to be applied to particular items. Witnesses noted the possibility that the overly-detailed approach of U.S. standard-setters may have delayed updating of necessary guidance and at the same time drawn the focus of auditors away from the overriding principle that a set of financial statements, taken as a whole, must fairly and completely reflect the economic results and operations of the company being audited.

To allow more careful consideration of the differences between various formulations of accounting standards, Section 108 requires the SEC to conduct a study of the adoption by the U.S. financial reporting system of a principles-based accounting system. The study must include an examination of:

- The extent to which principles-based accounting and financial reporting exists in the United States;
- The length of time required for change from a rules-based to a principles-based financial reporting system;
- The feasibility of and proposed methods by which a principles-based system may be implemented; and
- A thorough economic analysis of the implementation of a principles-based system.

The Commission must submit a report on the results of that study to Congress within one year of the law's enactment. (Sec. 108 at ¶ 1008.)

CHAPTER 3

AUDITOR INDEPENDENCE

The issue of auditor independence is at the center of the legislation. Public confidence in the integrity of financial statements of public companies is based on belief in the independence of the auditor from the audit client. Each of the federal securities laws requires comprehensive financial statements that must be prepared by an independent public or certified accountant.

The statutory independent audit requirement has two sides. It grants a franchise to the nation's public accountants since their services and certification must be secured before an issuer of securities can go to market, have the securities listed on the nation's stock exchanges, or comply with the reporting requirements of the securities laws. This is a source of significant private benefit to public accountants.

But the franchise is conditional. It comes in return for the CPA's assumption of a public duty and obligation. The U.S. Supreme Court has noted that, in certifying the public reports that collectively depict a company's financial status, the independent auditor assumes a public responsibility. That auditor owes ultimate allegiance to the company's creditors and stockholders, as well as to the investing public. This public watchdog function demands that the accountant maintain total independence from the client at all times and requires complete fidelity to the public trust. *United States v. Arthur Young*, (US Sup. Ct. 1984), 1983-84 CCH Dec. ¶ 99,721.

¶ 301 Non-Audit Services

Congress believes that there is arguably an inherent conflict in the fact that an auditor is paid by the company for which the audit is being performed. That conflict is implicit in the relationship between the auditor and the audit client. In the last fifteen years, however, the rapid growth in management consulting services offered by the major accounting firms has created a second and more substantial conflict that has eroded the independence that the auditor must bring to the audit function.

The Act defines "non-audit services" to mean any professional services provided to a company by a registered public accounting firm, other than those provided to a company in connection with an audit or a review of the financial statements of an issuer.

The Senate Banking Committee considered adopting a complete prohibition on non-audit services by accounting firms for their audit clients, but instead decided on a somewhat more flexible approach. The Act establishes the serious separation of the auditing function and other consulting functions that accountants can perform. Generally, under the Act, if you are going to be an auditor, you have to be an auditor, not an auditor and consultant. (See remarks of Sen. Jack Reed, Cong. Rec., July 11, 2002, p. S6617-6618.)

Under Section 201, it is unlawful for a public accounting firm registered with the oversight board that performs an audit for a public company to provide, contemporaneously with the audit, the following non-audit services:

- Bookkeeping or other services related to the accounting records or financial statements of the audit client;
- Financial information systems design and implementation;
- Appraisal or valuation services, fairness opinions, or contribution-in-kind reports;
- Actuarial services;
- Internal audit outsourcing services;
- Management functions or human resources;
- Broker or dealer, investment adviser, or investment banking services;
- Legal services and expert services unrelated to the audit; and
- Any other services that the public company accounting oversight board determines, by regulation, is impermissible.

The accounting oversight board may, on a case-by-case basis, exempt any person, company, public accounting firm, or transaction from the prohibition on the provision of non-audit services to the extent that such exemption is necessary or appropriate in the public interest and is consistent with the protection of investors. This exemptive power is subject to SEC review.

A registered public accounting firm may engage in any non-audit service, including tax services, that is not on the prohibited list for an audit client only if the activity is approved in advance by the company's audit committee. No limitations are placed on accounting firms in providing non-audit services to public companies that they do not audit or to any non-public companies.

While some had argued that standards for auditor independence should be left to the SEC and the new board, the approach adopted by the Act reflects Congress' belief that the issue of auditor independence is so fundamental to the problems currently being experienced in the financial markets that statutory standards are needed to assure the auditor's independence from the audit client. The Act adopts a strong, balanced approach to assure that, in return for the significant private benefits conferred on accounting firms by the securities laws, they maintain their independence from the companies they audit and fulfill their public trust.

The intention of this provision is to draw a clear line around a limited list of non-audit services that accounting firms may not provide to public company audit clients because their doing so creates a fundamental conflict of interest for the accounting firms. (See remarks of Sen. Paul Sarbanes, Cong. Rec, July 8, 2002, p. S6332.)

The list is based on simple principles. An accounting firm, in order to be independent of its audit client, should not audit its own work, which would be involved in providing bookkeeping services, financial information systems design, appraisal or valuation services, actuarial services, and internal audit outsourcing services to an audit client. The accounting firm should not function as part of management or as an employee of the audit client, which would be required if the accounting firm provides human resources services such as recruiting, hiring, and designing compensation packages for the officers, directors, and managers of an audit client. The accounting firm should not act as an advocate of the audit client, which would be involved in providing legal and expert services to an audit client in legal, administrative, or regulatory proceedings, or serving as a broker-dealer, investment adviser, or investment banker to an audit client, which places the auditor in the role of promoting a client's stock or other interests. (See remarks of Sen. Paul Sarbanes, Cong. Rec., July 8, 2002, p. S6332 and Senate Banking Committee Report No. 107-205.)

The accounting oversight board is given authority to make case-by-case exemptions in instances where the board believes an exemption is in the public interest and consistent with the protection of investors. Further, no limitations are placed on accounting firms in providing non-audit services to public companies that they do not audit or to any private companies. The purpose is to assure the audit's independence, not to put an end to the provision of non-audit services by accounting firms.

As explained by Sen. Sarbanes, if the accounting firm is not the auditor for the company, it can do any of these consulting services it wants. But if it is the auditor, thereby raising a conflict of interest problem, then Congress takes certain services and says those services you cannot do. And the reason is, in order to be independent, the auditor should not audit its own work, as it would do if it did financial information system design or appraisal evaluation services or actuarial services. They are the public company's auditors. They have a very defined responsibility as the auditors. The Act does not bar accounting firms from offering consulting services. It simply says that if a firm wants to audit the company, there are certain services it cannot perform. And even in that case, the Act provides the oversight board authority to grant case-by-case exceptions, so if a case could be made why an auditor's performing a consulting service ought to be permitted, there is some flexibility to permit it. (See remarks of Sen. Paul Sarbanes, Cong. Rec., July 8, 2002, p. S6332.)

See Act Section 201 at ¶ 1011

¶ 302 Audit Committee Pre-approval of Services

The Act requires that audit services, as well as non-audit services other than those proscribed by the Act, must be pre-approved by the audit committee of the company's board of directors. Congress believed the protection of investors warrants requiring a company's audit committee to approve in advance the services that the auditor will provide to the company (if those services are not explicitly prohibited under the Act). Thus, the audit committee must pre-approve all of the services, both audit and non-audit, provided to that company by a registered accounting firm. Note, however, that a company's audit committee need not to pre-approve non-audit services provided by an accounting firm that is not auditing the issuer.

The audit committee must pre-approve a non-audit service before it commences. The audit committee may pre-approve at any time in advance of the activity. For example, an audit committee may grant pre-approval at its March meeting for a non-audit service that would begin in August. However, the SEC, or the accounting oversight board under its general authority, may specify a maximum period of time in advance of which the approval may not be granted, such as, for example, requiring the pre-approval to be granted no earlier than one year prior to the commencement of the service.

The Act does not limit the number of non-audit services that the audit committee may pre-approve at one meeting or occasion. Congress intends, however, that each non-audit service be specifically identified in order to be approved by the audit committee. Congress does not intend for the statutory requirement to be satisfied by an audit committee voting, for example, to permit any service that management determines appropriate for the auditor to perform or all non-audit services permissible under law.

Congress decided to offer audit committees a delegation option in their administration of the pre-approval requirement. Thus, the Act permits the audit committee to delegate to one or more of its members (who are members of the board of directors) the authority to pre-approve non-audit services. After a delegated member has granted a pre-approval, he or she must report the decision at the next meeting of the full audit committee. This delegation of authority may be useful where, for example, the audit committee is asked to determine whether or not to permit the company's auditor to perform a new non-audit service within a short period of time.

Congress has also taken into account the atypical circumstance where an auditor is providing the company with a service that was anticipated to be an audit service within the scope of the engagement, but is later discovered to be a non-audit service. The Act provides that the pre-approval requirement is waived with respect to a non-audit service if:

- The service was not recognized by the company at the time of the audit engagement to be a non-audit service;
- The aggregate amount paid for all services described in (1) is not more than 5 percent of the total amount of revenues paid by the company to the auditor during the fiscal year when the non-audit services are performed;
- The service is promptly brought to the attention of the audit committee; and
- The audit committee approves the activity prior to the conclusion of the audit. This post-approval may be granted by the entire audit committee or by one or more audit committee members (who are members of the board of directors) to whom authority to grant such approvals has been delegated by the audit committee. This flexibility was suggested by Senator Enzi.

Audit committee approvals must be disclosed to investors in periodic reports filed with the SEC.

The Act specifically notes that audit services may entail providing comfort letters in connection with securities underwriting in order to make clear that providing such a comfort letter is an audit service. In addition, the conference committee inserted language to indicate that an audit of an insurance company required under state law is an auditing service.

Finally, the Act provides that if an audit committee approves an audit service within the scope of the engagement while carrying out its oversight work under new Exchange Act Section 10A(m)(2), the audit service will be deemed to have been pre-approved.

See Act Section 202 at ¶ 1012.

¶ 303 Audit Partner Rotation

While the Act does not require issuers to rotate their accounting firms, Congress recognizes the strong benefits that accrue for the company and its shareholders when a new accountant with fresh and skeptical eyes evaluates the company periodically. Accordingly, the Act requires a registered public accounting firm to rotate its lead or coordinating audit partner and its review partner on audits so that neither role is performed by the same accountant for the same company for more than five consecutive years.

The lead partner is the partner who is in charge of the audit engagement. The review partner refers to the outside partner brought in to review the work done by the lead partner and the audit team.

Congress also determined that the possibility of requiring audit firm rotation merits further study. The U.S. General Accounting Office must analyze the merits and potential effects of requiring mandatory rotation of auditors, and report its analysis to Congress within one year. For purposes of the study, mandatory rotation refers to the imposition of a limit on the period of years in which a particular registered public accounting firm may be the author of record for a particular issuer.

See Act Sections 203 and 207 at ¶ 1013 and 1017.

¶ 304 Report to Audit Committee

Congress believes that it is important for the audit committee to be aware of key assumptions underlying a company's financial statements and of disagreements that the auditor has with management. The audit committee should be informed in a timely manner of such disagreements, so that it can independently review them and intervene if it chooses to do so in order to assure the integrity of the audit.

Accordingly, the Act requires a registered independent public accounting firm performing an audit for a public company to report in a timely manner to that company's audit committee:

- The critical accounting policies and practices to be used;
- All alternative treatments of financial information within GAAP (generally accepted accounting principles) that have been discussed with management;
- Any accounting disagreements between the auditor and management; and
- Other material written communications between the auditor and management.

The requirement that auditors discuss specific accounting issues with the company's audit committee will not only increase the understanding of the company's board of directors, but also prevent directors from later claiming they were not informed about the company's accounting practices. (See remarks of Sen. Carl Levin, Cong. Rec., July 10, 2002, p. S6565.)

See Act Section 204 at ¶ 1014.

¶ 305 Cooling Off Period

The Act imposes a one-year cooling off period that would apply to an employee of the accounting firm who worked on the company's audit and subsequently seeks to be employed by that company in a senior management capacity. Thus, an accounting firm may not provide audit services for a public company if that company's chief executive officer, controller, chief financial officer, chief accounting officer, or other individual serving in an equivalent position, was employed by the accounting firm during the one year before the start of the audit services.

The cooling off period does not take effect if the CEO or other senior official worked for the auditor but did not work on the company's audit or if a member of the audit team is hired by the company for a position other than CEO, CFO, controller, chief accounting officer, or an equivalent position. However, if a company hires an accountant from the audit team as its CEO, for example, it would be required to change auditors.

Congress imposed the cooling off period as part of an effort to protect the independence of the audit. Concerned about the movement of audit firm personnel to the public company client, Congress imposed a one-year cooling off period with respect to the top positions in the company so that the company cannot hold out to the audit team the immediate prospect of an important position in the company. (See remarks of Sen. Paul Sarbanes, Cong. Rec., July 8, 2002, p. S6332.)

See Act Section 206 at ¶ 1016.

¶ 306 State Standards

Titles I and II of the Act apply only to accounting firms that audit public companies. They do not apply to audits of private companies. Nonetheless, some have raised the concern that the Act could lead state regulatory authorities to impose similar requirements for audits of private companies.

Congress does not intend that state regulatory authorities should find the Act controlling in their regulation of non-registered accountants. It is the intention of the Act that, in supervising non-registered accounting firms, state regulatory authorities should make an independent determination of the proper standards, and should not presume the standards applied by the accounting oversight board to be applicable to small- and medium-sized non-registered accounting firm.

See Act Section 209 at ¶ 1019.

CHAPTER 4

CORPORATE GOVERNANCE AND RESPONSIBILITY

In further response to recent corporate failures, Title III of the Act makes a number of changes to improve the responsibility of public companies for their financial disclosures.

Recent events have highlighted the failure of companies' internal audit committees to properly police their auditors and have raised awareness of the need for strong, competent audit committees with real authority. Several witnesses at hearings suggested that Congress make changes in the role of audit committees in order to enhance the audit process. In response, the Act directs the SEC to draft rules directing national securities exchanges and associations to require listed companies to comply with a number of enumerated provisions regarding audit committees. Congress believes that the Act's approach to strengthening audit committees will help avoid future auditing breakdowns.

The Act also contains a number of provisions aimed at corporate management. Defects in procedures for monitoring financial results and controls have been blamed for recent corporate failures. The Act therefore requires CEOs and CFOs to certify their companies' financial reports, outlaws fraud and deception by managers in the auditing process, prevents CEOs and CFOs from benefiting from profits they receive as a result of misstatements of their company's financials, and facilitates the imposition of judicial bars against officers and directors who have violated the securities laws. Finally, Title III includes a provision intended to prevent employees from being required to hold company stock in their retirement accounts while officers and directors are free to sell their shares.

¶ 401 Audit Committees

In light of recent events, Congress believes that a number of audit committee provisions should be codified in the securities laws in order to help rectify auditing misconduct and to enhance the effectiveness of audit committee oversight of public company audits.

The auditing process may be compromised when auditors view their main responsibility as serving the company's management rather than its full board of directors or its audit committee. For this reason, the Act requires audit committees to be directly responsible for the appointment, compensation, and oversight of the work of auditors, and requires auditors to report directly to the audit committee.

The Act mandates that audit committee members be independent and then enhances audit committee independence by barring audit committee members from accepting consulting fees or being affiliated persons of the company or its subsidiaries other than in the member's capacity as a member of the board of directors or any board committee. The SEC is authorized to exempt particular relationships with respect to audit committee members as it determines appropriate in light of the circumstances.

The Act contains several additional provisions regarding audit committees. The Act requires audit committees to have in place procedures to receive and address complaints regarding accounting, internal control, or auditing issues. Further, it provides protection for corporate whistle blowers by specifying that audit committees must establish procedures for employees' anonymous submission of concerns regarding accounting or auditing matters.

The Act also requires public companies to provide their audit committees with authority and funding to engage independent counsel and other advisers as they determine necessary in order to carry out their duties.

The Act defines "audit committee" to mean a committee established by and amongst a company's board of directors for the purpose of overseeing the accounting and financial reporting processes of the company and audits of its financial statements. If no such committee exists with respect to a company, the Act designates the entire board of directors as the audit committee.

See Act Section 301 at ¶ 1021.

¶ 402 Certification of Financial Statements

Congress believes that management should be held responsible for the financial representations of their companies. The Act therefore clearly establishes that CEOs and CFOs are responsible for the presentation of material in their company's financial reports. Under one of the recommendations put forward by the President on March 7, CEOs would personally attest each quarter that the financial statements and company disclosures accurately and fairly disclose the information of which the CEO is aware that a reasonable investor should have to make an informed investment decision.

In effect, the Act adopts this proposal by requiring CEOs and CFOs to certify, in periodic reports containing financial statements filed with the Commission the appropriateness of financial statements and disclosures contained therein, and that those financials and disclosures fairly present the company's operations and financial condition. These provisions reflect concern regarding the reliability of companies' audited financial statements.

Foreign reincorporations will have no effect on the certification required from CEOs and CFOs. It will still be required after the transfer of a company's domicile from inside the U.S. to outside the U.S.

More specifically, the Act requires that the principal executive officer and the principal financial officer must certify in each annual or quarterly report that:

(1) the signing officer has reviewed the report;

(2) based on the officer's knowledge, the report does not contain any untrue statement of a material fact or omit to state a material fact necessary in order to make the statements made, in light of the circumstances under which such statements were made, not misleading;

(3) based on such officer's knowledge, the financial statements, and other financial information included in the report, fairly present in all material respects the financial condition and results of operations of the issuer as of, and for, the periods presented in the report;

(4) the signing officers are responsible for establishing and maintaining internal controls and have designed such internal controls to ensure that material information relating to the company and its consolidated subsidiaries is made known to such officers by others within those entities, particularly during the period in which the periodic reports are being prepared. They must also have evaluated the effectiveness of the company's internal controls as of a date within 90 days prior to the report and presented their conclusions about the effectiveness of their internal controls based on their evaluation as of that date.

(5) the signing officers have disclosed to the company's auditors and the audit committee all significant deficiencies in the design or operation of internal controls which could adversely affect the company's ability to

record, process, summarize, and report financial data and have identified for the auditors any material weaknesses in internal controls; and any fraud, whether or not material, that involves management or other employees who have a significant role in the issuer's internal controls; and

(6) the signing officers have indicated in the report whether or not there were significant changes in internal controls or in other factors that could significantly affect internal controls subsequent to the date of their evaluation, including any corrective actions with regard to significant deficiencies and material weaknesses.

SEC rules implementing these provisions must be effective within 30 days of enactment.

Criminal Penalties

In Section 906 of the Act, Congress provides that the periodic reports must be accompanied by a written statement by the company's chief executive officer and chief financial officer (or equivalent thereof) certifying that information contained in the periodic report fairly presents, in all material respects, the financial condition and results of operations of the company. A person certifying a statement knowing that the periodic report accompanying the statement does not comport with all the requirements set forth in this section will be fined not more than $1 million or imprisoned not more than 10 years, or both. In addition, willfully certifying a statement knowing that the periodic report accompanying the statement does not comport with all the requirements set forth in this section carries a fine of up to $5 million or 20-years imprisonment, or both.

Federal Income Tax

Section 1001 declares that it is the sense of the Senate that the Federal income tax return of a corporation should be signed by its chief executive officer.

See Act Sections 302, 906, and 1001 at ¶ 1022, 1064, and 1065.

¶ 403 Improper Influence on Audits

The Act makes it unlawful for any corporate officer or director, or person acting under their direction, to fraudulently influence, coerce, manipulate, or mislead any accountant engaged in preparing an audit of that company, for the purpose of rendering the audit report misleading. The Commission is provided with exclusive authority to enforce this section. The Act establishes a 90-day deadline for proposed rules or regulations by the Commission under this section, and a 270-day deadline for final rules or regulations.

See Act Section 303 at ¶ 1023.

¶ 404 Forfeiture of Bonuses and Profits

The Act includes provisions designed to prevent CEOs or CFOs from making large profits by selling company stock, or receiving company bonuses, while management is misleading the public and regulators about the poor health of the company. The Act requires that in the case of accounting restatements that result from material non-compliance with SEC financial reporting requirements, CEOs and CFOs must disgorge bonuses and other incentive-based compensation and profits on stock sales, if the non-compliance results from misconduct. The required disgorgement applies to amounts received for the 12 months after the first public issuance or filing of a financial document embodying such financial reporting requirement. Under this section, the SEC may exempt any person from this requirement, as it deems necessary and appropriate.

See Act Section 304 at ¶ 1024.

¶ 405 Officer and Director Bars

The Act also empowers the SEC to bar persons from serving as officers or directors if they committed a securities law violation and their conduct demonstrated unfitness to serve as an officer or a director. Under current law, only a federal court can issue an order prohibiting a person from acting as an officer or director of a public company. These court orders are generally issued in SEC enforcement actions. The amendment gives the SEC the ability to bar an officer or director, who has committed an unlawful act, where the Commission has not yet instituted an enforcement action. (See remarks of Sen. Orrin Hatch, Cong. Rec. July 10, 2002, p. S6550.)

Similarly, currently it must be proved that an officer or director has both violated the securities laws, and has shown substantial unfitness to serve before a bar can be imposed. The Commission has argued that the substantial unfitness standard for imposing bars is inordinately high, causing courts to refrain from imposing bars even in cases of egregious misconduct. The Act rectifies this deficiency by modifying the standard governing imposition of officer and director bars from substantial unfitness to unfitness.

See Act Sections 305 and 1105 at ¶ 1025 and 1071.

¶ 406 Equitable Relief

The Commission has also suggested that it should be allowed to obtain additional relief in enforcement cases. For a securities law violation, currently an individual may be ordered to disgorge funds that he or she received as a result of the violation. Rather than limiting disgorgement to these gains, the Act will permit courts to impose any equitable relief necessary or appropriate to protect, and mitigate harm to, investors.

See Act Section 305 at ¶ 1025.

¶ 407 Insider Trades During Blackout Periods

In some cases, officers and directors have profited by selling off large portions of company stock during a time when employees were prevented from selling company stock in their Section 401(k) retirement plans. To address this problem, the Act prohibits key individuals from engaging in transactions involving any equity security of the issuer during a blackout period when at least half of the issuer's individual account plan participants are not permitted to purchase, sell, or otherwise transfer their interest in that equity security. This section applies to directors and executive officers in order to ensure that the prohibition is limited to individuals in policy-making positions.

The Act provides added protection for participants in retirement plans by requiring that they be provided with written notice at least 30 days before a blackout period. Two exceptions to the 30-day notice are provided. First, an exception is allowed in cases where a deferral of the blackout period to comply with the 30-day notice requirement would violate ERISA provisions that require fiduciaries to act exclusively on behalf of participants, and those that require trustees to act prudently in their decisions regarding plan assets. Second, an exception may be provided where the inability to provide the notice is due to unforeseeable events or circumstances beyond the reasonable control of the plan administrator.

Congress provided a 30-day notice requirement prior to a blackout so that workers and executives alike would know when the insider trading prohibition would be effective. (See remarks of Sen. Phil Gramm, Cong. Rec., July 15, 2002, p. S6757.) There appears to be broad consensus that pension plan administrators should be required to provide 30-days notice to affected plan participants before limiting their ability to exercise the rights provided through their pension plans. Congress believes that these advance blackout notices will become integral requirements for how pension plans will operate in the future. (See remarks of Sen. Charles Grassley, Cong. Rec., July 15, 2002, p. S6757.)

See Act Section 306 at ¶ 1026.

¶ 408 Attorney Professional Responsibility

Pursuant to an amendment offered by Sen. John Edwards, the Act makes lawyers notify company directors of management misconduct that top officers refuse to rectify. It would require the SEC to issue rules of professional conduct for lawyers. A lawyer who learned of a legal violation by a corporation would have to report that violation to corporate senior officers. If managers failed to correct a legal problem, lawyers then would have to inform the company board of directors.

More specifically, the SEC must adopt rules establishing minimum standards of professional conduct for attorneys appearing and practicing before the Commission in any way in the representation of public companies. This includes a rule requiring an attorney to report evidence of a material violation of securities law or breach of fiduciary duty or similar violation by the company or one of its agents to the chief legal counsel or the chief executive officer of the company. If the counsel or officer does not appropriately respond to the evidence (adopting, as necessary, appropriate remedial measures or sanctions with respect to the violation), the attorney must report the evidence to the board's audit committee or to another board committee comprised solely of directors not employed directly or indirectly by the company, or to the board of directors. The SEC must adopt the rules within 180 days of enactment.

As explained by Sen. Edwards, the SEC must establish rules to protect investors from unprofessional conduct by lawyers, conduct that violates the legal standards of the profession. The SEC must make one rule in particular, a rule with two parts. First, a lawyer with evidence of a material violation of the law has to report that evidence either to the chief legal counsel or the chief executive officer of the company. Second, if the person to whom that lawyer reports does not respond appropriately by remedying the violation, by doing something that makes sure it is cured, that lawyer has an obligation to go to the audit committee or to the board.

In addition, the duty to report applies only to evidence of a material violation of the law. That means no reporting is required for piddling violations or violations that do not amount to anything. The obligation to report is triggered only by violations that are material, that is, violations that a reasonable investor would want to know about. Also, when the evidence is reported within the company, the Act does not specify how a CEO or a general counsel should act to rectify the violation. That is because the appropriate response to cure the problem will vary dramatically, depending on the circumstances. If the CEO can do a short investigation, for example, and figure out that no violation occurred, then the obligation stops there. But if there is a serious violation of the law, the CEO has to act promptly to remedy the violation. If he or she does not, the lawyer has to go to the board. Finally, Sen. Edwards assured that nothing in the Act gives anybody a right to file a private lawsuit against anybody. Only the SEC can enforce the amendment. (See remarks of Sen. John Edwards, Cong. Rec., July 10, 2002, p. 6552.)

See Act Section 307 at ¶ 1027.

¶ 409 Funds for Investors

Section 308 of the Act take the civil penalties levied by the SEC as a result of any judicial or administrative action and directs them to a disgorgement fund for the benefit of harmed investors. It also authorizes the SEC to accept gifts and bequests for the disgorgement fund.

Section 308 also requires the SEC to develop methods to improve collection rates. The Commission must review and analyze enforcement actions over the last five years that have included proceedings to obtain civil penalties or disgorgements to identify areas where such proceedings may be utilized to efficiently and fairly provide restitution for injured investors; as well as other methods to more effectively provide restitution to injured investors, including methods to improve the collection rates for civil penalties and disgorgements.

The SEC must report its findings to Congress within 180 days after enactment, and must use the findings to revise its rules and regulations as necessary. The report must include a discussion of regulatory or legislative actions that are recommended or that may be necessary to address concerns identified in the study.

See Act Section 308 at ¶ 1028.

CHAPTER 5

ISSUER AND MANAGEMENT DISCLOSURE

¶ 501 Disclosures in Periodic Reports

Congress believes that it is an imperative for investors to have accurate and full financial information available on a timely basis in order to make informed investment decisions. Thus, for example, Section 401 requires financial statements filed with the SEC to reflect any material adjustments under GAAP that the auditor identifies.

In addition, Section 401 requires annual and quarterly reports filed with the SEC to disclose all material off-balance sheet transactions, arrangements, obligations (including contingent obligations), and other relationships of the company with unconsolidated entities or other persons that may have a material current or future effect on financial condition, changes in financial condition, results of operations, liquidity, capital expenditures, capital resources, or significant components of revenues or expenses. The SEC must complete rulemaking in this area within 180 days of enactment.

Pro Forma Disclosures

Congress also sought to address problems attendant to pro forma financial disclosures by requiring the SEC to adopt rules requiring that companies publish pro forma data with a reconciliation to comparable financial data calculated according to GAAP and in a way that is not misleading and does not contain untrue statements. The reconciliation presumes, and would require, the company to publish financial data calculated according to GAAP at the same time as it publishes pro forma data. This should enable investors to, at the least, simultaneously compare the pro forma financial data with the same types of financial disclosures, such as earnings, calculated according to GAAP for the comparable reporting period. The SEC must complete rulemaking in this area within 180 days of enactment.

Study on Special Purpose Entities

The Act directs the SEC to conduct a comprehensive study of all aspects of special purpose entities, including the extent of their use, the potential exposure faced by investors due to SPEs, whether SPEs should be disclosed on company balance sheets, if the material participation requirements are adequate, and if FASB's guidelines on SPEs are sufficient to protect investors. The SEC must make recommendations to Congress on SPEs to provide transparency and protection to investors if it determines that FASB's rules are insufficient.

See Act Section 401 at ¶ 1029.

¶ 502 Loans to Officers and Directors

Section 402 prohibits loans by a public company to any of its directors or executive officers. Originally, the Sarbanes bill would have mandated the disclosure of loans made by the company to its executive officers and directors. The Senate, however, adopted an amendment offered by Sen. Charles Schumer that makes it unlawful for any public company to make loans to its executive officers and directors. The loan prohibition is designed to sharply limit the types of hidden compensation that can be offered to executives without being fully disclosed to shareholders. (See remarks of Sen. Diane Feinstein, Cong. Rec., July 15, 2002, p. S6762.)

The Act ensures that the prohibition on loans to corporate executives will not apply retroactively to loans currently outstanding. Also, credit and charge cards issued by businesses to their employees will not be subject to the loan prohibition, nor will margin loans for personal securities brokerage accounts held by employees of a brokerage firm. This last was needed because the NYSE requires employees of securities firms to maintain margin loan accounts only with their own firm. There are also exceptions for home improvement and manufactured home loans. Finally, loans by financial institutions to their employees that are already subject to regulation by the Federal Reserve are exempted.

See Act Section 402 at ¶ 1030.

¶ 503 Insider Transactions

At present, Exchange Act Section 16(a) requires insiders to report trades by the tenth day of the month following the month in which the transaction was executed. Congress recognized that some investors find trades by insiders to be probative of whether investing in a company is desirable and feel that, in today's markets, the current deadline imposed by Section 16(a) allows too long a delay in reporting.

The Act amends Section 16(a) to require directors, officers and 10 percent equity holders to report their purchases and sales of securities more promptly, that is, by the end of the second day following the transaction, or such other time established by the SEC where the two-day period is not feasible. The purpose is to make available to investor's information about insider transactions more promptly so they can make better informed investment decisions. The changes take effect thirty days after enactment.

Within one year of enactment, Sarbanes-Oxley mandates three items:

(1) The two-day statement reporting insider trades must be filed electronically.

(2) The SEC must provide the two-day statement on a publicly accessible Internet site by the end of the business day following the filing.

(3) The company, if it maintains a corporate website, must provide the statement on that website by the end of the business day following the filing.

See Act Section 403 at ¶ 1031.

¶ 504 Management Assessment of Internal Controls

To enhance the quality of reporting and increase investor confidence, the Act requires that annual reports filed with the SEC must be accompanied by a statement by company management that management is responsible for creating and maintaining adequate internal controls. Management must also present its assessment of the effectiveness of those controls. A similar requirement was enacted in 1991 and has been imposed on depository institutions through Section 36 of the Federal Deposit Insurance Act.

In addition, the company's auditor must report on and attest to management's assessment of the company's internal controls. In requiring the registered public accounting firm preparing the audit report to attest to and report on management's assessment of internal controls, Congress does not intend that the auditor's evaluation be the subject of a separate engagement or the basis for increased charges or fees. High quality audits typically incorporate extensive internal control testing. Congress intends that the auditor's assessment of the company's system of internal controls should be considered to be a core responsibility of the auditor and an integral part of the audit report.

See Act Section 404 at ¶ 1032.

¶ 505 Investment Companies

The Act exempts registered investment companies from certain disclosure requirements. Thus, investment companies do not have to make a management statement assessing the effectiveness of internal controls, nor do they have to disclose material off-balance sheet transactions. Similarly, SEC rules mandated by Section 401 on pro forma financial information will not apply to investment companies. Congress believes that the objectives of those disclosure sections are adequately addressed by existing federal securities laws and the rules thereunder affecting investment companies. Finally, the ban on loans to directors or executive officers contained in Section 402 will not apply to investment companies.

See Act Section 405 at ¶ 1033.

¶ 506 Financial Officer Code of Ethics

Congress believes that investors have a legitimate interest in knowing whether a public company holds its financial officers to certain ethical standards in their financial dealings. Thus, the Act requires companies to disclose whether or not they have adopted a code of ethics for senior financial officers and, if not, why not.

In addition, it requires immediate disclosure of any change in or waiver of the company's code of ethics. Disclosure may be by filing a Form 8-K with the SEC, by the Internet or by other electronic means.

The Act states that the term code of ethics means such standards as are reasonably necessary to promote:

- Honest and ethical conduct, including the ethical handling of actual or apparent conflicts of interest between personal and professional relationships;

- Full, fair, accurate, timely, and understandable disclosure in the periodic reports required to be filed by the issuer; and

- Compliance with applicable governmental rules and regulations.

The Commission must propose rules to implement this section within 90 days of enactment and issue final rules within 180 days of enactment.

See Act Section 406 at ¶ 1034.

¶ 507 Audit Committee Financial Expert

It is axiomatic that audit committees play a pivotal role in corporate governance. Congress believes the effectiveness of the audit committee depends in part on its members' knowledge of and experience in auditing and financial matters. Investors may find it relevant in making their investment decisions whether a company's audit committee has at least one member who has relevant, sophisticated financial expertise with which to discharge his or her duties.

Thus, Section 407 requires the SEC to adopt rules requiring companies to disclose whether their audit committees include among their members at least one financial expert. In defining financial expert, the SEC must consider whether a person understands GAAP and financial statements, has experience preparing or auditing financial statements, has experience with internal accounting controls, and understands audit committee functions. The SEC must propose rules implementing this mandate within 90 days of enactment, and adopt final rules within 180 days of enactment.

See Act Section 407 at ¶ 1035.

¶ 508 Enhanced SEC Review of Disclosures

The SEC must regularly and systematically review corporate filings. Section 408 minimally requires SEC review of a company at least once every three years. In scheduling the reviews, the SEC must consider the following factors:

- Companies that have issued material misstatements of financial results;
- Companies with a stock price that has experienced significant volatility;
- Companies with the largest market capitalization;
- Emerging companies with disparities in price to earnings ratios;
- Companies whose operations significantly affect a material sector of the economy; and
- Any other relevant factors.

See Act Section 408 at ¶ 1036.

¶ 509 Real-Time Disclosures

Section 409 requires companies to disclose additional information concerning material changes in their financial conditions or operations on a rapid and current basis. These disclosures must be in plain English, which may include trend and qualitative information and graphic presentations, as the SEC determines is necessary or useful for the protection of investors and in the public interest. This provision empowers the SEC to determine the most effective way this disclosure should be made in order to be useful for the protection of investors.

See Act Section 409 at ¶ 1037.

CHAPTER 6

ANALYST CONFLICTS OF INTEREST

¶ 601 In General

Congress intended the Act to eliminate certain pressures on analysts that could compromise their objectivity and to provide disclosure to investors of certain conflicts of interest that can also influence the objectivity of the analyst in preparing a research report. Section 501 requires the Commission or a registered securities association or national securities exchange, within one year, to adopt rules designed to address conflicts of interest facing securities analysts.

The rules must be designed to foster greater public confidence in securities research and protect the objectivity and independence of stock analysts who publish research intended for the public by:

- Restricting the pre-publication clearance of such research or recommendations by investment banking or other staff not directly responsible for investment research;

- Limiting the supervision and compensatory evaluation of such research personnel to officials who are not engaged in investment banking activities; and

- Protecting securities analysts from retaliation or threats of retaliation by investment banking staff because of negative or otherwise unfavorable research reports that might adversely affect investment banking relations with the company described in the report, provided that the rules cannot limit the authority of a broker or dealer to discipline a securities analyst for causes other than such report in accordance with the firm's policies and procedures.

The rules must also define periods during which broker-dealers who participate in a public offering of securities as underwriters or dealers cannot publish research or recommendations about the company's securities. The booster shot is a type of situation that the SEC and the self-regulatory organizations should consider in framing such rules.

The rules must also define periods during which brokers or dealers participating in a public offering as underwriters or dealers should not distribute research reports relating to the issuer's securities.

Finally, the rules must establish structural and institutional safeguards within broker-dealers to assure that securities analysts preparing research reports are separated by appropriate informational partitions from the review, pressure, or oversight of those whose involvement in investment banking activities might potentially bias their judgment or supervision. As a catchall, the rules must address such other issues as the SEC or the SROs deem appropriate.

¶ 602 Disclosure of Conflicts

The Act also requires the SEC or a registered securities association or national securities exchange to adopt rules requiring disclosures about conflicts of interest in reports and public appearances. These disclosures must include:

- The extent to which the analyst holds securities in the company that is the subject of the research report.

- Whether compensation has been received from the company, subject to such exemptions as the SEC may determine appropriate and necessary to prevent disclosure of material non-public information regarding specific potential future investment banking transactions as is appropriate in the public interest and consistent with investor protection.

  In determining whether to grant an exemption, the Commission must consider the importance that Congress places on providing investors with this information for making investment decisions and the likelihood that stating an affirmative response would divulge material non-public information that would be understood by investors, particularly in light of the size and complexity of the brokerage firm. For example, a complex brokerage firm that has received money from an issuer may be far less likely to disclose material nonpublic information simply by responding 'yes,' and therefore not merit an exception, than a small firm that only is engaged to find buyers for an issuer and has received compensation. (See Senate Banking Committee Report No, 107-205.)

- Whether the company is or has recently been a client of the analyst's firm, and if so, the types of services provided. Note that the Act requires a description of the types of services provided, rather than a list of all specific services. This requirement is to enable the investor to assess whether the relationship is likely to influence the objectivity of the subjective portions of the research report.

- Whether the analyst received compensation based on an affiliate's investment banking revenues. Thus, the Act, while not eliminating deal-based pay, requires disclosure of whether the analyst received compensation based on an affiliate's investment banking revenues from the subject of any research report.

- Such other disclosures of conflicts of interest that are material to investors, research analysts, or the broker as the SEC or the SROs deem appropriate.

As explained by Sen. Sarbanes, if you are doing an analysis and if you are doing a report and a recommendation, you ought to disclose whether you own the company stocks or bonds, whether you have received compensation from the company, whether your firm has a client relationship with the company, and whether you are receiving compensation based on investment banking revenues from the company. These are not prohibitions, they are just disclosures. Elaborating further, Sen. Sarbanes noted:

> [I]f you are an investor and an analyst is making a recommendation and he puts up front in his analysis that he owns the company stock, or that he is receiving compensation from the company, or that his firm has a client relationship with the company, or that he is receiving compensation based on investment banking revenues received from the company, someone is going to look at this and say: wait a second. I have to take his recommendation in the context of his involvement. (See remarks of Sen. Paul Sarbanes, Cong., Rec., July 8, 2002, p. 6333.)

¶ 603 Anti-Retaliation Protections

When considering this legislation, Congress heard testimony about the serious problem of retaliation against analysts who wrote negative research reports. Acting on this, Congress inserted a provision in the Act requiring rules to protect securities analysts from retaliation or intimidation because of negative, or otherwise unfavorable, research reports, subject to the proviso that such rules may not limit a broker-dealer from disciplining a securities analyst in accordance with firm policies and procedures for causes other than writing such a research report.

The exception is intended to make certain that writing a negative research report does not protect an analyst who is, for example, incompetent or otherwise deficient. However, it is not intended to be used to permit a broker-dealer to discipline a good analyst for writing a negative report using a false pretext.

In adopting a proposed rule, the Senate Banking Committee said that the SEC or a self-regulatory organization should consider the recommendations of Professor John Coffee. In testimony of March 5, 2002, Professor Coffee recommended that a no-retaliation rule should not bar staff reductions or reduced bonuses based on economic downturns or individualized performance assessments.

¶ 604 Other Considerations

The Act authorizes the Commission, or a registered securities association or exchange at the Commission's direction, to create rules to address such other issues as it determines appropriate and to require such other disclosures of conflicts of interest that are material to investors, research analysts, or the broker or dealer as it deems appropriate. The prohibition of specific activities identified in the Act is not an exhaustive solution to the analyst conflicts problem, and Congress expects the Commission and the self-regulatory organizations to use their authority to apply such additional rules as they deem appropriate.

"Securities Analyst" Defined

Section 501 defines "securities analyst" to mean any associated person of a brokerage firm that is principally responsible for, and any associated person who reports to a securities analyst in connection with, the preparation of the substance of a research report, whether or not the person has the job title of "securities analyst." "Research report" is defined to mean a written or electronic communication that includes an analysis of equity securities of individual companies or industries, and that provides information reasonably sufficient on which to base an investment decision.

Rulemaking Deadline

The Act requires that rules be adopted within one year. Existing rules that satisfy the requirements of the Act do not have to be reproposed or readopted. Existing rules that do not contradict the Act or that impose requirements that are not imposed by the Act do not have to be withdrawn or reproposed. For example, self-regulatory organization rules that require disclosure of statistics regarding analyst ratings or of the securities holdings of an analyst's family members in a subject company are not adversely affected by this Act.

See Act Section 501 at ¶ 1039.

CHAPTER 7

SEC RESOURCES AND AUTHORITY

¶ 701 SEC Appropriations

Congress determined that it is necessary to increase the resources available to the SEC. Thus, Section 601 authorizes an appropriation of $776 million for the SEC for fiscal year 2003. This includes $102,700,000 to fund pay on a par with the federal bank regulators for SEC employees' salaries as well as their fringe benefits, as authorized by the Investor and Capital Markets Fee Relief Act.

The appropriation also includes $108,400,000 to fund enhanced information technology, security enhancements, and recovery and mitigation activities. Finally, the Act provides $98 million to fund at least 200 professionals to oversee auditors and auditing services, and additional staff to improve SEC investigative and disciplinary efforts and strengthen the SEC's oversight and regulation of market participants and of company disclosure, securities markets, and investment companies.

See Act Section 601 at ¶ 1041.

¶ 702 Discipline of Professionals

The SEC has a procedure to discipline professionals, including accountants, who lack the requisite qualifications to practice before the Commission. The Act codifies the SEC's authority in Rule 102(e) to censure or deny, temporarily or permanently, the privilege of appearing or practicing before it to any person whom the SEC, after notice and opportunity for hearing, finds: (1) does not possess the requisite qualifications to represent others; (2) is lacking in character or integrity or has engaged in unethical or improper professional conduct; or (3) has willfully violated, or willfully aided and abetted the violation of, any provision of the federal securities laws or the rules and regulations thereunder.

See Act Section 602 at ¶ 1042.

¶ 703 Penny Stock Bar

Under current law, the penny stock bar is available only in administrative proceedings. However, the Commission frequently brings cases involving serious microcap or penny stock fraud in federal district court in order to obtain injunctive relief. In such a case, if the SEC also wishes to obtain a penny stock bar, it must bring a separate administrative proceeding, typically after the district court case is concluded. The Commission would be able to obtain all necessary relief more efficiently if the district courts had the authority to order penny stock bars. Thus, the Act authorizes federal courts to impose penny stock bars, or conditionally or unconditionally and temporarily or permanently prohibit a person from participating in a penny stock offering. The Commission requested this authority in order to deal more swiftly with penny stock fraud.

See Act Section 603 at ¶ 1043.

¶ 704 Securities Industry Bar

In recent years, there has been a growing perception that fraud artists are able to exploit gaps in federal and state regulatory systems and to move from one sector of the financial services industry to another without sufficient impediment. The SEC lacks the enforcement authority to bar individuals from coming into the securities industry who have been found by other financial regulators to have engaged in fraudulent, deceptive, or dishonest conduct in other financial industries. The Act gives the SEC this power. In order to reduce the migration of fraud perpetrators into the securities industry, the SEC is authorized to bar from the securities industry persons who have been suspended or barred by a state securities, banking, or insurance regulator because of fraudulent, manipulative, or deceptive conduct.

See Act Section 604 at ¶ 1044.

¶ 705 Freeze Authority

The SEC would be allowed, during an investigation, to seek an order in federal court imposing a 45-day freeze on extraordinary payments to corporate executives. The order could be extended upon a showing of good cause. The targeted payments would be placed in escrow, ensuring that corporate assets are not improperly taken from an executive's personal benefit. If an executive is charged with violations of federal securities laws prior to the expiration of the court order, the escrow would continue until the conclusion of legal proceedings, again, with court approval.

The provision is designed to prevent corporate executives from enriching themselves while a company is subject to an SEC investigation, but before the SEC has gathered sufficient evidence to file formal charges. (See remarks of Sen. Orrin Hatch, Cong. Rec., July 10, 2002, p. S6550.)

See Act Section 1103 at ¶ 1069.

¶ 706 Rulemaking Power

The Act generally gives the SEC authority to promulgate rules consistent with the Act and provides that a violation of the Act, or of any rule of the Commission or of the new public company accounting oversight board will be treated for all purposes as a violation of the Exchange Act and the rules thereunder. Similarly, the new board will be treated as if it were a self-regulatory organization under the 1934 Act for purposes of the Commission's investigative and enforcement authority. It should be emphasized that the new board's own authority is limited to the work of accountants in auditing public companies; the board has no jurisdiction with respect to the work of accountants in performing audits of other companies.

The Act thus confirms that the Commission will have the authority to enforce the Act directly. It is also made clear that nothing in the Act or the rules of the new board limits the Commission's own authority over accounting firms and their personnel, or accounting, auditing, independence, or other standards relating to auditors' reports.

See Act Section 3 at ¶ 1000B.

Chapter 8

Studies and Reports

¶ 801 Consolidation of Accounting Firms

The Act directs that a number of studies be conducted and reports filed. For example, Section 701 directs the Comptroller General, in consultation with the SEC, similar regulatory agencies of the other G-7 nations, and the Department of Justice, to conduct a study identifying the factors that have led to the consolidation of public accounting firms since 1989, the impact of such consolidation, and solutions to any problems caused by such consolidation. The study must also examine the problems faced by businesses as a result of limited competition among public accounting firms, and consider whether federal or state regulations impede competition among public accounting firms. A report is to be submitted to Congress within one year of enactment.

This study is necessary to evaluate the impact that consolidation has had on quality of audit services, audit costs, auditor independence, or other problems for businesses. In addition, the study is necessary to determine what can be done to increase competition among accounting firms and whether federal or state regulations impede competition. (See remarks of Sen. Daniel Akaka, Cong. Rec., July 15, 2002, p. S6760.)

See Act Section 701 at ¶ 1045.

¶ 802 Credit Rating Agencies

In addition, Section 702 directs the SEC to conduct a study of the role of credit rating agencies in the operation of the securities market, including an examination of the role of credit rating agencies in the evaluation of issuers, the importance of that role to investors, any impediments to the rating agencies' accurate appraisal of issuers, any barriers to entry into the business of acting as a credit rating agency, measures to improve the dissemination of information about issuers when credit rating agencies announce credit ratings, and any conflicts of interest in the operation of credit rating agencies. A report must be submitted to the President and Congress within 180 days of enactment.

See Act Section 702 at ¶ 1046.

¶ 803 Aiding and Abetting

An amendment to the Senate bill offered by Sen. Richard Shelby has been codified as Section 703 of Sarbanes-Oxley. It calls for a study of aiding and abetting liability. Specifically, the SEC must conduct a study to determine in a specified four-year period the number of securities professionals who have been found to have aided and abetted a violation of the federal securities laws, but who have not been sanctioned, disciplined, or otherwise penalized as a primary violator in any administrative action or civil proceeding and who have been found to have been primary violators of the federal securities laws. The study must also include a description of the federal securities laws violations committed by aiders and abettors and by primary violators, including:

- The specific provisions of the federal securities laws violated;
- The specific sanctions and penalties imposed on such aiders and abettors and primary violators, including the amount of any monetary penalties assessed and collected from them;
- The occurrence of multiple violations by the same person or persons either as an aider or abettor or as a primary violator; and
- Whether as to each such violator disciplinary sanctions have been imposed, including any censure, suspension, temporary bar, or permanent bar to practice before the Commission.

Similarly, the study must also include the amount of disgorgement, restitution or any other fines or payments the SEC has assessed and collected from, aiders and abettors and from primary violators.

For purposes of the study, the Act defines securities professionals to mean public accountants, public accounting firms, investment bankers, investment advisers, brokers, dealers, attorneys, and other securities professionals practicing before the Commission. The four-year period specified for the study is from January 1, 1998 until December 31, 2001. A report based on the study must be submitted to Congress within six months of enactment.

See Act Section 703 at ¶ 1047.

¶ 804 Enforcement Actions

Section 704 requires the Commission to review and analyze all of its enforcement actions involving violations of securities law reporting requirements and all restatements of financial statements over the past five years. The purpose of the review is to identify the areas of reporting most susceptible to fraud, inappropriate manipulation or inappropriate earnings management, such as revenue recognition and the accounting treatment of off-balance sheet special purpose entities. The Commission must report its findings to Congress within 180 days of enactment, and use its findings to revise rules and regulations as necessary.

See Act Section 704 at ¶ 1048.

¶ 805 Investment Banks

Section 705 directs the General Accounting Office (GAO) to conduct a study on the role of investment banks and financial advisers in assisting public companies in manipulating their earnings and obfuscating their true financial condition. The statute directs the GAO to address the role of investment banks in the bankruptcy of Enron Corporation, the failure of Global Crossing, and in the creation and marketing of transactions designed to obfuscate a company's financial picture. The GAO must report to Congress within 180 days of the law's enactment.

Regarding the collapse of the Enron Corporation, the study should include the design and implementation of derivatives transactions, transactions involving special purpose vehicles, and other financing arrangements that may have had the effect of altering the company's reported financial statements in ways that obscured the company's true financial picture.

See Act Section 705 at ¶ 1049.

Chapter 9

Fraud and Criminal Penalties

The Act contains provisions generally designed to restore accountability by punishing and preventing fraud, preserving the evidence of fraud, and protecting victims of fraud.

¶ 901 Securities Fraud Felony

Section 807 creates a new federal felony for securities fraud with a 25-year maximum penalty. The provision makes it easier, in a limited class of cases, to prove securities fraud. Currently prosecutors are forced to resort to a patchwork of technical offenses and regulations that criminalize particular violations of securities law, or to treat the cases as generic mail or wire fraud. This new provision would criminalize any scheme or artifice to defraud persons in connection with securities of public companies or to obtain their money or property.

Addressing concerns that it may be hard to define a scheme or artifice to defraud, Sen. John McCain pointed out that full and honest disclosure of material dealings and accounting treatments is the best way for corporate officers to protect themselves and those who invest in their companies. He emphasized that, when criminal charges are pursued, it is not necessarily the firm that should be charged but senior corporate officers who should be prosecuted. (See Cong. Rec., July 10, 2002, p. S. 6528.)

See Act Section 807 at ¶ 1057.

¶ 902 Corporate Audit Records

The Act also creates two new anti-shredding penalties, which set clear requirements for preserving financial audit guides and close loopholes in current anti-shredding laws. These provisions set a clear requirement that corporate audit documents must be saved for five years, a time period selected because it happens to be the statute of limitation for most federal crimes.

More specifically, the Act creates two new criminal statutes that would clarify current criminal laws relating to the destruction or fabrication of evidence and the preservation of financial and audit records. There will be a 20-year criminal penalty for the destruction or creation of evidence with the intent to obstruct a federal investigation. There will be a new ten-year criminal penalty for the willful failure to preserve, for a minimum of five years, audit or review work papers of companies that issue securities.

The SEC must adopt rules, within 180 days, relating to the retention of relevant records such as work papers, documents that form the basis of an audit or review, memoranda, correspondence, communications, other documents, and records (including electronic records) that are created, sent, or received in connection with an audit or review and contain conclusions, opinions, analyses, or financial data relating to such an audit or review, which is conducted by any accountant who conducts an audit of an issuer of securities to which Exchange Act Section 10A(a) applies.

See Section 802 at ¶ 1052.

¶ 903 Statute of Limitations

Section 804 lengthens the statute of limitation for securities fraud by extending it from the current earlier of from one year after the fraud was discovered but no more than three years from the date of the fraud regardless of when it was discovered to two years from discovery or five years from the fraud. The new limitations period will apply to all proceedings commenced on or after enactment.

The previous limitations period of one year after discovery of the facts constituting the violation and within three years after the violation was established in 1991 by the U.S. Supreme Court in *Lampf, Pleva, Lipkind, Prupis & Petigrow v. Gilbertson*, 1991 CCH Dec. ¶ 96,034. Prior to the Court's 1991 ruling, federal courts generally borrowed and applied the most analogous state limitations period.

See Act Section 804 at ¶ 1054.

¶ 904 Bankruptcy Discharges

The Act protects victims of securities fraud by amending the bankruptcy code to make judgments and settlements based on securities law violations nondischargeable. Section 803 is designed to prevent the corporate wrongdoer, the CEO or CFO, from sheltering their assets under the umbrella of bankruptcy and protecting them from judgments and settlements arising from federal and state securities law violations. (See remarks of Sen. John McCain, Cong. Rec., July 10, 2002, p. S6529.)

See Act Section 803 at ¶ 1053.

¶ 905 Obstruction of Justice

The Act strengthens an existing federal offense that is often used to prosecute document shredding and other forms of obstruction of justice. Section 1520 of Title 18 of the United States Code currently prohibits individuals from persuading others to engage in obstructive conduct. However, it does not prohibit an act of destruction committed by a defendant acting alone. While other existing obstruction of justice statutes cover acts of destruction that are committed by and individual acting alone, such statutes have been interpreted as applying only where a proceeding is pending, and a subpoena has been issued for the evidence that is destroyed.

This amendment closes this loophole by broadening the scope of Section 1512. The Act permits the government to prosecute an individual who acts alone in destroying evidence, even where the evidence is destroyed prior to the issuance of a grand jury subpoena.

A person who acts with the intent to obstruct an investigation should be criminally liable even if he or she acts alone in destroying or altering documents. This amendment will ensure that individuals acting alone would be liable for such criminal acts. (See remarks of Sen. Orrin Hatch, Cong. Rec. July 10, 2002, p. 6550.)

See Act Section 1102 at ¶ 1068.

¶ 906 Mail and Wire Fraud

The Act increases the maximum prison term for mail and wire fraud offenses, from 5 years to 20 years. Because prosecutors frequently use the mail and wire statutes to charge acts of corporate misconduct, Congress believed it was important to ensure that the penalties that apply to such offenses are sufficiently severe to deter and punish corporate wrongdoers. (See remarks of Sen. Orrin Hatch, Cong. Rec., July 10, 2002, p. S6550.)

See Act Section 903 at ¶ 1061.

¶ 907 Sentencing Guidelines

The Act directs the U.S. Sentencing Commission to review the sentencing guidelines that apply to acts of corporate misconduct and to enhance the prison time that would apply to criminal frauds committed by corporate officers and directors. Congress enacted this enhancement because corporate leaders who hold high offices and breach their duties of trust should face stiff penalties. (See remarks of Sen. Orrin Hatch, Cong. Rec., July 10, 2002, p. 6550.)

See Act Section 1104 at ¶ 1070.

¶ 908 Whisteblower Protections

The Act creates federal protection for whistle blowers. It provides whistleblower protection to employees of public companies when they act lawfully to disclose information about fraudulent activities within their company.

The statute specifically protects employees when they take lawful acts to disclose information or otherwise assist criminal investigators, federal regulators, Congress, supervisors (or other proper people within a corporation), or parties in a judicial proceeding in detecting and stopping fraud. If the employer does take illegal action in retaliation for lawful and protected conduct, the statute allows the employee to file a complaint with the Department of Labor.

The employee can bring the matter to federal court only if the Department of Labor does not resolve the matter in 180 days (and there is no showing that such delay is due to the bad faith of the claimant) as a normal case in law or equity, with no amount in controversy requirement. With regard to remedies, the statute provides for the reinstatement of the whistle blower, backpay, and compensatory damages to make a victim whole, including reasonable attorney fees and costs, as remedies if the claimant prevails. (See Senate Report No. 107-146.)

This provision was part of the Corporate and Criminal Fraud Accountability Act of 2002 (S. 2010) and was placed into the Sarbanes-Oxley Act pursuant to an amendment offered by Sen. Patrick Leahy.

Criminal Penalty

In Section 1107, the Act provides that whoever knowingly, with the intent to retaliate, takes any action harmful to any person, including interference with the lawful employment or livelihood of any person, for providing to a law enforcement officer any truthful information relating to the commission or possible commission of any federal offense, will be subject to up to 10 years in prison.

See Act Sections 806 and 1107 at ¶ 1056 and 1073.

¶ 909 Exchange Act Penalties

The Act amends Exchange Act Section 32(a) to increase the criminal penalties for those who file false statements with the SEC to a maximum penalty of $5 million and 20 years in prison. This is up from $1 million and ten years in prison. If a corporation files a false statement those fines can increase up to a maximum of $25 million. Under prior law, the maximum corporate fine was $2,500,000.

See Act Section 1106 at ¶ 1072.

¶ 910 ERISA Penalties

Under the Employment Retirement Security Act of 1974, a violation for essentially squandering someone's pension to the tune of tens of millions, maybe billions, of dollars is a misdemeanor with a maximum penalty of one year. The Act increases the penalty for criminal violation of ERISA to 1 to 10 years, based on the value of what is stolen in ERISA. If the loss in ERISA is a $20,000 pension versus several billion dollars' worth, the Sentencing Commission can make that judgment, as they do now, to have the penalty be from one but up to 10 years. Monetary penalties are also increased. (See remarks of Sen. Joseph Biden, Cong. Rec., July 10, 2002, p. S6546.)

See Act Section 904 at ¶ 1062.

PART II LAW TEXT—SARBANES-OXLEY ACT OF 2002

One Hundred Seventh Congress of the United States of America

AT THE SECOND SESSION

Begun and held at the City of Washington on Wednesday, the twenty-third day of January, two thousand and two

An Act

To protect and investors by improving the accuracy and reliability of corporate disclosures made pursuant to the securities laws, and for other purposes

Be it enacted by the Senate and House of Representatives of the United States of America in Congress assembled

[¶ 1000] Section 1—SHORT TITLE; TABLE OF CONTENTS.

(a) SHORT TITLE—This Act may be cited as the 'Sarbanes-Oxley Act of 2002'.

(b) TABLE OF CONTENTS—The table of contents for this Act is as follows:

TITLE I—PUBLIC COMPANY ACCOUNTING OVERSIGHT BOARD

TITLE II—AUDITOR INDEPENDENCE

TITLE III—CORPORATE RESPONSIBILITY

TITLE IV—ENHANCED FINANCIAL DISCLOSURES

TITLE V—ANALYST CONFLICTS OF INTEREST

TITLE VI—COMMISSION RESOURCES AND AUTHORITY

TITLE VII—STUDIES AND REPORTS

TITLE VIII—CORPORATE AND CRIMINAL FRAUD ACCOUNTABILITY

TITLE IX—WHITE-COLLAR CRIME PENALTY ENHANCEMENTS

TITLE X—CORPORATE TAX RETURNS

TITLE XI—CORPORATE FRAUD AND ACCOUNTABILITY

[¶ 1000A] Section 2—DEFINITIONS.

(a) IN GENERAL—In this Act, the following definitions shall apply:

(1) APPROPRIATE STATE REGULATORY AUTHORITY—The term 'appropriate State regulatory authority' means the State agency or other authority responsible for the licensure or other regulation of the practice of accounting in the State or States having jurisdiction over a registered public accounting firm or associated person thereof, with respect to the matter in question.

(2) AUDIT—The term 'audit' means an examination of the financial statements of any issuer by an independent public accounting firm in accordance with the rules of the Board or the Commission (or, for the period preceding the adoption of applicable rules of the Board under section 103, in accordance with then-applicable generally accepted auditing and related standards for such purposes), for the purpose of expressing an opinion on such statements.

(3) AUDIT COMMITTEE—The term 'audit committee' means—

(A) a committee (or equivalent body) established by and amongst the board of directors of an issuer for the purpose of overseeing the accounting and financial reporting processes of the issuer and audits of the financial statements of the issuer; and

(B) if no such committee exists with respect to an issuer, the entire board of directors of the issuer.

(4) AUDIT REPORT—The term 'audit report' means a document or other record—

(A) prepared following an audit performed for purposes of compliance by an issuer with the requirements of the securities laws; and

(B) in which a public accounting firm either—

(i) sets forth the opinion of that firm regarding a financial statement, report, or other document; or

(ii) asserts that no such opinion can be expressed.

(5) BOARD—The term 'Board' means the Public Company Accounting Oversight Board established under section 101.

(6) COMMISSION—The term 'Commission' means the Securities and Exchange Commission.

(7) ISSUER—The term 'issuer' means an issuer (as defined in section 3 of the Securities Exchange Act of 1934 (15 U.S.C. 78c)), the securities of which are registered under section 12 of that Act (15 U.S.C. 78l), or that is required to file reports under section 15(d) (15 U.S.C. 78o(d)), or that files or has filed a registration statement that has not yet become effective under the Securities Act of 1933 (15 U.S.C. 77a et seq.), and that it has not withdrawn.

(8) NON-AUDIT SERVICES—The term 'non-audit services' means any professional services provided to an issuer by a registered public accounting firm, other than those provided to an issuer in connection with an audit or a review of the financial statements of an issuer.

(9) PERSON ASSOCIATED WITH A PUBLIC ACCOUNTING FIRM—

(A) IN GENERAL—The terms 'person associated with a public accounting firm' (or with a 'registered public accounting firm') and 'associated person of a public accounting firm' (or of a 'registered public accounting firm') mean any individual proprietor, partner, shareholder, principal, accountant, or other professional employee of a public accounting firm, or any other independent contractor or entity that, in connection with the preparation or issuance of any audit report—

(i) shares in the profits of, or receives compensation in any other form from, that firm; or

(ii) participates as agent or otherwise on behalf of such accounting firm in any activity of that firm.

(B) EXEMPTION AUTHORITY—The Board may, by rule, exempt persons engaged only in ministerial tasks from the definition in subparagraph (A), to the extent that the Board determines that any such exemption is consistent with the purposes of this Act, the public interest, or the protection of investors.

(10) PROFESSIONAL STANDARDS—The term 'professional standards' means—

(A) accounting principles that are—

(i) established by the standard setting body described in section 19(b) of the Securities Act of 1933, as amended by this Act, or prescribed by the Commission under section 19(a) of that Act (15 U.S.C. 17a(s)) or section 13(b) of the Securities Exchange Act of 1934 (15 U.S.C. 78a(m)); and

(ii) relevant to audit reports for particular issuers, or dealt with in the quality control system of a particular registered public accounting firm; and

(B) auditing standards, standards for attestation engagements, quality control policies and procedures, ethical and competency standards, and independence standards (including rules implementing title II) that the Board or the Commission determines—

(i) relate to the preparation or issuance of audit reports for issuers; and

(ii) are established or adopted by the Board under section 103(a), or are promulgated as rules of the Commission.

(11) PUBLIC ACCOUNTING FIRM—The term 'public accounting firm' means—

(A) a proprietorship, partnership, incorporated association, corporation, limited liability company, limited liability partnership, or other legal entity that is engaged in the practice of public accounting or preparing or issuing audit reports; and

(B) to the extent so designated by the rules of the Board, any associated person of any entity described in subparagraph (A).

(12) REGISTERED PUBLIC ACCOUNTING FIRM—The term 'registered public accounting firm' means a public accounting firm registered with the Board in accordance with this Act.

(13) RULES OF THE BOARD—The term 'rules of the Board' means the bylaws and rules of the Board (as submitted to, and approved, modified, or amended by the Commission, in accordance with section 107), and those stated policies, practices, and interpretations of the Board that the Commission, by rule, may deem to be rules of the Board, as necessary or appropriate in the public interest or for the protection of investors.

(14) SECURITY—The term 'security' has the same meaning as in section 3(a) of the Securities Exchange Act of 1934 (15 U.S.C. 78c(a)).

(15) SECURITIES LAWS—The term 'securities laws' means the provisions of law referred to in section 3(a)(47) of the Securities Exchange Act of 1934 (15 U.S.C. 78c(a)(47)), as amended by this Act, and includes the rules, regulations, and orders issued by the Commission thereunder.

(16) STATE—The term 'State' means any State of the United States, the District of Columbia, Puerto Rico, the Virgin Islands, or any other territory or possession of the United States.

(b) CONFORMING AMENDMENT—Section 3(a)(47) of the Securities Exchange Act of 1934 (15 U.S.C. 78c(a)(47)) is amended by inserting 'the Sarbanes-Oxley Act of 2002,' before 'the Public'.

[¶ 1000B] Section 3—COMMISSION RULES AND ENFORCEMENT.

(a) REGULATORY ACTION—The Commission shall promulgate such rules and regulations, as may be necessary or appropriate in the public interest or for the protection of investors, and in furtherance of this Act.

(b) ENFORCEMENT—

(1) IN GENERAL—A violation by any person of this Act, any rule or regulation of the Commission issued under this Act, or any rule of the Board shall be treated for all purposes in the same manner as a violation of the Securities Exchange Act of 1934 (15 U.S.C. 78a et seq.) or the rules and regulations issued thereunder, consistent with the provisions of this Act, and

any such person shall be subject to the same penalties, and to the same extent, as for a violation of that Act or such rules or regulations.

(2) INVESTIGATIONS, INJUNCTIONS, AND PROSECUTION OF OFFENSES—Section 21 of the Securities Exchange Act of 1934 (15 U.S.C. 78u) is amended—

(A) in subsection (a)(1), by inserting 'the rules of the Public Company Accounting Oversight Board, of which such person is a registered public accounting firm or a person associated with such a firm,' after 'is a participant,';

(B) in subsection (d)(1), by inserting 'the rules of the Public Company Accounting Oversight Board, of which such person is a registered public accounting firm or a person associated with such a firm,' after 'is a participant,';

(C) in subsection (e), by inserting 'the rules of the Public Company Accounting Oversight Board, of which such person is a registered public accounting firm or a person associated with such a firm,' after 'is a participant,'; and

(D) in subsection (f), by inserting 'or the Public Company Accounting Oversight Board' after 'self-regulatory organization' each place that term appears.

(3) CEASE-AND-DESIST PROCEEDINGS—Section 21C(c)(2) of the Securities Exchange Act of 1934 (15 U.S.C. 78u-3(c)(2)) is amended by inserting 'registered public accounting firm (as defined in section 2 of the Sarbanes-Oxley Act of 2002),' after 'government securities dealer,'.

(4) ENFORCEMENT BY FEDERAL BANKING AGENCIES—Section 12(i) of the Securities Exchange Act of 1934 (15 U.S.C. 78l(i)) is amended by—

(A) striking 'sections 12,' each place it appears and inserting 'sections 10A(m), 12,'; and

(B) striking 'and 16,' each place it appears and inserting 'and 16 of this Act, and sections 302, 303, 304, 306, 401(b), 404, 406, and 407 of the Sarbanes-Oxley Act of 2002,'.

(c) EFFECT ON COMMISSION AUTHORITY—Nothing in this Act or the rules of the Board shall be construed to impair or limit—

(1) the authority of the Commission to regulate the accounting profession, accounting firms, or persons associated with such firms for purposes of enforcement of the securities laws;

(2) the authority of the Commission to set standards for accounting or auditing practices or auditor independence, derived from other provisions of the securities laws or the rules or regulations thereunder, for purposes of the preparation and issuance of any audit report, or otherwise under applicable law; or

(3) the ability of the Commission to take, on the initiative of the Commission, legal, administrative, or disciplinary action against any registered public accounting firm or any associated person thereof.

TITLE I—PUBLIC COMPANY ACCOUNTING OVERSIGHT BOARD

[¶ 1001] Section 101—ESTABLISHMENT; ADMINISTRATIVE PROVISIONS.

(a) ESTABLISHMENT OF BOARD—There is established the Public Company Accounting Oversight Board, to oversee the audit of public companies that are subject to the securities laws, and related matters, in order to protect the interests of investors and further the public interest in the preparation of informative, accurate, and independent audit reports for companies the securities of which are sold to, and held by and for, public investors. The Board shall be a body corporate, operate as a nonprofit corporation, and have succession until dissolved by an Act of Congress.

(b) STATUS—The Board shall not be an agency or establishment of the United States Government, and, except as otherwise provided in this Act, shall be subject to, and have all the powers conferred upon a nonprofit corporation by, the District of Columbia Nonprofit Corporation Act. No member or person employed by, or agent for, the Board shall be deemed to be an officer or employee of or agent for the Federal Government by reason of such service.

(c) DUTIES OF THE BOARD—The Board shall, subject to action by the Commission under section 107, and once a determination is made by the Commission under subsection (d) of this section—

(1) register public accounting firms that prepare audit reports for issuers, in accordance with section 102;

(2) establish or adopt, or both, by rule, auditing, quality control, ethics, independence, and other standards relating to the preparation of audit reports for issuers, in accordance with section 103;

(3) conduct inspections of registered public accounting firms, in accordance with section 104 and the rules of the Board;

(4) conduct investigations and disciplinary proceedings concerning, and impose appropriate sanctions where justified upon, registered public accounting firms and associated persons of such firms, in accordance with section 105;

(5) perform such other duties or functions as the Board (or the Commission, by rule or order) determines are necessary or appropriate to promote high professional standards among, and improve the quality of audit services offered by, registered public accounting firms and associated persons thereof, or otherwise to carry out this Act, in order to protect investors, or to further the public interest;

(6) enforce compliance with this Act, the rules of the Board, professional standards, and the securities laws relating to the preparation and issuance of audit reports and the obligations and liabilities of accountants with respect thereto, by registered public accounting firms and associated persons thereof; and

(7) set the budget and manage the operations of the Board and the staff of the Board.

(d) COMMISSION DETERMINATION—The members of the Board shall take such action (including hiring of staff, proposal of rules, and adoption of initial and transitional auditing and other professional standards) as may be necessary or appropriate to enable the Commission to determine, not later than 270 days after the date of enactment of this Act, that the Board is so organized and has the capacity to carry out the requirements of this title, and to enforce compliance with this title by registered public accounting firms and associated persons thereof. The Commission shall be responsible, prior to the appointment of the Board, for the planning for the establishment and administrative transition to the Board's operation.

(e) BOARD MEMBERSHIP—

(1) COMPOSITION—The Board shall have 5 members, appointed from among prominent individuals of integrity and reputation who have a demonstrated commitment to the interests of investors and the public, and an understanding of the responsibilities for and nature of the financial disclosures required of issuers under the securities laws and the obligations of accountants with respect to the preparation and issuance of audit reports with respect to such disclosures.

(2) LIMITATION—Two members, and only 2 members, of the Board shall be or have been certified public accountants pursuant to the laws of 1 or more States, provided that, if 1 of those 2 members is the chairperson, he or she may not have been a practicing certified public accountant for at least 5 years prior to his or her appointment to the Board.

(3) FULL-TIME INDEPENDENT SERVICE—Each member of the Board shall serve on a full-time basis, and may not, concurrent with service on the Board, be employed by any other person or engage in any other professional or business activity. No member of the Board may share in any of the profits of, or receive payments from, a public accounting firm (or any other person, as determined by rule of the Commission), other than fixed continuing payments, subject to such conditions as the Commission may impose, under standard arrangements for the retirement of members of public accounting firms.

(4) APPOINTMENT OF BOARD MEMBERS—

(A) INITIAL BOARD—Not later than 90 days after the date of enactment of this Act, the Commission, after consultation with the Chairman of the Board of Governors of the Federal Reserve System and the Secretary of the Treasury, shall appoint the chairperson and other initial members of the Board, and shall designate a term of service for each.

(B) VACANCIES—A vacancy on the Board shall not affect the powers of the Board, but shall be filled in the same manner as provided for appointments under this section.

(5) TERM OF SERVICE—

(A) IN GENERAL—The term of service of each Board member shall be 5 years, and until a successor is appointed, except that—

(i) the terms of office of the initial Board members (other than the chairperson) shall expire in annual increments, 1 on each of the first 4 anniversaries of the initial date of appointment; and

(ii) any Board member appointed to fill a vacancy occurring before the expiration of the term for which the predecessor was appointed shall be appointed only for the remainder of that term.

(B) TERM LIMITATION—No person may serve as a member of the Board, or as chairperson of the Board, for more than 2 terms, whether or not such terms of service are consecutive.

(6) REMOVAL FROM OFFICE—A member of the Board may be removed by the Commission from office, in accordance with section 107(d)(3), for good cause shown before the expiration of the term of that member.

(f) POWERS OF THE BOARD—In addition to any authority granted to the Board otherwise in this Act, the Board shall have the power, subject to section 107—

(1) to sue and be sued, complain and defend, in its corporate name and through its own counsel, with theapproval of the Commission, in any Federal, State, or other court;

(2) to conduct its operations and maintain offices, and to exercise all other rights and powers authorized by this Act, in any State, without regard to any qualification, licensing, or other provision of law in effect in such State (or a political subdivision thereof);

(3) to lease, purchase, accept gifts or donations of or otherwise acquire, improve, use, sell, exchange, or convey, all of or an interest in any property, wherever situated;

(4) to appoint such employees, accountants, attorneys, and other agents as may be necessary or appropriate, and to determine their qualifications, define their duties, and fix their salaries or other compensation (at a level that is comparable to private sector self-regulatory, accounting, technical, supervisory, or other staff or management positions);

(5) to allocate, assess, and collect accounting support fees established pursuant to section 109, for the Board, and other fees and charges imposed under this title; and

(6) to enter into contracts, execute instruments, incur liabilities, and do any and all other acts and things necessary, appropriate, or incidental to the conduct of its operations and the exercise of its obligations, rights, and powers imposed or granted by this title.

(g) RULES OF THE BOARD—The rules of the Board shall, subject to the approval of the Commission—

(1) provide for the operation and administration of the Board, the exercise of its authority, and the performance of its responsibilities under this Act;

(2) permit, as the Board determines necessary or appropriate, delegation by the Board of any of its functions to an individual member or employee of the Board, or to a division of the Board, including functions with respect to hearing, determining, ordering, certifying, reporting, or otherwise acting as to any matter, except that—

(A) the Board shall retain a discretionary right to review any action pursuant to any such delegated function, upon its own motion;

(B) a person shall be entitled to a review by the Board with respect to any matter so delegated, and the decision of the Board upon such review shall be deemed to be the action of the Board for all purposes (including appeal or review thereof); and

(C) if the right to exercise a review described in subparagraph (A) is declined, or if no such review is sought within the time stated in the rules of the Board, then the action taken by the holder of such delegation shall for all purposes, including appeal or review thereof, be deemed to be the action of the Board;

(3) establish ethics rules and standards of conduct for Board members and staff, including a bar on practice before the Board (and the Commission, with respect to Board-related matters) of 1 year for former members of the Board, and appropriate periods (not to exceed 1 year) for former staff of the Board; and

(4) provide as otherwise required by this Act.

(h) ANNUAL REPORT TO THE COMMISSION—The Board shall submit an annual report (including its audited financial statements) to the Commission, and the Commission shall transmit a copy of that report to the Committee on Banking, Housing, and Urban Affairs of the Senate, and the Committee on Financial Services of the House of Representatives, not later than 30 days after the date of receipt of that report by the Commission.

[¶ 1002] Section 102—REGISTRATION WITH THE BOARD.

(a) MANDATORY REGISTRATION—Beginning 180 days after the date of the determination of the Commission under section 101(d), it shall be unlawful for any person that is not a registered public accounting firm to prepare or issue, or to participate in the preparation or issuance of, any audit report with respect to any issuer.

(b) APPLICATIONS FOR REGISTRATION—

(1) FORM OF APPLICATION—A public accounting firm shall use such form as the Board may prescribe, by rule, to apply for registration under this section.

(2) CONTENTS OF APPLICATIONS—Each public accounting firm shall submit, as part of its application for registration, in such detail as the Board shall specify—

(A) the names of all issuers for which the firm prepared or issued audit reports during the immediately preceding calendar year, and for which the firm expects to prepare or issue audit reports during the current calendar year;

(B) the annual fees received by the firm from each such issuer for audit services, other accounting services, and non-audit services, respectively;

(C) such other current financial information for the most recently completed fiscal year of the firm as the Board may reasonably request;

(D) a statement of the quality control policies of the firm for its accounting and auditing practices;

(E) a list of all accountants associated with the firm who participate in or contribute to the preparation of audit reports, stating the license or certification number of each such person, as well as the State license numbers of the firm itself;

(F) information relating to criminal, civil, or administrative actions or disciplinary proceedings pending against the firm or any associated person of the firm in connection with any audit report;

(G) copies of any periodic or annual disclosure filed by an issuer with the Commission during the immediately preceding calendar year which discloses accounting disagreements between such issuer and the firm in connection with an audit report furnished or prepared by the firm for such issuer; and

(H) such other information as the rules of the Board or the Commission shall specify as necessary or appropriate in the public interest or for the protection of investors.

(3) CONSENTS—Each application for registration under this subsection shall include—

(A) a consent executed by the public accounting firm to cooperation in and compliance with any request for testimony or the production of documents made by the Board in the furtherance of its authority and responsibilities under this title (and an agreement to secure and enforce similar consents from each of the associated persons of the public accounting firm as a condition of their continued employment by or other association with such firm); and

(B) a statement that such firm understands and agrees that cooperation and compliance, as described in the consent required by subparagraph (A), and the securing and enforcement of such consents from its associated persons, in accordance with the rules of the Board, shall be a condition to the continuing effectiveness of the registration of the firm with the Board.

(c) ACTION ON APPLICATIONS—

(1) TIMING—The Board shall approve a completed application for registration not later than 45 days after the date of receipt of the application, in accordance with the rules of the Board, unless the Board, prior to such date, issues a written notice of disapproval to, or requests more information from, the prospective registrant.

(2) TREATMENT—A written notice of disapproval of a completed application under paragraph (1) for registration shall be treated as a disciplinary sanction for purposes of sections 105(d) and 107(c).

(d) PERIODIC REPORTS—Each registered public accounting firm shall submit an annual report to the Board, and may be required to report more frequently, as necessary to update the information contained in its application for registration under this section, and to provide to the Board such additional information as the Board or the Commission may specify, in accordance with subsection (b)(2).

(e) PUBLIC AVAILABILITY—Registration applications and annual reports required by this subsection, or such portions of such applications or reports as may be designated under rules of the Board, shall be made available for public inspection, subject to rules of the Board or the Commission, and to applicable laws relating to the confidentiality of proprietary, personal, or other information contained in such applications or reports, provided that, in all events, the Board shall protect from public disclosure information reasonably identified by the subject accounting firm as proprietary information.

(f) REGISTRATION AND ANNUAL FEES—The Board shall assess and collect a registration fee and an annual fee from each registered public accounting firm, in amounts that are sufficient to recover the costs of processing and reviewing applications and annual reports.

[¶ 1003] Section 103—AUDITING, QUALITY CONTROL, AND INDEPENDENCE STANDARDS AND RULES.

(a) AUDITING, QUALITY CONTROL, AND ETHICS STANDARDS—

(1) IN GENERAL—The Board shall, by rule, establish, including, to the extent it determines appropriate, through adoption of standards proposed by 1 or more professional groups of accountants designated pursuant to paragraph (3)(A) or advisory groups convened pursuant to paragraph (4), and amend or otherwise modify or alter, such auditing and related attestation standards, such quality control standards, and such ethics standards to be used by registered public accounting firms in the preparation and issuance of audit reports, as required by this Act or the rules of the Commission, or as may be necessary or appropriate in the public interest or for the protection of investors.

(2) RULE REQUIREMENTS—In carrying out paragraph (1), the Board—

(A) shall include in the auditing standards that it adopts, requirements that each registered public accounting firm shall—

(i) prepare, and maintain for a period of not less than 7 years, audit work papers, and other information related to any audit report, in sufficient detail to support the conclusions reached in such report;

(ii) provide a concurring or second partner review and approval of such audit report (and other related information), and concurring approval in its issuance, by a qualified person (as prescribed by the Board) associated with the public accounting firm, other than the person in charge of the audit, or by an independent reviewer (as prescribed by the Board); and

(iii) describe in each audit report the scope of the auditor's testing of the internal control structure and procedures of the issuer, required by section 404(b), and present (in such report or in a separate report)—

(I) the findings of the auditor from such testing;

(II) an evaluation of whether such internal control structure and procedures—

(aa) include maintenance of records that in reasonable detail accurately and fairly reflect the transactions and dispositions of the assets of the issuer;

(bb) provide reasonable assurance that transactions are recorded as necessary to permit preparation of financial statements in accordance with generally accepted accounting principles, and that receipts and expenditures of the issuer are being made only in accordance with authorizations of management and directors of the issuer; and

(III) a description, at a minimum, of material weaknesses in such internal controls, and of any material noncompliance found on the basis of such testing.

(B) shall include, in the quality control standards that it adopts with respect to the issuance of audit reports, requirements for every registered public accounting firm relating to—

(i) monitoring of professional ethics and independence from issuers on behalf of which the firm issues audit reports;

(ii) consultation within such firm on accounting and auditing questions;

(iii) supervision of audit work;

(iv) hiring, professional development, and advancement of personnel;

(v) the acceptance and continuation of engagements;

(vi) internal inspection; and

(vii) such other requirements as the Board may prescribe, subject to subsection (a)(1).

(3) AUTHORITY TO ADOPT OTHER STANDARDS—

(A) IN GENERAL—In carrying out this subsection, the Board—

(i) may adopt as its rules, subject to the terms of section 107, any portion of any statement of auditing standards or other professional standards that the Board determines satisfy the requirements of paragraph (1), and that were proposed by 1 or more professional groups of accountants that shall be designated or recognized by the Board, by rule, for such purpose, pursuant to this paragraph or 1 or more advisory groups convened pursuant to paragraph (4); and

(ii) notwithstanding clause (i), shall retain full authority to modify, supplement, revise, or subsequently amend, modify, or repeal, in whole or in part, any portion of any statement described in clause (i).

(B) INITIAL AND TRANSITIONAL STANDARDS—The Board shall adopt standards described in subparagraph (A)(i) as initial or transitional standards, to the extent the Board determines necessary, prior to a determination of the Commission under section 101(d), and such standards shall be separately approved by the Commission at the time of that determination, without regard to the procedures required by section 107 that otherwise would apply to the approval of rules of the Board.

(4) ADVISORY GROUPS—The Board shall convene, or authorize its staff to convene, such expert advisory groups as may be appropriate, which may include practicing accountants and other experts, as well as representatives of other interested groups, subject to such rules as the Board may prescribe to prevent conflicts of interest, to make recommendations concerning the content (including proposed drafts) of auditing, quality control, ethics, independence, or other standards required to be established under this section.

(b) INDEPENDENCE STANDARDS AND RULES—The Board shall establish such rules as may be necessary or appropriate in the public interest or for the protection of investors, to implement, or as authorized under, title II of this Act.

(c) COOPERATION WITH DESIGNATED PROFESSIONAL GROUPS OF ACCOUNTANTS AND ADVISORY GROUPS—

(1) IN GENERAL—The Board shall cooperate on an ongoing basis with professional groups of accountants designated under subsection (a)(3)(A) and advisory groups convened under subsection (a)(4) in the examination of the need for changes in any standards subject to its authority under subsection (a), recommend issues for inclusion on the agendas of such designated professional groups of accountants or advisory groups, and take such other steps as it deems appropriate to increase the effectiveness of the standard setting process.

(2) BOARD RESPONSES—The Board shall respond in a timely fashion to requests from designated professional groups of accountants and advisory groups referred to inparagraph (1) for any changes in standards over which the Board has authority.

(d) EVALUATION OF STANDARD SETTING PROCESS—The Board shall include in the annual report required by section 101(h) the results of its standard setting responsibilities during the period to which the report relates, including a discussion of the work of the Board with any designated professional groups of accountants and advisory groups described in paragraphs (3)(A) and (4) of subsection (a), and its pending issues agenda for future standard setting projects.

[¶ 1004] Section 104—INSPECTIONS OF REGISTERED PUBLIC ACCOUNTING FIRMS.

(a) IN GENERAL—The Board shall conduct a continuing program of inspections to assess the degree of compliance of each registered public accounting firm and associated persons of that firm with this Act, the rules of the Board, the rules of the Commission, or professional standards, in connection with its performance of audits, issuance of audit reports, and related matters involving issuers.

(b) INSPECTION FREQUENCY—

(1) IN GENERAL—Subject to paragraph (2), inspections required by this section shall be conducted—

(A) annually with respect to each registered public accounting firm that regularly provides audit reports for more than 100 issuers; and

(B) not less frequently than once every 3 years with respect to each registered public accounting firm that regularly provides audit reports for 100 or fewer issuers.

(2) ADJUSTMENTS TO SCHEDULES—The Board may, by rule, adjust the inspection schedules set under paragraph (1) if the Board finds that different inspection schedules are consistent with the purposes of this Act, the public interest, and the protection of investors. The Board may conduct special inspections at the request of the Commission or upon its own motion.

(c) PROCEDURES—The Board shall, in each inspection under this section, and in accordance with its rules for such inspections—

(1) identify any act or practice or omission to act by the registered public accounting firm, or by any associated person thereof, revealed by such inspection that may be in violation of this Act, the rules of the Board, the rules of the Commission, the firm's own quality control policies, or professional standards;

(2) report any such act, practice, or omission, if appropriate, to the Commission and each appropriate State regulatory authority; and

(3) begin a formal investigation or take disciplinary action, if appropriate, with respect to any such violation, in accordance with this Act and the rules of the Board.

(d) CONDUCT OF INSPECTIONS—In conducting an inspection of a registered public accounting firm under this section, the Board shall—

(1) inspect and review selected audit and review engagements of the firm (which may include audit engagements that are the subject of ongoing litigation or other controversy between the firm and 1 or more third parties), performed at various offices and by various associated persons of the firm, as selected by the Board;

(2) evaluate the sufficiency of the quality control system of the firm, and the manner of the documentation and communication of that system by the firm; and

(3) perform such other testing of the audit, supervisory, and quality control procedures of the firm as are necessary or appropriate in light of the purpose of the inspection and the responsibilities of the Board.

(e) RECORD RETENTION—The rules of the Board may require the retention by registered public accounting firms for inspection purposes of records whose retention is not otherwise required by section 103 or the rules issued thereunder.

(f) PROCEDURES FOR REVIEW—The rules of the Board shall provide a procedure for the review of and response to a draft inspection report by the registered public accounting firm under inspection. The Board shall take such action with respect to such response as it considers appropriate (including revising the draft report or continuing or supplementing its inspection activities before issuing a final report), but the text of any such response, appropriately redacted to protect information reasonably identified by the accounting firm as confidential, shall be attached to and made part of the inspection report.

(g) REPORT—A written report of the findings of the Board for each inspection under this section, subject to subsection (h), shall be—

(1) transmitted, in appropriate detail, to the Commission and each appropriate State regulatory authority, accompanied by any letter or comments by the Board or the inspector, and any letter of response from the registered public accounting firm; and

(2) made available in appropriate detail to the public (subject to section 105(b)(5)(A), and to the protection of such confidential and proprietary information as the Board may determine to be appropriate, or as may be required by law), except that no portions of the inspection report that deal with criticisms of or potential defects in the quality control systems of the firm under inspection shall be made public if those criticisms or defects are addressed by the firm, to the satisfaction of the Board, not later than 12 months after the date of the inspection report.

(h) INTERIM COMMISSION REVIEW—

(1) REVIEWABLE MATTERS—A registered public accounting firm may seek review by the Commission, pursuant to such rules as the Commission shall promulgate, if the firm—

(A) has provided the Board with a response, pursuant to rules issued by the Board under subsection (f), to the substance of particular items in a draft inspection report, and disagrees with the assessments contained in any final report prepared by the Board following such response; or

(B) disagrees with the determination of the Board that criticisms or defects identified in an inspection report have not been addressed to the satisfaction of the Board within 12 months of the date of the inspection report, for purposes of subsection (g)(2).

(2) TREATMENT OF REVIEW—Any decision of the Commission with respect to a review under paragraph (1) shall not be reviewable under section 25 of the Securities Exchange Act of 1934 (15 U.S.C. 78y), or deemed to be 'final agency action' for purposes of section 704 of title 5, United States Code.

(3) TIMING—Review under paragraph (1) may be sought during the 30-day period following the date of the event giving rise to the review under subparagraph (A) or (B) of paragraph (1).

[¶ 1005] Section 105—INVESTIGATIONS AND DISCIPLINARY PROCEEDINGS.

(a) IN GENERAL—The Board shall establish, by rule, subject to the requirements of this section, fair procedures for the investigation and disciplining of registered public accounting firms and associated persons of such firms.

(b) INVESTIGATIONS—

(1) AUTHORITY—In accordance with the rules of the Board, the Board may conduct an investigation of any act or practice, or omission to act, by a registered public accounting firm, any associated person of such firm, or both, that may violate any provision of this Act, the rules of the Board, the provisions of the securities laws relating to the preparation and issuance of audit reports and the obligations and liabilities of accountants with respect thereto, including the rules of the Commission issued under this Act, or professional standards, regardless of how the act, practice, or omission is brought to the attention of the Board.

(2) TESTIMONY AND DOCUMENT PRODUCTION—In addition to such other actions as the Board determines to be necessary or appropriate, the rules of the Board may—

(A) require the testimony of the firm or of any person associated with a registered public accounting firm, with respect to any matter that the Board considers relevant or material to an investigation;

(B) require the production of audit work papers and any other document or information in the possession of a registered public accounting firm or any associated person thereof, wherever domiciled, that the Board considers relevant or material to the investigation, and may inspect the books and records of such firm or associated person to verify the accuracy of any documents or information supplied;

(C) request the testimony of, and production of any document in the possession of, any other person, including any client of a registered public accounting firm that the Board considers relevant or material to an investigation under this section, with appropriate notice, subject to the needs of the investigation, as permitted under the rules of the Board; and

(D) provide for procedures to seek issuance by the Commission, in a manner established by the Commission, of a subpoena to require the testimony of, and production of any document in the possession of, any person, including any client of a registered public accounting firm, that the Board considers relevant or material to an investigation under this section.

(3) NONCOOPERATION WITH INVESTIGATIONS—

(A) IN GENERAL—If a registered public accounting firm or any associated person thereof refuses to testify, produce documents, or otherwise cooperate with the Board in connection with an investigation under this section, the Board may—

(i) suspend or bar such person from being associated with a registered public accounting firm, or require the registered public accounting firm to end such association;

(ii) suspend or revoke the registration of the public accounting firm; and

(iii) invoke such other lesser sanctions as the Board considers appropriate, and as specified by rule of the Board.

(B) PROCEDURE—Any action taken by the Board under this paragraph shall be subject to the terms of section 107(c).

(4) COORDINATION AND REFERRAL OF INVESTIGATIONS—

(A) COORDINATION—The Board shall notify the Commission of any pending Board investigation involving a potential violation of the securities laws, and thereafter coordinate its work with the work of the Commission's Division of Enforcement, as necessary to protect an ongoing Commission investigation.

(B) REFERRAL—The Board may refer an investigation under this section—

(i) to the Commission;

(ii) to any other Federal functional regulator (as defined in section 509 of the Gramm-Leach-Bliley Act (15 U.S.C. 6809)), in the case of an investigation that concerns an audit report for an institution that is subject to the jurisdiction of such regulator; and

(iii) at the direction of the Commission, to—

(I) the Attorney General of the United States;

(II) the attorney general of 1 or more States; and

(III) the appropriate State regulatory authority.

(5) USE OF DOCUMENTS—

(A) CONFIDENTIALITY—Except as provided in subparagraph (B), all documents and information prepared or received by or specifically for the Board, and deliberations of the Board and its employees and agents, in connection with an inspection under section 104 or with an investigation under this section, shall be confidential and privileged as an evidentiary matter (and shall not be subject to civil discovery or other legal process) in any proceeding in any Federal or State court or administrative agency, and shall be exempt from disclosure, in the hands of an agency or establishment of the Federal Government, under the Freedom of Information Act (5 U.S.C. 552a), or otherwise, unless and until presented in connection with a public proceeding or released in accordance with subsection (c).

(B) AVAILABILITY TO GOVERNMENT AGENCIES—Without the loss of its status as confidential and privileged in the hands of the Board, all information referred to in subparagraph (A) may—

(i) be made available to the Commission; and

(ii) in the discretion of the Board, when determined by the Board to be necessary to accomplish the purposes of this Act or to protect investors, be made available to—

(I) the Attorney General of the United States;

(II) the appropriate Federal functional regulator (as defined in section 509 of the Gramm-Leach-Bliley Act (15 U.S.C. 6809)), other than the Commission, with respect to an audit report for an institution subject to the jurisdiction of such regulator;

(III) State attorneys general in connection with any criminal investigation; and

(IV) any appropriate State regulatory authority, each of which shall maintain such information as confidential and privileged.

(6) IMMUNITY—Any employee of the Board engaged in carrying out an investigation under this Act shall be immune from any civil liability arising out of such investigation in the same manner and to the same extent as an employee of the Federal Government in similar circumstances.

(c) DISCIPLINARY PROCEDURES—

(1) NOTIFICATION; RECORDKEEPING—The rules of the Board shall provide that in any proceeding by the Board to determine whether a registered public accounting firm, or an associated person thereof, should be disciplined, the Board shall—

(A) bring specific charges with respect to the firm or associated person;

(B) notify such firm or associated person of, and provide to the firm or associated person an opportunity to defend against, such charges; and

(C) keep a record of the proceedings.

(2) PUBLIC HEARINGS—Hearings under this section shall not be public, unless otherwise ordered by the Board for good cause shown, with the consent of the parties to such hearing.

(3) SUPPORTING STATEMENT—A determination by the Board to impose a sanction under this subsection shall be supported by a statement setting forth—

(A) each act or practice in which the registered public accounting firm, or associated person, has engaged (or omitted to engage), or that forms a basis for all or a part of such sanction;

(B) the specific provision of this Act, the securities laws, the rules of the Board, or professional standards which the Board determines has been violated; and

(C) the sanction imposed, including a justification for that sanction.

(4) SANCTIONS—If the Board finds, based on all of the facts and circumstances, that a registered public accounting firm or associated person thereof has engaged in any act or practice, or omitted to act, in violation of this Act, the rules of the Board, the provisions of the securities laws relating to the preparation and issuance of audit reports and the obligations and liabilities of accountants with respect thereto, including the rules of the Commission issued under this Act, or professional standards, the Board may impose such disciplinary or remedial sanctions as it determines appropriate, subject to applicable limitations under paragraph (5), including—

(A) temporary suspension or permanent revocation of registration under this title;

(B) temporary or permanent suspension or bar of a person from further association with any registered public accounting firm;

(C) temporary or permanent limitation on the activities, functions, or operations of such firm or person (other than in connection with required additional professional education or training);

(D) a civil money penalty for each such violation, in an amount equal to—

(i) not more than $100,000 for a natural person or $2,000,000 for any other person; and

(ii) in any case to which paragraph (5) applies, not more than $750,000 for a natural person or $15,000,000 for any other person;

(E) censure;

(F) required additional professional education or training; or

(G) any other appropriate sanction provided for in the rules of the Board.

(5) INTENTIONAL OR OTHER KNOWING CONDUCT—The sanctions and penalties described in subparagraphs (A) through (C) and (D)(ii) of paragraph (4) shall only apply to—

(A) intentional or knowing conduct, including reckless conduct, that results in violation of the applicable statutory, regulatory, or professional standard; or

(B) repeated instances of negligent conduct, each resulting in a violation of the applicable statutory, regulatory, or professional standard.

(6) FAILURE TO SUPERVISE—

(A) IN GENERAL—The Board may impose sanctions under this section on a registered accounting firm or upon the supervisory personnel of such firm, if the Board finds that—

(i) the firm has failed reasonably to supervise an associated person, either as required by the rules of the Board relating to auditing or quality control standards, or otherwise, with a view to preventing violations of this Act, the rules of the Board, the provisions of the securities laws relating to the preparation and issuance of audit reports and the obligations and liabilities of accountants with respect thereto, including the rules of the Commission under this Act, or professional standards; and

(ii) such associated person commits a violation of this Act, or any of such rules, laws, or standards.

(B) RULE OF CONSTRUCTION—No associated person of a registered public accounting firm shall be deemed to have failed reasonably to supervise any other person for purposes of subparagraph (A), if—

(i) there have been established in and for that firm procedures, and a system for applying such procedures, that comply with applicable rules of the Board and that would reasonably be expected to prevent and detect any such violation by such associated person; and

(ii) such person has reasonably discharged the duties and obligations incumbent upon that person by reason of such procedures and system, and had no reasonable cause to believe that such procedures and system were not being complied with.

(7) EFFECT OF SUSPENSION—

(A) ASSOCIATION WITH A PUBLIC ACCOUNTING FIRM—It shall be unlawful for any person that is suspended or barred from being associated with a registered public accounting firm under this subsection willfully to become or remain associated with any registered public accounting firm, or for any registered public accounting firm that knew, or, in the exercise of reasonable care should have known, of the suspension or bar, to permit such an association, without the consent of the Board or the Commission.

(B) ASSOCIATION WITH AN ISSUER—It shall be unlawful for any person that is suspended or barred from being associated with an issuer under this subsection willfully to become or remain associated with any issuer in an accountancy or a financial management capacity, and for any issuer that knew, or in the exercise of reasonable care should have known, of such suspension or bar, to permit such an association, without the consent of the Board or the Commission.

(d) REPORTING OF SANCTIONS—

(1) RECIPIENTS—If the Board imposes a disciplinary sanction, in accordance with this section, the Board shall report the sanction to—

(A) the Commission;

(B) any appropriate State regulatory authority or any foreign accountancy licensing board with which such firm or person is licensed or certified; and

(C) the public (once any stay on the imposition of such sanction has been lifted).

(2) CONTENTS—The information reported under paragraph (1) shall include—

(A) the name of the sanctioned person;

(B) a description of the sanction and the basis for its imposition; and

(C) such other information as the Board deems appropriate.

(e) STAY OF SANCTIONS—

(1) IN GENERAL—Application to the Commission for review, or the institution by the Commission of review, of any disciplinary action of the Board shall operate as a stay of any such disciplinary action, unless and until the Commission orders (summarily or after notice and opportunity for hearing on the question of a stay, which hearing may consist solely of the submission of affidavits or presentation of oral arguments) that no such stay shall continue to operate.

(2) EXPEDITED PROCEDURES—The Commission shall establish for appropriate cases an expedited procedure for consideration and determination of the question of the duration of a stay pending review of any disciplinary action of the Board under this subsection.

[¶ 1006] Section 106—FOREIGN PUBLIC ACCOUNTING FIRMS.

(a) APPLICABILITY TO CERTAIN FOREIGN FIRMS—

(1) IN GENERAL—Any foreign public accounting firm that prepares or furnishes an audit report with respect to any issuer, shall be subject to this Act and the rules of the Board and the Commission issued under this Act, in the same manner and to the same extent as a public accounting firm that is organized and operates under the laws of the United States or any State, except that registration pursuant to section 102 shall not by itself provide a basis for subjecting such a foreign public accounting firm to the jurisdiction of the Federal or State courts, other than with respect to controversies between such firms and the Board.

(2) BOARD AUTHORITY—The Board may, by rule, determine that a foreign public accounting firm (or a class of such firms) that does not issue audit reports nonetheless plays such a substantial role in the preparation and furnishing of such reports for particular issuers, that it is necessary or appropriate, in light of the purposes of this Act and in the public interest or for the protection of investors, that such firm (or class of firms) should be treated as a public accounting firm (or firms) for purposes of registration under, and oversight by the Board in accordance with, this title.

(b) PRODUCTION OF AUDIT WORKPAPERS—

(1) CONSENT BY FOREIGN FIRMS—If a foreign public accounting firm issues an opinion or otherwise performs material services upon which a registered public accounting firm relies in issuing all or part of any audit report or any opinion contained in an audit report, that foreign public accounting firm shall be deemed to have consented—

(A) to produce its audit workpapers for the Board or the Commission in connection with any investigation by either body with respect to that audit report; and

(B) to be subject to the jurisdiction of the courts of the United States for purposes of enforcement of any request for production of such workpapers.

(2) CONSENT BY DOMESTIC FIRMS—A registered public accounting firm that relies upon the opinion of a foreign public accounting firm, as described in paragraph (1), shall be deemed—

(A) to have consented to supplying the audit workpapers of that foreign public accounting firm in response to a request for production by the Board or the Commission; and

(B) to have secured the agreement of that foreign public accounting firm to such production, as a condition of its reliance on the opinion of that foreign public accounting firm.

(c) EXEMPTION AUTHORITY—The Commission, and the Board, subject to the approval of the Commission, may, by rule, regulation, or order, and as the Commission (or Board) determines necessary or appropriate in the public interest or for the protection of investors, either unconditionally or upon specified terms and conditions exempt any foreign public accounting firm, or any class of such firms, from any provision of this Act or the rules of the Board or the Commission issued under this Act.

(d) DEFINITION—In this section, the term 'foreign public accounting firm' means a public accounting firm that is organized and operates under the laws of a foreign government or political subdivision thereof.

[¶ 1007] Section 107—COMMISSION OVERSIGHT OF THE BOARD.

(a) GENERAL OVERSIGHT RESPONSIBILITY—The Commission shall have oversight and enforcement authority over the Board, as provided in this Act. The provisions of section 17(a)(1) of the Securities Exchange Act of 1934 (15 U.S.C. 78q(a)(1)), and of section 17(b)(1) of the Securities Exchange Act of 1934 (15 U.S.C. 78q(b)(1)) shall apply to the Board as fully as if the Board were a 'registered securities association' for purposes of those sections 17(a)(1) and 17(b)(1).

(b) RULES OF THE BOARD—

(1) DEFINITION—In this section, the term 'proposed rule' means any proposed rule of the Board, and any modification of any such rule.

(2) PRIOR APPROVAL REQUIRED—No rule of the Board shall become effective without prior approval of the Commission in accordance with this section, other than as provided in section 103(a)(3)(B) with respect to initial or transitional standards.

(3) APPROVAL CRITERIA—The Commission shall approve a proposed rule, if it finds that the rule is consistent with the requirements of this Act and the securities laws, or is necessary or appropriate in the public interest or for the protection of investors.

(4) PROPOSED RULE PROCEDURES—The provisions of paragraphs (1) through (3) of section 19(b) of the Securities Exchange Act of 1934 (15 U.S.C. 78s(b)) shall govern the proposed rules of the Board, as fully as if the Board were a 'registered securities association' for purposes of that section 19(b), except that, for purposes of this paragraph—

(A) the phrase 'consistent with the requirements of this title and the rules and regulations thereunder applicable to such organization' in section 19(b)(2) of that Act shall be deemed to read 'consistent with the requirements of title I of the Sarbanes-Oxley Act of 2002, and the rules and regulations issued thereunder applicable to such organization, or as necessary or appropriate in the public interest or for the protection of investors'; and

(B) the phrase 'otherwise in furtherance of the purposes of this title' in section 19(b)(3)(C) of that Act shall be deemed to read 'otherwise in furtherance of the purposes of title I of the Sarbanes-Oxley Act of 2002'.

(5) COMMISSION AUTHORITY TO AMEND RULES OF THE BOARD—The provisions of section 19(c) of the Securities Exchange Act of 1934 (15 U.S.C. 78s(c)) shall govern the abrogation, deletion, or addition to portions of the rules of the Board by the Commission as fully as if the Board were a 'registered securities association' for purposes of that section 19(c), except that the phrase 'to conform its rules to the requirements of this title and the rules and regulations thereunder applicable to such organization, or otherwise in furtherance of the purposes of this title' in section 19(c) of that Act shall, for purposes of this paragraph, be deemed to read 'to assure the fair administration of the Public Company Accounting Oversight Board, conform the rules promulgated by that Board to the requirements of title I of the Sarbanes-Oxley Act of 2002, or otherwise further the purposes of that Act, the securities laws, and the rules and regulations thereunder applicable to that Board'.

(c) COMMISSION REVIEW OF DISCIPLINARY ACTION TAKEN BY THE BOARD—

(1) NOTICE OF SANCTION—The Board shall promptly file notice with the Commission of any final sanction on any registered public accounting firm or on any associated person thereof, in such form and containing such information as the Commission, by rule, may prescribe.

(2) REVIEW OF SANCTIONS—The provisions of sections 19(d)(2) and 19(e)(1) of the Securities Exchange Act of 1934 (15 U.S.C. 78s (d)(2) and (e)(1)) shall govern the review by the Commission of final disciplinary sanctions imposed by the Board (including sanctions imposed under section 105(b)(3) of this Act for noncooperation in an investigation of the Board), as fully as if the Board were a self-regulatory organization and the Commission were the appropriate regulatory agency for such organization for purposes of those sections 19(d)(2) and 19(e)(1), except that, for purposes of this paragraph—

(A) section 105(e) of this Act (rather than that section 19(d)(2)) shall govern the extent to which application for, or institution by the Commission on its own motion of, review of any disciplinary action of the Board operates as a stay of such action;

(B) references in that section 19(e)(1) to 'members' of such an organization shall be deemed to be references to registered public accounting firms;

(C) the phrase 'consistent with the purposes of this title' in that section 19(e)(1) shall be deemed to read 'consistent with the purposes of this title and title I of the Sarbanes-Oxley Act of 2002';

(D) references to rules of the Municipal Securities Rulemaking Board in that section 19(e)(1) shall not apply; and

(E) the reference to section 19(e)(2) of the Securities Exchange Act of 1934 shall refer instead to section 107(c)(3) of this Act.

(3) COMMISSION MODIFICATION AUTHORITY—The Commission may enhance, modify, cancel, reduce, or require the remission of a sanction

imposed by the Board upon a registered public accounting firm or associated person thereof, if the Commission, having due regard for the public interest and the protection of investors, finds, after a proceeding in accordance with this subsection, that the sanction—

(A) is not necessary or appropriate in furtherance of this Act or the securities laws; or

(B) is excessive, oppressive, inadequate, or otherwise not appropriate to the finding or the basis on which the sanction was imposed.

(d) CENSURE OF THE BOARD; OTHER SANCTIONS—

(1) RESCISSION OF BOARD AUTHORITY—The Commission, by rule, consistent with the public interest, the protection of investors, and the other purposes of this Act and the securities laws, may relieve the Board of any responsibility to enforce compliance with any provision of this Act, the securities laws, the rules of the Board, or professional standards.

(2) CENSURE OF THE BOARD; LIMITATIONS—The Commission may, by order, as it determines necessary or appropriate in the public interest, for the protection of investors, or otherwise in furtherance of the purposes of this Act or the securities laws, censure or impose limitations upon the activities, functions, and operations of the Board, if the Commission finds, on the record, after notice and opportunity for a hearing, that the Board—

(A) has violated or is unable to comply with any provision of this Act, the rules of the Board, or the securities laws; or

(B) without reasonable justification or excuse, has failed to enforce compliance with any such provision or rule, or any professional standard by a registered public accounting firm or an associated person thereof.

(3) CENSURE OF BOARD MEMBERS; REMOVAL FROM OFFICE—The Commission may, as necessary or appropriate in the public interest, for the protection of investors, or otherwise in furtherance of the purposes of this Act or the securities laws, remove from office or censure any member of the Board, if the Commission finds, on the record, after notice and opportunity for a hearing, that such member—

(A) has willfully violated any provision of this Act, the rules of the Board, or the securities laws;

(B) has willfully abused the authority of that member; or

(C) without reasonable justification or excuse, has failed to enforce compliance with any such provision or rule, or any professional standard by any registered public accounting firm or any associated person thereof.

[¶ 1008] Section 108—ACCOUNTING STANDARDS.

(a) AMENDMENT TO SECURITIES ACT OF 1933—Section 19 of the Securities Act of 1933 (15 U.S.C. 77s) is amended—

(1) by redesignating subsections (b) and (c) as subsections (c) and (d), respectively; and

(2) by inserting after subsection (a) the following:

'(b) RECOGNITION OF ACCOUNTING STANDARDS—

'(1) IN GENERAL—In carrying out its authority under subsection (a) and under section 13(b) of the Securities Exchange Act of 1934, the Commission may recognize, as 'generally accepted' for purposes of the securities laws, any accounting principles established by a standard setting body—

'(A) that—

'(i) is organized as a private entity;

'(ii) has, for administrative and operational purposes, a board of trustees (or equivalent body) serving in the public interest, the majority of whom are not, concurrent with their service on such board, and have not been during the 2-year period preceding such service, associated persons of any registered public accounting firm;

'(iii) is funded as provided in section 109 of the Sarbanes-Oxley Act of 2002;

'(iv) has adopted procedures to ensure prompt consideration, by majority vote of its members, of changes to accounting principles necessary to reflect emerging accounting issues and changing business practices; and

'(v) considers, in adopting accounting principles, the need to keep standards current in order to reflect changes in the business environment, the extent to which international convergence on high quality accounting standards is necessary or appropriate in the public interest and for the protection of investors; and

'(B) that the Commission determines has the capacity to assist the Commission in fulfilling the requirements of subsection (a) and section 13(b) of the Securities Exchange Act of 1934, because, at a minimum, the standard setting body is capable of improving the accuracy and effectiveness of financial reporting and the protection of investors under the securities laws.

'(2) ANNUAL REPORT—A standard setting body described in paragraph (1) shall submit an annual report to the Commission and the public, containing audited financial statements of that standard setting body.'.

(b) COMMISSION AUTHORITY—The Commission shall promulgate such rules and regulations to carry out section 19(b) of the Securities Act of 1933, as added by this section, as it deems necessary or appropriate in the public interest or for the protection of investors.

(c) NO EFFECT ON COMMISSION POWERS—Nothing in this Act, including this section and the amendment made by this section, shall be construed to impair or limit the authority of the Commission to establish accounting principles or standards for purposes of enforcement of the securities laws.

(d) STUDY AND REPORT ON ADOPTING PRINCIPLES-BASED ACCOUNTING—

(1) STUDY—

(A) IN GENERAL—The Commission shall conduct a study on the adoption by the United States financial reporting system of a principles-based accounting system.

(B) STUDY TOPICS—The study required by subparagraph (A) shall include an examination of—

(i) the extent to which principles-based accounting and financial reporting exists in the United States;

(ii) the length of time required for change from a rules-based to a principles-based financial reporting system;

(iii) the feasibility of and proposed methods by which a principles-based system may be implemented; and

(iv) a thorough economic analysis of the implementation of a principles-based system.

(2) REPORT—Not later than 1 year after the date of enactment of this Act, the Commission shall submit a report on the results of the study required by paragraph (1) to the Committee on Banking, Housing, and Urban Affairs of the Senate and the Committee on Financial Services of the House of Representatives.

[¶ 1009] Section 109—FUNDING.

(a) IN GENERAL—The Board, and the standard setting body designated pursuant to section 19(b) of the Securities Act of 1933, as amended by section 108, shall be funded as provided in this section.

(b) ANNUAL BUDGETS—The Board and the standard setting body referred to in subsection (a) shall each establish a budget for each fiscal year, which shall be reviewed and approved according to their respective internal procedures not less than 1 month prior to the commencement of the fiscal year to which the budget pertains (or at the beginning of the Board's first fiscal year, which may be a short fiscal year). The budget of the Board shall be subject to approval by the Commission. The budget for the first fiscal year of the Board shall be prepared and approved promptly following the appointment of the initial five Board members, to permit action by the Board of the organizational tasks contemplated by section 101(d).

(c) SOURCES AND USES OF FUNDS—

(1) RECOVERABLE BUDGET EXPENSES—The budget of the Board (reduced by any registration or annual fees received under section 102(e) for the year preceding the year for which the budget is being computed), and all of the budget of the standard setting body referred to in subsection (a), for each fiscal year of each of those 2 entities, shall be payable from annual accounting support fees, in accordance with subsections (d) and (e). Accounting support fees and other receipts of the Board and of suchstandard-setting body shall not be considered public monies of the United States.

(2) FUNDS GENERATED FROM THE COLLECTION OF MONETARY PENALTIES—Subject to the availability in advance in an appropriations Act, and notwithstanding subsection (i), all funds collected by the Board as a result of the assessment of monetary penalties shall be used to fund a merit scholarship program for undergraduate and graduate students enrolled in accredited accounting degree programs, which program is to be administered by the Board or by an entity or agent identified by the Board.

(d) ANNUAL ACCOUNTING SUPPORT FEE FOR THE BOARD—

(1) ESTABLISHMENT OF FEE—The Board shall establish, with the approval of the Commission, a reasonable annual accounting support fee (or a

formula for the computation thereof), as may be necessary or appropriate to establish and maintain the Board. Such fee may also cover costs incurred in the Board's first fiscal year (which may be a short fiscal year), or may be levied separately with respect to such short fiscal year.

(2) ASSESSMENTS—The rules of the Board under paragraph (1) shall provide for the equitable allocation, assessment, and collection by the Board (or an agent appointed by the Board) of the fee established under paragraph (1), among issuers, in accordance with subsection (g), allowing for differentiation among classes of issuers, as appropriate.

(e) ANNUAL ACCOUNTING SUPPORT FEE FOR STANDARD SETTING BODY—The annual accounting support fee for the standard setting body referred to in subsection (a)—

(1) shall be allocated in accordance with subsection (g), and assessed and collected against each issuer, on behalf of the standard setting body, by 1 or more appropriate designated collection agents, as may be necessary or appropriate to pay for the budget and provide for the expenses of that standard setting body, and to provide for an independent, stable source of funding for such body, subject to review by the Commission; and

(2) may differentiate among different classes of issuers.

(f) LIMITATION ON FEE—The amount of fees collected under this section for a fiscal year on behalf of the Board or the standards setting body, as the case may be, shall not exceed the recoverable budget expenses of the Board or body, respectively (which may include operating, capital, and accrued items), referred to in subsection (c)(1).

(g) ALLOCATION OF ACCOUNTING SUPPORT FEES AMONG ISSUERS—Any amount due from issuers (or a particular class of issuers) under this section to fund the budget of the Board or the standard setting body referred to in subsection (a) shall be allocated among and payable by each issuer (or each issuer in a particular class, as applicable) in an amount equal to the total of such amount, multiplied by a fraction—

(1) the numerator of which is the average monthly equity market capitalization of the issuer for the 12-month period immediately preceding the beginning of the fiscal year to which such budget relates; and

(2) the denominator of which is the average monthly equity market capitalization of all such issuers for such 12-month period.

(h) CONFORMING AMENDMENTS—Section 13(b)(2) of the Securities Exchange Act of 1934 (15 U.S.C. 78m(b)(2)) is amended—

(1) in subparagraph (A), by striking 'and' at the end; and

(2) in subparagraph (B), by striking the period at the end and inserting the following: '; and

'(C) notwithstanding any other provision of law, pay the allocable share of such issuer of a reasonable annual accounting support fee or fees, determined in accordance with section 109 of the Sarbanes-Oxley Act of 2002.'.

(i) RULE OF CONSTRUCTION—Nothing in this section shall be construed to render either the Board, the standard setting body referred to in subsection (a), or both, subject to procedures in Congress to authorize or appropriate public funds, or to prevent such organization from utilizing additional sources of revenue for its activities, such as earnings from publication sales, provided that each additional source of revenue shall not jeopardize, in the judgment of the Commission, the actual and perceived independence of such organization.

(j) START-UP EXPENSES OF THE BOARD—From the unexpended balances of the appropriations to the Commission for fiscal year 2003, the Secretary of the Treasury is authorized to advance to the Board not to exceed the amount necessary to cover the expenses of the Board during its first fiscal year (which may be a short fiscal year).

Title II AUDITOR INDEPENDENCE

[¶ 1011] Section 201—SERVICES OUTSIDE THE SCOPE OF PRACTICE OF AUDITORS.

(a) PROHIBITED ACTIVITIES—Section 10A of the Securities Exchange Act of 1934 (15 U.S.C. 78j-1) is amended by adding at the end the following:

'(g) PROHIBITED ACTIVITIES—Except as provided in subsection (h), it shall be unlawful for a registered public accounting firm (and any associated person of that firm, to the extent determined appropriate by the Commission) that performs for any issuer any audit required by this title or the rules of the Commission under this title or, beginning 180 days after the date of commencement of the operations of the Public Company Accounting Oversight Board established under section 101 of the Sarbanes-Oxley Act of 2002 (in this section referred to as the 'Board'), the rules of the Board, to provide to that issuer, contemporaneously with the audit, any non-audit service, including—

'(1) bookkeeping or other services related to the accounting records or financial statements of the audit client;

'(2) financial information systems design and implementation;

'(3) appraisal or valuation services, fairness opinions, or contribution-in-kind reports;

'(4) actuarial services;

'(5) internal audit outsourcing services;

'(6) management functions or human resources;

'(7) broker or dealer, investment adviser, or investment banking services;

'(8) legal services and expert services unrelated to the audit; and

'(9) any other service that the Board determines, by regulation, is impermissible.

'(h) PREAPPROVAL REQUIRED FOR NON-AUDIT SERVICES—A registered public accounting firm may engage in any non-audit service, including tax services, that is not described in any of paragraphs (1) through (9) of subsection (g) for an audit client, only if the activity is approved in advance by the audit committee of the issuer, in accordance with subsection (i).'.

(b) EXEMPTION AUTHORITY—The Board may, on a case by case basis, exempt any person, issuer, public accounting firm, or transaction from the prohibition on the provision of services under section 10A(g) of the Securities Exchange Act of 1934 (as added by this section), to the extent that such exemption is necessary or appropriate in the public interest and is consistent with the protection of investors, and subject to review by the Commission in the same manner as for rules of the Board under section 107.

[¶ 1012] Section 202—PREAPPROVAL REQUIREMENTS.

Section 10A of the Securities Exchange Act of 1934 (15 U.S.C. 78j-1), as amended by this Act, is amended by adding at the end the following:

'(i) PREAPPROVAL REQUIREMENTS—

'(1) IN GENERAL—

'(A) AUDIT COMMITTEE ACTION—All auditing services (which may entail providing comfort letters in connection with securities underwritings or statutory audits required for insurance companies for purposes ofState law) and non-audit services, other than as provided in subparagraph (B), provided to an issuer by the auditor of the issuer shall be preapproved by the audit committee of the issuer.

'(B) DE MINIMUS EXCEPTION—The preapproval requirement under subparagraph (A) is waived with respect to the provision of non-audit services for an issuer, if—

'(i) the aggregate amount of all such non-audit services provided to the issuer constitutes not more than 5 percent of the total amount of revenues paid by the issuer to its auditor during the fiscal year in which the nonaudit services are provided;

'(ii) such services were not recognized by the issuer at the time of the engagement to be non-audit services; and

'(iii) such services are promptly brought to the attention of the audit committee of the issuer and approved prior to the completion of the audit by the audit committee or by 1 or more members of the audit committee who are members of the board of directors to whom authority to grant such approvals has been delegated by the audit committee.

'(2) DISCLOSURE TO INVESTORS—Approval by an audit committee of an issuer under this subsection of a non-audit service to be performed by the auditor of the issuer shall be disclosed to investors in periodic reports required by section 13(a).

'(3) DELEGATION AUTHORITY—The audit committee of an issuer may delegate to 1 or more designated members of the audit committee who are independent directors of the board of directors, the authority to grant preapprovals required by this subsection. The decisions of any member to whom authority is delegated under this paragraph to preapprove an activity under this subsection shall be presented to the full audit committee at each of its scheduled meetings.

'(4) APPROVAL OF AUDIT SERVICES FOR OTHER PURPOSES—In carrying out its duties under subsection (m)(2), if the audit committee of an issuer approves an audit service within the scope of the engagement of the auditor, such audit service shall be deemed to have been preapproved for purposes of this subsection.'.

[¶ 1013] Section 203—AUDIT PARTNER ROTATION.

Section 10A of the Securities Exchange Act of 1934 (15 U.S.C. 78j-1), as amended by this Act, is amended by adding at the end the following:

'(j) AUDIT PARTNER ROTATION—It shall be unlawful for a registered public accounting firm to provide audit services to an issuer if the lead (or coordinating) audit partner (having primary responsibility for the audit), or the audit partner responsible for reviewing the audit, has performed audit services for that issuer in each of the 5 previous fiscal years of that issuer.'.

[¶ 1014] Section 204—AUDITOR REPORTS TO AUDIT COMMITTEES.

Section 10A of the Securities Exchange Act of 1934 (15 U.S.C. 78j-1), as amended by this Act, is amended by adding at the end the following:

'(k) REPORTS TO AUDIT COMMITTEES—Each registered public accounting firm that performs for any issuer any audit required by this title shall timely report to the audit committee of the issuer—

'(1) all critical accounting policies and practices to be used;

'(2) all alternative treatments of financial information within generally accepted accounting principles that have been discussed with management officials of the issuer, ramifications of the use of such alternative disclosures and treatments, and the treatment preferred by the registered public accounting firm; and

'(3) other material written communications between the registered public accounting firm and the management of the issuer, such as any management letter or schedule of unadjusted differences.'.

[¶ 1015] Section 205—CONFORMING AMENDMENTS.

(a) DEFINITIONS—Section 3(a) of the Securities Exchange Act of 1934 (15 U.S.C. 78c(a)) is amended by adding at the end the following:

'(58) AUDIT COMMITTEE—The term 'audit committee' means—

'(A) a committee (or equivalent body) established by and amongst the board of directors of an issuer for the purpose of overseeing the accounting and financial reporting processes of the issuer and audits of the financial statements of the issuer; and

'(B) if no such committee exists with respect to an issuer, the entire board of directors of the issuer.

'(59) REGISTERED PUBLIC ACCOUNTING FIRM—The term 'registered public accounting firm' has the same meaning as in section 2 of the Sarbanes-Oxley Act of 2002.'.

(b) AUDITOR REQUIREMENTS—Section 10A of the Securities Exchange Act of 1934 (15 U.S.C. 78j-1) is amended—

(1) by striking 'an independent public accountant' each place that term appears and inserting 'a registered public accounting firm';

(2) by striking 'the independent public accountant' each place that term appears and inserting 'the registered public accounting firm';

(3) in subsection (c), by striking 'No independent public accountant' and inserting 'No registered public accounting firm'; and

(4) in subsection (b)—

(A) by striking 'the accountant' each place that term appears and inserting 'the firm';

(B) by striking 'such accountant' each place that term appears and inserting 'such firm'; and

(C) in paragraph (4), by striking 'the accountant's report' and inserting 'the report of the firm'.

(c) OTHER REFERENCES—The Securities Exchange Act of 1934 (15 U.S.C. 78a et seq.) is amended—

(1) in section 12(b)(1) (15 U.S.C. 78l(b)(1)), by striking 'independent public accountants' each place that term appears and inserting 'a registered public accounting firm'; and

(2) in subsections (e) and (i) of section 17 (15 U.S.C. 78q), by striking 'an independent public accountant' each place that term appears and inserting 'a registered public accounting firm'.

(d) CONFORMING AMENDMENT—Section 10A(f) of the Securities Exchange Act of 1934 (15 U.S.C. 78k(f)) is amended—

(1) by striking 'DEFINITION' and inserting 'DEFINITIONS'; and

(2) by adding at the end the following: 'As used in this section, the term 'issuer' means an issuer (as defined in section 3), the securities of which are registered under section 12, or that is required to file reports pursuant to section 15(d), or that files or has filed a registration statement that has not yet become effective under the Securities Act of 1933 (15 U.S.C. 77a et seq.), and that it has not withdrawn.'.

[¶ 1016] Section 206—CONFLICTS OF INTEREST.

Section 10A of the Securities Exchange Act of 1934 (15 U.S.C. 78j-1), as amended by this Act, is amended by adding at the end the following:

'(l) CONFLICTS OF INTEREST—It shall be unlawful for a registered public accounting firm to perform for an issuer any audit service required by this title, if a chief executive officer, controller, chief financial officer, chief accounting officer, or any person serving in an equivalent position for the issuer, was employed by that registered independent public accounting firm and participated in any capacity in the audit of that issuer during the 1-year period preceding the date of the initiation of the audit.'.

[¶ 1017] Section 207—STUDY OF MANDATORY ROTATION OF REGISTERED PUBLIC ACCOUNTING FIRMS.

(a) STUDY AND REVIEW REQUIRED—The Comptroller General of the United States shall conduct a study and review of the potential effects of requiring the mandatory rotation of registered public accounting firms.

(b) REPORT REQUIRED—Not later than 1 year after the date of enactment of this Act, the Comptroller General shall submit a report to the Committee on Banking, Housing, and Urban Affairs of the Senate and the Committee on Financial Services of the House of Representatives on the results of the study and review required by this section.

(c) DEFINITION—For purposes of this section, the term 'mandatory rotation' refers to the imposition of a limit on the period of years in which a particular registered public accounting firm may be the auditor of record for a particular issuer.

[¶ 1018] Section 208—COMMISSION AUTHORITY.

(a) COMMISSION REGULATIONS—Not later than 180 days after the date of enactment of this Act, the Commission shall issue final regulations to carry out each of subsections (g) through (l) of section 10A of the Securities Exchange Act of 1934, as added by this title.

(b) AUDITOR INDEPENDENCE—It shall be unlawful for any registered public accounting firm (or an associated person thereof, as applicable) to prepare or issue any audit report with respect to any issuer, if the firm or associated person engages in any activity with respect to that issuer prohibited by any of subsections (g) through (l) of section 10A of the Securities Exchange Act of 1934, as added by this title, or any rule or regulation of the Commission or of the Board issued thereunder.

[¶ 1019] Section 209—CONSIDERATIONS BY APPROPRIATE STATE REGULATORY AUTHORITIES.

In supervising nonregistered public accounting firms and their associated persons, appropriate State regulatory authorities should make an independent determination of the proper standards applicable, particularly taking into consideration the size and nature of the business of the accounting firms they supervise and the size and nature of the business of the clients of those firms. The standards applied by the Board under this Act should not be presumed to be applicable for purposes of this section for small and medium sized nonregistered public accounting firms.

TITLE III CORPORATE RESPONSIBILITY

[¶ 1021] Section 301—PUBLIC COMPANY AUDIT COMMITTEES.

Section 10A of the Securities Exchange Act of 1934 (15 U.S.C. 78f) is amended by adding at the end the following:

'(m) STANDARDS RELATING TO AUDIT COMMITTEES—

'(1) COMMISSION RULES—

'(A) IN GENERAL—Effective not later than 270 days after the date of enactment of this subsection, the Commission shall, by rule, direct the national securities exchanges and national securities associations to prohibit the listing of any security of an issuer that is not in compliance with the requirements of any portion of paragraphs (2) through (6).

(B) OPPORTUNITY TO CURE DEFECTS—The rules of the Commission under subparagraph (A) shall provide for appropriate procedures for an issuer to have an opportunity to cure any defects that would be the basis for a prohibition under subparagraph (A), before the imposition of such prohibition.

'(2) RESPONSIBILITIES RELATING TO REGISTERED PUBLIC ACCOUNTING FIRMS—The audit committee of each issuer, in its capacity as a committee of the board of directors, shall be directly responsible for the appointment, compensation, and oversight of the work of any registered public accounting firm employed by that issuer (including resolution of disagreements between management and the auditor regarding financial reporting) for the purpose of preparing or issuing an audit report or related work, and each such registered public accounting firm shall report directly to the audit committee.

'(3) INDEPENDENCE—

'(A) IN GENERAL—Each member of the audit committee of the issuer shall be a member of the board of directors of the issuer, and shall otherwise be independent.

'(B) CRITERIA—In order to be considered to be independent for purposes of this paragraph, a member of an audit committee of an issuer may not, other than in his or her capacity as a member of the audit committee, the board of directors, or any other board committee—

'(i) accept any consulting, advisory, or other compensatory fee from the issuer; or

'(ii) be an affiliated person of the issuer or any subsidiary thereof.

'(C) EXEMPTION AUTHORITY—The Commission may exempt from the requirements of subparagraph (B) a particular relationship with respect to audit committee members, as the Commission determines appropriate in light of the circumstances.

'(4) COMPLAINTS—Each audit committee shall establish procedures for—

'(A) the receipt, retention, and treatment of complaints received by the issuer regarding accounting, internal accounting controls, or auditing matters; and

'(B) the confidential, anonymous submission by employees of the issuer of concerns regarding questionable accounting or auditing matters.

'(5) AUTHORITY TO ENGAGE ADVISERS—Each audit committee shall have the authority to engage independent counsel and other advisers, as it determines necessary to carry out its duties.

'(6) FUNDING—Each issuer shall provide for appropriate funding, as determined by the audit committee, in its capacity as a committee of the board of directors, for payment of compensation—

'(A) to the registered public accounting firm employed by the issuer for the purpose of rendering or issuing an audit report; and

'(B) to any advisers employed by the audit committee under paragraph (5).'.

[¶ 1022] Section 302—CORPORATE RESPONSIBILITY FOR FINANCIAL REPORTS.

(a) REGULATIONS REQUIRED—The Commission shall, by rule, require, for each company filing periodic reports under section 13(a) or 15(d) of the Securities Exchange Act of 1934 (15 U.S.C. 78m, 78o(d)), that the principal executive officer or officers and the principal financial officer or officers, or persons performing similar functions, certify in each annual or quarterly report filed or submitted under either such section of such Act that—

(1) the signing officer has reviewed the report;

(2) based on the officer's knowledge, the report does not contain any untrue statement of a material fact or omit to state a material fact necessary in order to make the statements made, in light of the circumstances under which such statements were made, not misleading;

(3) based on such officer's knowledge, the financial statements, and other financial information included in the report, fairly present in all material respects the financial condition and results of operations of the issuer as of, and for, the periods presented in the report;

(4) the signing officers—

(A) are responsible for establishing and maintaining internal controls;

(B) have designed such internal controls to ensure that material information relating to the issuer and its consolidated subsidiaries is made known to such officers by others within those entities, particularly during the period in which the periodic reports are being prepared;

(C) have evaluated the effectiveness of the issuer's internal controls as of a date within 90 days prior to the report; and

(D) have presented in the report their conclusions about the effectiveness of their internal controls based on their evaluation as of that date;

(5) the signing officers have disclosed to the issuer's auditors and the audit committee of the board of directors (or persons fulfilling the equivalent function)—

(A) all significant deficiencies in the design or operation of internal controls which could adversely affect the issuer's ability to record, process, summarize, and report financial data and have identified for the issuer's auditors any material weaknesses in internal controls; and

(B) any fraud, whether or not material, that involves management or other employees who have a significant role in the issuer's internal controls; and

(6) the signing officers have indicated in the report whether or not there were significant changes in internal controls or in other factors that could significantly affect internal controls subsequent to the date of their evaluation, including any corrective actions with regard to significant deficiencies and material weaknesses.

(b) FOREIGN REINCORPORATIONS HAVE NO EFFECT—Nothing in this section 302 shall be interpreted or applied in any way to allow any issuer to lessen the legal force of the statement required under this section 302, by an issuer having reincorporated or having engaged in any other transaction that resulted in the transfer of the corporate domicile or offices of the issuer from inside the United States to outside of the United States.

(c) DEADLINE—The rules required by subsection (a) shall be effective not later than 30 days after the date of enactment of this Act.

[¶ 1023] Section 303—IMPROPER INFLUENCE ON CONDUCT OF AUDITS.

(a) RULES TO PROHIBIT—It shall be unlawful, in contravention of such rules or regulations as the Commission shall prescribe as necessary and appropriate in the public interest or for the protection of investors, for any officer or director of an issuer, or any other person acting under the direction thereof, to take any action to fraudulently influence, coerce, manipulate, or mislead any independent public or certified accountant engaged in the performance of an audit of the financial statements of that issuer for the purpose of rendering such financial statements materially misleading.

(b) ENFORCEMENT—In any civil proceeding, the Commission shall have exclusive authority to enforce this section and any rule or regulation issued under this section.

(c) NO PREEMPTION OF OTHER LAW—The provisions of subsection (a) shall be in addition to, and shall not supersede or preempt, any other provision of law or any rule or regulation issued thereunder.

(d) DEADLINE FOR RULEMAKING—The Commission shall—

(1) propose the rules or regulations required by this section, not later than 90 days after the date of enactment of this Act; and

(2) issue final rules or regulations required by this section, not later than 270 days after that date of enactment.

[¶ 1024] Section 304—FORFEITURE OF CERTAIN BONUSES AND PROFITS.

(a) ADDITIONAL COMPENSATION PRIOR TO NONCOMPLIANCE WITH COMMISSION FINANCIAL REPORTING REQUIREMENTS—If an issuer is required to prepare an accounting restatement due to the material noncompliance of the issuer, as a result of misconduct, with any financial reporting requirement under the securities laws, the chief executive officer and chief financial officer of the issuer shall reimburse the issuer for—

(1) any bonus or other incentive-based or equity-based compensation received by that person from the issuer during the 12-month period following the first public issuance or filing with the Commission (whichever first occurs) of the financial document embodying such financial reporting requirement; and

(2) any profits realized from the sale of securities of the issuer during that 12-month period.

(b) COMMISSION EXEMPTION AUTHORITY—The Commission may exempt any person from the application of subsection (a), as it deems necessary and appropriate.

[¶ 1025] Section 305—OFFICER AND DIRECTOR BARS AND PENALTIES.

(a) UNFITNESS STANDARD—

(1) SECURITIES EXCHANGE ACT OF 1934—Section 21(d)(2) of the Securities Exchange Act of 1934 (15 U.S.C. 78u(d)(2)) is amended by striking 'substantial unfitness' and inserting 'unfitness'.

(2) SECURITIES ACT OF 1933—Section 20(e) of the Securities Act of 1933 (15 U.S.C. 77t(e)) is amended by striking 'substantial unfitness' and inserting 'unfitness'.

(b) EQUITABLE RELIEF—Section 21(d) of the Securities Exchange Act of 1934 (15 U.S.C. 78u(d)) is amended by adding at the end the following:

'(5) EQUITABLE RELIEF—In any action or proceeding brought or instituted by the Commission under any provision of the securities laws, the Commission may seek, and any Federal court may grant, any equitable relief that may be appropriate or necessary for the benefit of investors.'.

[¶ 1026] Section 306—INSIDER TRADES DURING PENSION FUND BLACKOUT PERIODS.

(a) PROHIBITION OF INSIDER TRADING DURING PENSION FUND BLACKOUT PERIODS—

(1) IN GENERAL—Except to the extent otherwise provided by rule of the Commission pursuant to paragraph (3), it shall be unlawful for any director or executive officer of an issuer of any equity security (other than an exempted security), directly or indirectly, to purchase, sell, or otherwise acquire or transfer any equity security of the issuer (other than an exempted security) during any blackout period with respect to such equity security if such director or officer acquires such equity security in connection with his or her service or employment as a director or executive officer.

(2) REMEDY—

(A) IN GENERAL—Any profit realized by a director or executive officer referred to in paragraph (1) from any purchase, sale, or other acquisition or transfer in violation of this subsection shall inure to and be recoverable by the issuer, irrespective of any intention on the part of such director or executive officer in entering into the transaction.

(B) ACTIONS TO RECOVER PROFITS—An action to recover profits in accordance with this subsection may be instituted at law or in equity in any court of competent jurisdiction by the issuer, or by the owner of any security of the issuer in the name and in behalf of the issuer if the issuer fails or refuses to bring such action within 60 days after the date of request, or fails diligently to prosecute the action thereafter, except that no such suit shall be brought more than 2 years after the date on which such profit was realized.

(3) RULEMAKING AUTHORIZED—The Commission shall, in consultation with the Secretary of Labor, issue rules to clarify the application of this subsection and to prevent evasion thereof. Such rules shall provide for the application of the requirements of paragraph (1) with respect to entities treated as a single employer with respect to an issuer under section 414(b), (c), (m), or (o) of the Internal Revenue Code of 1986 to the extent necessary to clarify the application of such requirements and to prevent evasion thereof. Such rules may also provide for appropriate exceptions from the requirements of this subsection, including exceptions for purchases pursuant to an automatic dividend reinvestment program or purchases or sales made pursuant to an advance election.

(4) BLACKOUT PERIOD—For purposes of this subsection, the term 'blackout period', with respect to the equity securities of any issuer—

(A) means any period of more than 3 consecutive business days during which the ability of not fewer than 50 percent of the participants or beneficiaries under all individual account plans maintained by the issuer to purchase, sell, or otherwise acquire or transfer an interest in any equity of such issuer held in such an individual account plan is temporarily suspended by the issuer or by a fiduciary of the plan; and

(B) does not include, under regulations which shall be prescribed by the Commission—

(i) a regularly scheduled period in which the participants and beneficiaries may not purchase, sell, or otherwise acquire or transfer an interest in any equity of such issuer, if such period is—

(I) incorporated into the individual account plan; and

(II) timely disclosed to employees before becoming participants under the individual account plan or as a subsequent amendment to the plan; or

(ii) any suspension described in subparagraph (A) that is imposed solely in connection with persons becoming participants or beneficiaries, or ceasing to be participants or beneficiaries, in an individual account plan by reason of a corporate merger, acquisition, divestiture, or similar transaction involving the plan or plan sponsor.

(5) INDIVIDUAL ACCOUNT PLAN—For purposes of this subsection, the term 'individual account plan' has the meaning provided in section 3(34) of the Employee Retirement Income Security Act of 1974 (29 U.S.C. 1002(34), except that such term shall not include a one-participant retirement plan (within the meaning of section 101(i)(8)(B) of such Act (29 U.S.C. 1021(i)(8)(B))).

(6) NOTICE TO DIRECTORS, EXECUTIVE OFFICERS, AND THE COMMISSION—In any case in which a director or executive officer is subject to the requirements of this subsection in connection with a blackout period (as defined in paragraph (4)) with respect to any equity securities, the issuer of such equity securities shall timely notify such director or officer and the Securities and Exchange Commission of such blackout period.

(b) NOTICE REQUIREMENTS TO PARTICIPANTS AND BENEFICIARIES UNDER ERISA—

(1) IN GENERAL—Section 101 of the Employee Retirement Income Security Act of 1974 (29 U.S.C. 1021) is amended by redesignating the second subsection (h) as subsection (j), and by inserting after the first subsection (h) the following new subsection:

'(i) NOTICE OF BLACKOUT PERIODS TO PARTICIPANT OR BENEFICIARY UNDER INDIVIDUAL ACCOUNT PLAN—

'(1) DUTIES OF PLAN ADMINISTRATOR—In advance of the commencement of any blackout period with respect to an individual account plan, the plan administrator shall notify the plan participants and beneficiaries who are affected by such action in accordance with this subsection.

'(2) NOTICE REQUIREMENTS—

'(A) IN GENERAL—The notices described in paragraph (1) shall be written in a manner calculated to be understood by the average plan participant and shall include—

'(i) the reasons for the blackout period,

'(ii) an identification of the investments and other rights affected,

'(iii) the expected beginning date and length of the blackout period,

'(iv) in the case of investments affected, a statement that the participant or beneficiary should evaluate the appropriateness of their current investment decisions in light of their inability to direct or diversify assets credited to their accounts during the blackout period, and

'(v) such other matters as the Secretary may require by regulation.

'(B) NOTICE TO PARTICIPANTS AND BENEFICIARIES—Except as otherwise provided in this subsection, notices described in paragraph (1) shall be furnished to all participants and beneficiaries under the plan to whom the blackout period applies at least 30 days in advance of the blackout period.

'(C) EXCEPTION TO 30-DAY NOTICE REQUIREMENT—In any case in which—

'(i) a deferral of the blackout period would violate the requirements of subparagraph (A) or (B) of section 404(a)(1), and a fiduciary of the plan reasonably so determines in writing, or

'(ii) the inability to provide the 30-day advance notice is due to events that were unforeseeable or circumstances beyond the reasonable control of the plan administrator, and a fiduciary of the plan reasonably so determines in writing,

subparagraph (B) shall not apply, and the notice shall be furnished to all participants and beneficiaries under the plan to whom the blackout period applies as soon as reasonably possible under the circumstances unless such a notice in advance of the termination of the blackout period is impracticable.

'(D) WRITTEN NOTICE—The notice required to be provided under this subsection shall be in writing, except that such notice may be in electronic or other form to the extent that such form is reasonably accessible to the recipient.

'(E) NOTICE TO ISSUERS OF EMPLOYER SECURITIES SUBJECT TO BLACKOUT PERIOD—In the case of any blackout period in connection with an individual account plan, the plan administrator shall provide timely notice of such blackout period to the issuer of any employer securities subject to such blackout period.

'(3) EXCEPTION FOR BLACKOUT PERIODS WITH LIMITED APPLICABILITY—In any case in which the blackout period applies only to 1 or more participants or beneficiaries in connection with a merger, acquisition, divestiture, or similar transaction involving the plan or plan sponsor and occurs solely in connection with becoming or ceasing to be a participant or beneficiary under the plan by reason of such merger, acquisition, divestiture, or transaction, the requirement of this subsection that the notice be provided to all participants and beneficiaries shall be treated as met if the notice required under paragraph (1) is provided to such participants or beneficiaries to whom the blackout period applies as soon as reasonably practicable.

'(4) CHANGES IN LENGTH OF BLACKOUT PERIOD—If, following the furnishing of the notice pursuant to this subsection, there is a change in the beginning date or length of the blackout period (specified in such notice pursuant to paragraph (2)(A)(iii)), the administrator shall provide affected participants and beneficiaries notice of the change as soon as reasonably practicable. In relation to the extended blackout period, such notice shall meet the requirements of paragraph (2)(D) and shall specify any material change in the matters referred to in clauses (i) through (v) of paragraph (2)(A).

'(5) REGULATORY EXCEPTIONS—The Secretary may provide by regulation for additional exceptions to the requirements of this subsection which the Secretary determines are in the interests of participants and beneficiaries.

'(6) GUIDANCE AND MODEL NOTICES—The Secretary shall issue guidance and model notices which meet the requirements of this subsection.

'(7) BLACKOUT PERIOD—For purposes of this subsection—

'(A) IN GENERAL—The term 'blackout period' means, in connection with an individual account plan, any period for which any ability of participants or beneficiaries under the plan, which is otherwiseavailable under the terms of such plan, to direct or diversify assets credited to their accounts, to obtain loans from the plan, or to obtain distributions from the plan is temporarily suspended, limited, or restricted, if such suspension, limitation, or restriction is for any period of more than 3 consecutive business days.

'(B) EXCLUSIONS—The term 'blackout period' does not include a suspension, limitation, or restriction—

'(i) which occurs by reason of the application of the securities laws (as defined in section 3(a)(47) of the Securities Exchange Act of 1934),

'(ii) which is a change to the plan which provides for a regularly scheduled suspension, limitation, or restriction which is disclosed to participants or beneficiaries through any summary of material modifications, any materials describing specific investment alternatives under the plan, or any changes thereto, or

'(iii) which applies only to 1 or more individuals, each of whom is the participant, an alternate payee (as defined in section 206(d)(3)(K)), or any other beneficiary pursuant to a qualified domestic relations order (as defined in section 206(d)(3)(B)(i)).

'(8) INDIVIDUAL ACCOUNT PLAN—

'(A) IN GENERAL—For purposes of this subsection, the term 'individual account plan' shall have the meaning provided such term in section 3(34), except that such term shall not include a one-participant retirement plan.

'(B) ONE-PARTICIPANT RETIREMENT PLAN—For purposes of subparagraph (A), the term 'one-participant retirement plan' means a retirement plan that—

'(i) on the first day of the plan year—

'(I) covered only the employer (and the employer's spouse) and the employer owned the entire business (whether or not incorporated), or

'(II) covered only one or more partners (and their spouses) in a business partnership (including partners in an S or C corporation (as defined in section 1361(a) of the Internal Revenue Code of 1986)),

'(ii) meets the minimum coverage requirements of section 410(b) of the Internal Revenue Code of 1986 (as in effect on the date of the enactment of this paragraph) without being combined with any other plan of the business that covers the employees of the business,

'(iii) does not provide benefits to anyone except the employer (and the employer's spouse) or the partners (and their spouses),

'(iv) does not cover a business that is a member of an affiliated service group, a controlled group of corporations, or a group of businesses under common control, and

'(v) does not cover a business that leases employees.'.

(2) ISSUANCE OF INITIAL GUIDANCE AND MODEL NOTICE—The Secretary of Labor shall issue initial guidance and a model notice pursuant to section 101(i)(6) of the Employee Retirement Income Security Act of 1974 (as added by this subsection) not later than January 1, 2003. Not later than 75 days after the date of the enactment of this Act, the Secretary shall promulgate interim final rules necessary to carry out the amendments made by this subsection.

(3) CIVIL PENALTIES FOR FAILURE TO PROVIDE NOTICE—Section 502 of such Act (29 U.S.C. 1132) is amended—

(A) in subsection (a)(6), by striking '(5), or (6)' and inserting '(5), (6), or (7)';

(B) by redesignating paragraph (7) of subsection (c) as paragraph (8); and

(C) by inserting after paragraph (6) of subsection (c) the following new paragraph:

'(7) The Secretary may assess a civil penalty against a plan administrator of up to $100 a day from the date of the plan administrator's failure or refusal to provide notice to participants and beneficiaries in accordance with section 101(i). For purposes of this paragraph, each violation with respect to any single participant or beneficiary shall be treated as a separate violation.'.

(3) PLAN AMENDMENTS—If any amendment made by this subsection requires an amendment to any plan, such plan amendment shall not be required to be made before the first plan year beginning on or after the effective date of this section, if—

(A) during the period after such amendment made by this subsection takes effect and before such first plan year, the plan is operated in good faith compliance with the requirements of such amendment made by this subsection, and

(B) such plan amendment applies retroactively to the period after such amendment made by this subsection takes effect and before such first plan year.

(c) EFFECTIVE DATE—The provisions of this section (including the amendments made thereby) shall take effect 180 days after the date of the enactment of this Act. Good faith compliance with the requirements of such provisions in advance of the issuance of applicable regulations thereunder shall be treated as compliance with such provisions.

[¶ 1027] Section 307—RULES OF PROFESSIONAL RESPONSIBILITY FOR ATTORNEYS.

Not later than 180 days after the date of enactment of this Act, the Commission shall issue rules, in the public interest and for the protection of investors, setting forth minimum standards of professional conduct for attorneys appearing and practicing before the Commission in any way in the representation of issuers, including a rule—

(1) requiring an attorney to report evidence of a material violation of securities law or breach of fiduciary duty or similar violation by the company or any agent thereof, to the chief legal counsel or the chief executive officer of the company (or the equivalent thereof); and

(2) if the counsel or officer does not appropriately respond to the evidence (adopting, as necessary, appropriate remedial measures or sanctions with respect to the violation), requiring the attorney to report the evidence to the audit committee of the board of directors of the issuer or to another committee of the board of directors comprised solely of directors not employed directly or indirectly by the issuer, or to the board of directors.

[¶ 1028] Section 308—FAIR FUNDS FOR INVESTORS.

(a) CIVIL PENALTIES ADDED TO DISGORGEMENT FUNDS FOR THE RELIEF OF VICTIMS—If in any judicial or administrative action brought by the Commission under the securities laws (as such term is defined in section 3(a)(47) of the Securities Exchange Act of 1934 (15 U.S.C. 78c(a)(47)) the Commission obtains an order requiring disgorgement against any person for a violation of such laws or the rules or regulations thereunder, or such person agrees in settlement of any such action to such disgorgement, and the Commission also obtains pursuant to such laws a civil penalty against such person, the amount of such civil penalty shall, on the motion or at the direction of the Commission, be added to and become part of the disgorgement fund for the benefit of the victims of such violation.

(b) ACCEPTANCE OF ADDITIONAL DONATIONS—The Commission is authorized to accept, hold, administer, and utilize gifts, bequests and devises of property, both real and personal, to the United States for a disgorgement fund described in subsection (a). Such gifts, bequests, and devises of money and proceeds from sales of other property received as gifts, bequests, or devises shall be deposited in the disgorgement fund and shall be available for allocation in accordance with subsection (a).

(c) STUDY REQUIRED—

(1) SUBJECT OF STUDY—The Commission shall review and analyze—

(A) enforcement actions by the Commission over the five years preceding the date of the enactment of this Act that have included proceedings to obtain civil penalties or disgorgements to identify areas where such proceedings may be utilized to efficiently, effectively, and fairly provide restitution for injured investors; and

(B) other methods to more efficiently, effectively, and fairly provide restitution to injured investors, including methods to improve the collection rates for civil penalties and disgorgements.

(2) REPORT REQUIRED—The Commission shall report its findings to the Committee on Financial Services of the House of Representatives and the Committee on Banking, Housing, and Urban Affairs of the Senate within 180 days after of the date of the enactment of this Act, and shall use such findings to revise its rules and regulations as necessary. The report shall include a discussion of regulatory or legislative actions that are recommended or that may be necessary to address concerns identified in the study.

(d) CONFORMING AMENDMENTS—Each of the following provisions is amended by inserting ', except as otherwise provided in section 308 of the Sarbanes-Oxley Act of 2002' after 'Treasury of the United States':

(1) Section 21(d)(3)(C)(i) of the Securities Exchange Act of 1934 (15 U.S.C. 78u(d)(3)(C)(i)).

(2) Section 21A(d)(1) of such Act (15 U.S.C. 78u-1(d)(1)).

(3) Section 20(d)(3)(A) of the Securities Act of 1933 (15 U.S.C. 77t(d)(3)(A)).

(4) Section 42(e)(3)(A) of the Investment Company Act of 1940 (15 U.S.C. 80a-41(e)(3)(A)).

(5) Section 209(e)(3)(A) of the Investment Advisers Act of 1940 (15 U.S.C. 80b-9(e)(3)(A)).

(e) DEFINITION—As used in this section, the term 'disgorgement fund' means a fund established in any administrative or judicial proceeding described in subsection (a).

TITLE IV ENHANCED FINANCIAL DISCLOSURES

[¶ 1029] Section 401—DISCLOSURES IN PERIODIC REPORTS.

(a) DISCLOSURES REQUIRED—Section 13 of the Securities Exchange Act of 1934 (15 U.S.C. 78m) is amended by adding at the end the following:

'(i) ACCURACY OF FINANCIAL REPORTS—Each financial report that contains financial statements, and that is required to be prepared in accordance with (or reconciled to) generally accepted accounting principles under this title and filed with the Commission shall reflect all material correcting adjustments that have been identified by a registered public accounting firm in accordance with generally accepted accounting principles and the rules and regulations of the Commission.

'(j) OFF-BALANCE SHEET TRANSACTIONS—Not later than 180 days after the date of enactment of the Sarbanes-Oxley Act of 2002, the Commission shall issue final rules providing that each annual and quarterly financial report required to be filed with the Commission shall disclose all material off-balance sheet transactions, arrangements, obligations (including contingent obligations), and other relationships of the issuer with unconsolidated entities or other persons, that may have a material current or future effect on financial condition, changes in financial condition, results of operations, liquidity, capital expenditures, capital resources, or significant components of revenues or expenses.'.

(b) COMMISSION RULES ON PRO FORMA FIGURES—Not later than 180 days after the date of enactment of the Sarbanes-Oxley Act fo 2002, the Commission shall issue final rules providing that pro forma financial information included in any periodic or other report filed with the Commission pursuant to the securities laws, or in any public disclosure or press or other release, shall be presented in a manner that—

(1) does not contain an untrue statement of a material fact or omit to state a material fact necessary in order to make the pro forma financial information, in light of the circumstances under which it is presented, not misleading; and

(2) reconciles it with the financial condition and results of operations of the issuer under generally accepted accounting principles.

(c) STUDY AND REPORT ON SPECIAL PURPOSE ENTITIES—

(1) STUDY REQUIRED—The Commission shall, not later than 1 year after the effective date of adoption of off-balance sheet disclosure rules required by section 13(j) of the Securities Exchange Act of 1934, as added by this section, complete a study of filings by issuers and their disclosures to determine—

(A) the extent of off-balance sheet transactions, including assets, liabilities, leases, losses, and the use of special purpose entities; and

(B) whether generally accepted accounting rules result in financial statements of issuers reflecting the economics of such off-balance sheet transactions to investors in a transparent fashion.

(2) REPORT AND RECOMMENDATIONS—Not later than 6 months after the date of completion of the study required by paragraph (1), the Commission shall submit a report to the President, the Committee on Banking, Housing, and Urban Affairs of the Senate, and the Committee on Financial Services of the House of Representatives, setting forth—

(A) the amount or an estimate of the amount of off-balance sheet transactions, including assets, liabilities, leases, and losses of, and the use of special purpose entities by, issuers filing periodic reports pursuant to section 13 or 15 of the Securities Exchange Act of 1934;

(B) the extent to which special purpose entities are used to facilitate off-balance sheet transactions;

(C) whether generally accepted accounting principles or the rules of the Commission result in financial statements of issuers reflecting the economics of such transactions to investors in a transparent fashion;

(D) whether generally accepted accounting principles specifically result in the consolidation of special purpose entities sponsored by an issuer in cases in which the issuer has the majority of the risks and rewards of the special purpose entity; and

(E) any recommendations of the Commission for improving the transparency and quality of reporting off-balance sheet transactions in the financial statements and disclosures required to be filed by an issuer with the Commission.

[¶ 1030] Section 402—ENHANCED CONFLICT OF INTEREST PROVISIONS.

(a) PROHIBITION ON PERSONAL LOANS TO EXECUTIVES—Section 13 of the Securities Exchange Act of 1934 (15 U.S.C. 78m), as amended by this Act, is amended by adding at the end the following:

'(k) PROHIBITION ON PERSONAL LOANS TO EXECUTIVES—

'(1) IN GENERAL—It shall be unlawful for any issuer (as defined in section 2 of the Sarbanes-Oxley Act of 2002), directly or indirectly, including through any subsidiary, to extend or maintain credit, to arrange for the extension of credit, or to renew an extension of credit, in the form of a personal loan to or for any director or executive officer (or equivalent thereof) of that issuer. An extension of credit maintained by the issuer on the date of enactment of this subsection shall not be subject to the provisions of this subsection, provided that there is no material modification to any term of any such extension of credit or any renewal of any such extension of credit on or after that date of enactment.

'(2) LIMITATION—Paragraph (1) does not preclude any home improvement and manufactured home loans (as that term is defined in section 5 of the Home Owners' Loan Act (12 U.S.C. 1464)), consumer credit (as defined in section 103 of the Truth in Lending Act (15 U.S.C. 1602)), or any extension of credit under an open end credit plan (as defined in section 103 of the Truth in Lending Act (15 U.S.C. 1602)), or a charge card (as defined in section 127(c)(4)(e) of the Truth in Lending Act (15 U.S.C. 1637(c)(4)(e)), or any extension of credit by a broker or dealer registered under section 15 of this title to an employee of that broker or dealer to buy, trade, or carry securities, that is permitted under rules or regulations of the Board of Governors of the Federal Reserve System pursuant to section 7 of this title (other than an extension of credit that would be used to purchase the stock of that issuer), that is—

'(A) made or provided in the ordinary course of the consumer credit business of such issuer;

'(B) of a type that is generally made available by such issuer to the public; and

'(C) made by such issuer on market terms, or terms that are no more favorable than those offered by the issuer to the general public for such extensions of credit.

'(3) RULE OF CONSTRUCTION FOR CERTAIN LOANS—Paragraph (1) does not apply to any loan made or maintained by an insured depository institution (as defined in section 3 of the Federal Deposit Insurance Act (12 U.S.C. 1813)), if the loan is subject to the insider lending restrictions of section 22(h) of the Federal Reserve Act (12 U.S.C. 375b).'.

[¶ 1031] Section 403—DISCLOSURES OF TRANSACTIONS INVOLVING MANAGEMENT AND PRINCIPAL STOCKHOLDERS.

(a) AMENDMENT—Section 16 of the Securities Exchange Act of 1934 (15 U.S.C. 78p) is amended by striking the heading of such section and subsection (a) and inserting the following:

'SEC. 16. DIRECTORS, OFFICERS, AND PRINCIPAL STOCKHOLDERS.

'(a) DISCLOSURES REQUIRED—

'(1) DIRECTORS, OFFICERS, AND PRINCIPAL STOCKHOLDERS REQUIRED TO FILE—Every person who is directly or indirectly the beneficial owner of more than 10 percent of any class of any equity security (other than an exempted security) which is registered pursuant to section 12, or who is a director or an officer of the issuer of such security, shall file the statements required by this subsection with the Commission (and, if such security is registered on a national securities exchange, also with the exchange).

'(2) TIME OF FILING—The statements required by this subsection shall be filed—

'(A) at the time of the registration of such security on a national securities exchange or by the effective date of a registration statement filed pursuant to section 12(g);

'(B) within 10 days after he or she becomes such beneficial owner, director, or officer;

'(C) if there has been a change in such ownership, or if such person shall have purchased or sold a security-based swap agreement (as defined in section 206(b) of the Gramm-Leach-Bliley Act (15 U.S.C. 78c note)) involving such equity security, before the end of the second business day following the day on which the subject transaction has been executed, or at such other time as the

Commission shall establish, by rule, in any case in which the Commission determines that such 2-day period is not feasible.

'(3) CONTENTS OF STATEMENTS—A statement filed—

'(A) under subparagraph (A) or (B) of paragraph (2) shall contain a statement of the amount of all equity securities of such issuer of which the filing person is the beneficial owner; and

'(B) under subparagraph (C) of such paragraph shall indicate ownership by the filing person at the date of filing, any such changes in such ownership, and such purchases and sales of the security-based swap agreements as have occurred since the most recent such filing under such subparagraph.

'(4) ELECTRONIC FILING AND AVAILABILITY—Beginning not later than 1 year after the date of enactment of the Sarbanes-Oxley Act of 2002—

'(A) a statement filed under subparagraph (C) of paragraph (2) shall be filed electronically;

'(B) the Commission shall provide each such statement on a publicly accessible Internet site not later than the end of the business day following that filing; and

'(C) the issuer (if the issuer maintains a corporate website) shall provide that statement on that corporate website, not later than the end of the business day following that filing.'.

(b) EFFECTIVE DATE—The amendment made by this section shall be effective 30 days after the date of the enactment of this Act.

[¶ 1032] Section 404—MANAGEMENT ASSESSMENT OF INTERNAL CONTROLS.

(a) RULES REQUIRED—The Commission shall prescribe rules requiring each annual report required by section 13(a) or 15(d) of the Securities Exchange Act of 1934 (15 U.S.C. 78m or 78o(d)) to contain an internal control report, which shall—

(1) state the responsibility of management for establishing and maintaining an adequate internal control structure and procedures for financial reporting; and

(2) contain an assessment, as of the end of the most recent fiscal year of the issuer, of the effectiveness of the internal control structure and procedures of the issuer for financial reporting.

(b) INTERNAL CONTROL EVALUATION AND REPORTING—With respect to the internal control assessment required by subsection (a), each registered public accounting firm that prepares or issues the audit report for the issuer shall attest to, and report on, the assessment made by the management of the issuer. An attestation made under this subsection shall be made in accordance with standards for attestation engagements issued or adopted by the Board. Any such attestation shall not be the subject of a separate engagement.

[¶ 1033] Section 405—EXEMPTION.

Nothing in section 401, 402, or 404, the amendments made by those sections, or the rules of the Commission under those sections shall apply to any investment company registered under section 8 of the Investment Company Act of 1940 (15 U.S.C. 80a-8).

[¶ 1034] Section 406—CODE OF ETHICS FOR SENIOR FINANCIAL OFFICERS.

(a) CODE OF ETHICS DISCLOSURE—The Commission shall issue rules to require each issuer, together with periodic reports required pursuant to section 13(a) or 15(d) of the Securities Exchange Act of 1934, to disclose whether or not, and if not, the reason therefor, such issuer has adopted a code of ethics for senior financial officers, applicable to its principal financial officer and comptroller or principal accounting officer, or persons performing similar functions.

(b) CHANGES IN CODES OF ETHICS—The Commission shall revise its regulations concerning matters requiring prompt disclosure on Form 8-K (or any successor thereto) to require the immediate disclosure, by means of the filing of such form, dissemination by the Internet or by other electronic means, by any issuer of any change in or waiver of the code of ethics for senior financial officers.

(c) DEFINITION—In this section, the term 'code of ethics' means such standards as are reasonably necessary to promote—

(1) honest and ethical conduct, including the ethical handling of actual or apparent conflicts of interest between personal and professional relationships;

(2) full, fair, accurate, timely, and understandable disclosure in the periodic reports required to be filed by the issuer; and

(3) compliance with applicable governmental rules and regulations.

(d) DEADLINE FOR RULEMAKING—The Commission shall—

(1) propose rules to implement this section, not later than 90 days after the date of enactment of this Act; and

(2) issue final rules to implement this section, not later than 180 days after that date of enactment.

[¶ 1035] Section 407—DISCLOSURE OF AUDIT COMMITTEE FINANCIAL EXPERT.

(a) RULES DEFINING 'FINANCIAL EXPERT'—The Commission shall issue rules, as necessary or appropriate in the public interest and consistent with the protection of investors, to require each issuer, together with periodic reports required pursuant to sections 13(a) and 15(d) of the Securities Exchange Act of 1934, to disclose whether or not, and if not, the reasons therefor, the audit committee of that issuer is comprised of at least 1 member who is a financial expert, as such term is defined by the Commission.

(b) CONSIDERATIONS—In defining the term 'financial expert' for purposes of subsection (a), the Commission shall consider whether a person has, through education and experience as a public accountant or auditor or a principal financial officer, comptroller, or principal accounting officer of an issuer, or from a position involving the performance of similar functions—

(1) an understanding of generally accepted accounting principles and financial statements;

(2) experience in—

(A) the preparation or auditing of financial statements of generally comparable issuers; and

(B) the application of such principles in connection with the accounting for estimates, accruals, and reserves;

(3) experience with internal accounting controls; and

(4) an understanding of audit committee functions.

(c) DEADLINE FOR RULEMAKING—The Commission shall—

(1) propose rules to implement this section, not later than 90 days after the date of enactment of this Act; and

(2) issue final rules to implement this section, not later than 180 days after that date of enactment.

[¶ 1036] Section 408—ENHANCED REVIEW OF PERIODIC DISCLOSURES BY ISSUERS.

(a) REGULAR AND SYSTEMATIC REVIEW—The Commission shall review disclosures made by issuers reporting under section 13(a) of the Securities Exchange Act of 1934 (including reports filed on Form 10-K), and which have a class of securities listed on a national securities exchange or traded on an automated quotation facility of a national securities association, on a regular and systematic basis for the protection of investors. Such review shall include a review of an issuer's financial statement.

(b) REVIEW CRITERIA—For purposes of scheduling the reviews required by subsection (a), the Commission shall consider, among other factors—

(1) issuers that have issued material restatements of financial results;

(2) issuers that experience significant volatility in their stock price as compared to other issuers;

(3) issuers with the largest market capitalization;

(4) emerging companies with disparities in price to earning ratios;

(5) issuers whose operations significantly affect any material sector of the economy; and

(6) any other factors that the Commission may consider relevant.

(c) MINIMUM REVIEW PERIOD—In no event shall an issuer required to file reports under section 13(a) or 15(d) of the Securities Exchange Act of 1934 be reviewed under this section less frequently than once every 3 years.

[¶ 1037] Section 409—REAL TIME ISSUER DISCLOSURES.

Section 13 of the Securities Exchange Act of 1934 (15 U.S.C. 78m), as amended by this Act, is amended by adding at the end the following:

'(l) REAL TIME ISSUER DISCLOSURES—Each issuer reporting under section 13(a) or 15(d) shall disclose to the public on a rapid and current basis such additional information concerning material changes in the financial condition or operations of the issuer, in plain English, which may include trend and qualitative information and graphic presentations, as the Commission determines, by rule, is necessary or useful for the protection of investors and in the public interest.'.

TITLE V ANALYST CONFLICTS OF INTEREST

[¶ 1039] Section 501—TREATMENT OF SECURITIES ANALYSTS BY REGISTERED SECURITIES ASSOCIATIONS AND NATIONAL SECURITIES EXCHANGES.

(a) RULES REGARDING SECURITIES ANALYSTS—The Securities Exchange Act of 1934 (15 U.S.C. 78a et seq.) is amended by inserting after section 15C the following new section:

'SEC. 15D. SECURITIES ANALYSTS AND RESEARCH REPORTS.

'(a) ANALYST PROTECTIONS—The Commission, or upon the authorization and direction of the Commission, a registered securities association or national securities exchange, shall have adopted, not later than 1 year after the date of enactment of this section, rules reasonably designed to address conflicts of interest that can arise when securities analysts recommend equity securities in research reports and public appearances, in order to improve the objectivity of research and provide investors with more useful and reliable information, including rules designed—

'(1) to foster greater public confidence in securities research, and to protect the objectivity and independence of securities analysts, by—

'(A) restricting the prepublication clearance or approval of research reports by persons employed by the broker or dealer who are engaged in investment banking activities, or persons not directly responsible for investment research, other than legal or compliance staff;

'(B) limiting the supervision and compensatory evaluation of securities analysts to officials employed by the broker or dealer who are not engaged in investment banking activities; and

'(C) requiring that a broker or dealer and persons employed by a broker or dealer who are involved with investment banking activities may not, directly or indirectly, retaliate against or threaten to retaliate against any securities analyst employed by that broker or dealer or its affiliates as a result of an adverse, negative, or otherwise unfavorable research report that may adversely affect the present or prospective investment banking relationship of the broker or dealer with the issuer that is the subject of the research report, except that such rules may not limit the authority of a broker or dealer to discipline a securities analyst for causes other than such research report in accordance with the policies and procedures of the firm;

'(2) to define periods during which brokers or dealers who have participated, or are to participate, in a public offering of securities as underwriters or dealers should not publish or otherwise distribute research reports relating to such securities or to the issuer of such securities;

'(3) to establish structural and institutional safeguards within registered brokers or dealers to assure that securities analysts are separated by appropriate informational partitions within the firm from the review, pressure, or oversight of those whose involvement in investment banking activities might potentially bias their judgment or supervision; and

'(4) to address such other issues as the Commission, or such association or exchange, determines appropriate.

'(b) DISCLOSURE—The Commission, or upon the authorization and direction of the Commission, a registered securities association or national securities exchange, shall have adopted, not later than 1 year after the date of enactment of this section, rules reasonably designed to require each securities analyst to disclose in public appearances, and each registered broker or dealer to disclose in each research report, as applicable, conflicts of interest that are known or should have been known by the securities analyst or the broker or dealer, to exist at the time of the appearance or the date of distribution of the report, including—

'(1) the extent to which the securities analyst has debt or equity investments in the issuer that is the subject of the appearance or research report;

'(2) whether any compensation has been received by the registered broker or dealer, or any affiliate thereof, including the securities analyst, from the issuer that is the subject of the appearance or research report, subject to such exemptions as the Commission may determine appropriate and necessary to prevent disclosure by virtue of this paragraph of material non-public information regarding specific potential future investment banking transactions of such issuer, as is appropriate in the public interest and consistent with the protection of investors;

'(3) whether an issuer, the securities of which are recommended in the appearance or research report, currently is, or during the 1-year period preceding the date of the appearance or date of distribution of the report has been, a client of the registered broker or dealer, and if so, stating the types of services provided to the issuer;

'(4) whether the securities analyst received compensation with respect to a research report, based upon (among any other factors) the investment banking revenues (either generally or specifically earned from the issuer being analyzed) of the registered broker or dealer; and

'(5) such other disclosures of conflicts of interest that are material to investors, research analysts, or the broker or dealer as the Commission, or such association or exchange, determines appropriate.

'(c) DEFINITIONS—In this section—

'(1) the term 'securities analyst' means any associated person of a registered broker or dealer that is principally responsible for, and any associated person who reports directly or indirectly to a securities analyst in connection with, the preparation of the substance of a research report, whether or not any such person has the job title of 'securities analyst'; and

'(2) the term 'research report' means a written or electronic communication that includes an analysis of equity securities of individual companies or industries, and that provides information reasonably sufficient upon which to base an investment decision.'.

(b) ENFORCEMENT—Section 21B(a) of the Securities Exchange Act of 1934 (15 U.S.C. 78u-2(a)) is amended by inserting '15D,' before '15B'.

(c) COMMISSION AUTHORITY—The Commission may promulgate and amend its regulations, or direct a registered securities association or national securities exchange to promulgate and amend its rules, to carry out section 15D of the Securities Exchange Act of 1934, as added by this section, as is necessary for the protection of investors and in the public interest.

Title VI COMMISSION RESOURCES AND AUTHORITY

[¶ 1041] Section 601—Authorization of Appropriations

Section 35 of the Securities Exchange Act of 1934 (15 U.S.C. 78kk) is amended to read as follows:

'SEC. 35. AUTHORIZATION OF APPROPRIATIONS.

'In addition to any other funds authorized to be appropriated to the Commission, there are authorized to be appropriated to carry out the functions, powers, and duties of the Commission, $776,000,000 for fiscal year 2003, of which—

'(1) $102,700,000 shall be available to fund additional compensation, including salaries and benefits, as authorized in the Investor and Capital Markets Fee Relief Act (Public Law 107-123; 115 Stat. 2390 et seq.);

'(2) $108,400,000 shall be available for information technology, security enhancements, and recovery and mitigation activities in light of the terrorist attacks of September 11, 2001; and

'(3) $98,000,000 shall be available to add not fewer than an additional 200 qualified professionals to provide enhanced oversight of auditors and audit services required by the Federal securities laws, and to improve Commission investigative and disciplinary efforts with respect to such auditors and services, as well as for additional professional support staff necessary to strengthen the programs of the Commission involving Full Disclosure and Prevention and Suppression of Fraud, risk management, industry technology review, compliance, inspections, examinations, market regulation, and investment management.'.

[¶ 1042] Section 602—APPEARANCE AND PRACTICE BEFORE THE COMMISSION.

The Securities Exchange Act of 1934 (15 U.S.C. 78a et seq.) is amended by inserting after section 4B the following:

'SEC. 4C. APPEARANCE AND PRACTICE BEFORE THE COMMISSION.

'(a) AUTHORITY TO CENSURE—The Commission may censure any person, or deny, temporarily or permanently, to any person the privilege of appearing or practicing before the Commission in any way, if that person is found by the Commission, after notice and opportunity for hearing in the matter—

'(1) not to possess the requisite qualifications to represent others;

'(2) to be lacking in character or integrity, or to have engaged in unethical or improper professional conduct; or

'(3) to have willfully violated, or willfully aided and abetted the violation of, any provision of the securities laws or the rules and regulations issued thereunder.

'(b) DEFINITION—With respect to any registered public accounting firm or associated person, for purposes of this section, the term 'improper professional conduct' means—

'(1) intentional or knowing conduct, including reckless conduct, that results in a violation of applicable professional standards; and

'(2) negligent conduct in the form of—

'(A) a single instance of highly unreasonable conduct that results in a violation of applicable professional standards in circumstances in which the registered public accounting firm or associated person knows, or should know, that heightened scrutiny is warranted; or

'(B) repeated instances of unreasonable conduct, each resulting in a violation of applicable professional standards, that indicate a lack of competence to practice before the Commission.'.

[¶ 1043] Section 603—FEDERAL COURT AUTHORITY TO IMPOSE PENNY STOCK BARS.

(a) Securities Exchange Act of 1934—Section 21(d) of the Securities Exchange Act of 1934 (15 U.S.C. 78u(d)), as amended by this Act, is amended by adding at the end the following:

'(6) AUTHORITY OF A COURT TO PROHIBIT PERSONS FROM PARTICIPATING IN AN OFFERING OF PENNY STOCK—

'(A) IN GENERAL—In any proceeding under paragraph (1) against any person participating in, or, at the time of the alleged misconduct who was participating in, an offering of penny stock, the court may prohibit that person from participating in an offering of penny stock, conditionally or unconditionally, and permanently or for such period of time as the court shall determine.

'(B) DEFINITION—For purposes of this paragraph, the term 'person participating in an offering of penny stock' includes any person engaging in activities with a broker, dealer, or issuer for purposes of issuing, trading, or inducing or attempting to induce the purchase or sale of, any penny stock. The Commission may, by rule or regulation, define such term to include other activities, and may, by rule, regulation, or order, exempt any person or class of persons, in whole or in part, conditionally or unconditionally, from inclusion in such term.'.

(b) Securities Act of 1933—Section 20 of the Securities Act of 1933 (15 U.S.C. 77t) is amended by adding at the end the following:

'(g) AUTHORITY OF A COURT TO PROHIBIT PERSONS FROM PARTICIPATING IN AN OFFERING OF PENNY STOCK—

'(1) IN GENERAL—In any proceeding under subsection (a) against any person participating in, or, at the time of the alleged misconduct, who was participating in, an offering of penny stock, the court may prohibit that person from participating in an offering of penny stock, conditionally or unconditionally, and permanently or for such period of time as the court shall determine.

'(2) DEFINITION—For purposes of this subsection, the term 'person participating in an offering of penny stock' includes any person engaging in activities with a broker, dealer, or issuer for purposes of issuing, trading, or inducing or attempting to induce the purchase or sale of, any penny stock. The Commission may, by rule or regulation, define such term to include other activities, and may, by rule, regulation, or order, exempt any person or class of persons, in whole or in part, conditionally or unconditionally, from inclusion in such term.'.

[¶ 1044] Section 604—QUALIFICATIONS OF ASSOCIATED PERSONS OF BROKERS AND DEALERS.

(a) BROKERS AND DEALERS—Section 15(b)(4) of the Securities Exchange Act of 1934 (15 U.S.C. 78o) is amended—

(1) by striking subparagraph (F) and inserting the following:

'(F) is subject to any order of the Commission barring or suspending the right of the person to be associated with a broker or dealer;'; and

(2) in subparagraph (G), by striking the period at the end and inserting the following: '; or

'(H) is subject to any final order of a State securities commission (or any agency or officer performing like functions), State authority that supervises or examines banks, savings associations, or credit unions, State insurance commission (or any agency or office performing like functions), an appropriate Federal banking agency (as defined in section 3 of the Federal Deposit Insurance Act (12 U.S.C. 1813(q))), or the National Credit Union Administration, that—

'(i) bars such person from association with an entity regulated by such commission, authority, agency, or officer, or from engaging in the business of securities, insurance, banking, savings association activities, or credit union activities; or '(ii) constitutes a final order based on violations of any laws or regulations that prohibit fraudulent, manipulative, or deceptive conduct.'.

(b) INVESTMENT ADVISERS—Section 203(e) of the Investment Advisers Act of 1940 (15 U.S.C. 80b-3(e)) is amended—

(1) by striking paragraph (7) and inserting the following:

'(7) is subject to any order of the Commission barring or suspending the right of the person to be associated with an investment adviser;';

(2) in paragraph (8), by striking the period at the end and inserting '; or'; and

(3) by adding at the end the following:

'(9) is subject to any final order of a State securities commission (or any agency or officer performing like functions), State authority that supervises or examines banks, savings associations, or credit unions, State insurance commission (or any agency or office performing like functions), an appropriate Federal banking agency (as defined in section 3 of the Federal Deposit Insurance Act (12 U.S.C. 1813(q))), or the National Credit Union Administration, that—

'(A) bars such person from association with an entity regulated by such commission, authority, agency, or officer, or from engaging in the business of securities, insurance, banking, savings association activities, or credit union activities; or

'(B) constitutes a final order based on violations of any laws or regulations that prohibit fraudulent, manipulative, or deceptive conduct.'.

(c) CONFORMING AMENDMENTS—

(1) SECURITIES EXCHANGE ACT OF 1934—The Securities Exchange Act of 1934 (15 U.S.C. 78a et seq.) is amended—

(A) in section 3(a)(39)(F) (15 U.S.C. 78c(a)(39)(F))—

(i) by striking 'or (G)' and inserting '(H), or (G)'; and

(ii) by inserting ', or is subject to an order or finding,' before 'enumerated';

(B) in each of section 15(b)(6)(A)(i) (15 U.S.C. 78o(b)(6)(A)(i)), paragraphs (2) and (4) of section 15B(c) (15 U.S.C. 78o-4(c)), and subparagraphs (A) and (C) of section 15C(c)(1) (15 U.S.C. 78o-5(c)(1))—

(i) by striking 'or (G)' each place that term appears and inserting '(H), or (G)'; and

(ii) by striking 'or omission' each place that term appears, and inserting ', or is subject to an order or finding,'; and

(C) in each of paragraphs (3)(A) and (4)(C) of section 17A(c) (15 U.S.C. 78q-1(c))—

(i) by striking 'or (G)' each place that term appears and inserting '(H), or (G)'; and

(ii) by inserting ', or is subject to an order or finding,' before 'enumerated' each place that term appears.

(2) INVESTMENT ADVISERS ACT OF 1940—Section 203(f) of the Investment Advisers Act of 1940 (15 U.S.C. 80b-3(f)) is amended—

(A) by striking 'or (8)' and inserting '(8), or (9)'; and

(B) by inserting 'or (3)' after 'paragraph (2)'.

Title VII STUDIES AND REPORTS

[¶ 1045] Section 701—GAO STUDY AND REPORT REGARDING CONSOLIDATION OF PUBLIC ACCOUNTING FIRMS.

(a) STUDY REQUIRED-The Comptroller General of the United States shall conduct a study—

(1) to identify—

(A) the factors that have led to the consolidation of public accounting firms since 1989 and the consequent reduction in the number of firms capable of providing audit services to large national and multi-national business organizations that are subject to the securities laws;

(B) the present and future impact of the condition described in subparagraph (A) on capital formation and securities markets, both domestic and international; and

(C) solutions to any problems identified under subparagraph (B), including ways to increase competition and the number of firms capable of providing audit services to large national and multinational business organizations that are subject to the securities laws;

(2) of the problems, if any, faced by business organizations that have resulted from limited competition among public accounting firms, including—

(A) higher costs;

(B) lower quality of services;

(C) impairment of auditor independence; or

(D) lack of choice; and

(3) whether and to what extent Federal or State regulations impede competition among public accounting firms.

(b) CONSULTATION—In planning and conducting the study under this section, the Comptroller General shall consult with—

(1) the Commission;

(2) the regulatory agencies that perform functions similar to the Commission within the other member countries of the Group of Seven Industrialized Nations;

(3) the Department of Justice; and

(4) any other public or private sector organization that the Comptroller General considers appropriate.

(c) REPORT REQUIRED—Not later than 1 year after the date of enactment of this Act, the Comptroller General shall submit a report on the results of the study required by this section to the Committee on Banking, Housing, and Urban Affairs of the Senate and the Committee on Financial Services of the House of Representatives.

[¶ 1046] Section 702—COMMISSION STUDY AND REPORT REGARDING CREDIT RATING AGENCIES.

(a) STUDY REQUIRED—

(1) IN GENERAL—The Commission shall conduct a study of the role and function of credit rating agencies in the operation of the securities market.

(2) AREAS OF CONSIDERATION—The study required by this subsection shall examine—

(A) the role of credit rating agencies in the evaluation of issuers of securities;

(B) the importance of that role to investors and the functioning of the securities markets;

(C) any impediments to the accurate appraisal by credit rating agencies of the financial resources and risks of issuers of securities;

(D) any barriers to entry into the business of acting as a credit rating agency, and any measures needed to remove such barriers;

(E) any measures which may be required to improve the dissemination of information concerning such resources and risks when credit rating agencies announce credit ratings; and

(F) any conflicts of interest in the operation of credit rating agencies and measures to prevent such conflicts or ameliorate the consequences of such conflicts.

(b) REPORT REQUIRED—The Commission shall submit a report on the study required by subsection (a) to the President, the Committee on Financial Services of the House of Representatives, and the Committee on Banking, Housing, and Urban Affairs of the Senate not later than 180 days after the date of enactment of this Act.

[¶ 1047] Section 703—STUDY AND REPORT ON VIOLATORS AND VIOLATIONS.

(a) STUDY—The Commission shall conduct a study to determine, based upon information for the period from January 1, 1998, to December 31, 2001—

(1) the number of securities professionals, defined as public accountants, public accounting firms, investment bankers, investment advisers, brokers, dealers, attorneys, and other securities professionals practicing before the Commission—

(A) who have been found to have aided and abetted a violation of the Federal securities laws, including rules or regulations promulgated thereunder (collectively referred to in this section as 'Federal securities laws'), but who have not been sanctioned, disciplined, or otherwise penalized as a primary violator in any administrative action or civil proceeding, including in any settlement of such an action or proceeding (referred to in this section as 'aiders and abettors'); and

(B) who have been found to have been primary violators of the Federal securities laws;

(2) a description of the Federal securities laws violations committed by aiders and abettors and by primary violators, including—

(A) the specific provision of the Federal securities laws violated;

(B) the specific sanctions and penalties imposed upon such aiders and abettors and primary violators, including the amount of any monetary penalties assessed upon and collected from such persons;

(C) the occurrence of multiple violations by the same person or persons, either as an aider or abettor or as a primary violator; and

(D) whether, as to each such violator, disciplinary sanctions have been imposed, including any censure, suspension, temporary bar, or permanent bar to practice before the Commission; and

(3) the amount of disgorgement, restitution, or any other fines or payments that the Commission has assessed upon and collected from, aiders and abettors and from primary violators.

(b) REPORT—A report based upon the study conducted pursuant to subsection (a) shall be submitted to the Committee on Banking, Housing, and Urban Affairs of the Senate, and the Committee on Financial Services of the House of Representatives not later than 6 months after the date of enactment of this Act.

[¶ 1048] Section 704—STUDY OF ENFORCEMENT ACTIONS.

(a) STUDY REQUIRED—The Commission shall review and analyze all enforcement actions by the Commission involving violations of reporting requirements imposed under the securities laws, and restatements of financial statements, over the 5-year period preceding the date of enactment of this Act, to identify areas of reporting that are most susceptible to fraud, inappropriate manipulation, or inappropriate earnings management, such as revenue recognition and the accounting treatment of off-balance sheet special purpose entities.

(b) REPORT REQUIRED—The Commission shall report its findings to the Committee on Financial Services of the House of Representatives and the Committee on Banking, Housing, and Urban Affairs of the Senate, not later than 180 days after the date of enactment of this Act, and shall use such findings to revise its rules and regulations, as necessary. The report shall include a discussion of regulatory or legislative steps that are recommended or that may be necessary to address concerns identified in the study.

[¶ 1049] Section 705—STUDY OF INVESTMENT BANKS.

(a) GAO STUDY—The Comptroller General of the United States shall conduct a study on whether investment banks and financial advisers assisted public companies in manipulating their earnings and obfuscating their true financial condition. The study should address the rule of investment banks and financial advisers—

(1) in the collapse of the Enron Corporation, including with respect to the design and implementation of derivatives transactions, transactions involving special purpose vehicles, and other financial arrangements that may have had the effect of altering the company's reported financial statements in ways that obscured the true financial picture of the company;

(2) in the failure of Global Crossing, including with respect to transactions involving swaps of fiberoptic cable capacity, in the designing transactions that may have had the effect of altering the company's reported financial statements in ways that obscured the true financial picture of the company; and

(3) generally, in creating and marketing transactions which may have been designed solely to enable companies to manipulate revenue streams, obtain loans, or move liabilities off balance sheets without altering the economic and business risks faced by the companies or any other mechanism to obscure a company's financial picture.

(b) REPORT—The Comptroller General shall report to Congress not later than 180 days after the date of enactment of this Act on the results of the study required by this section. The report shall include a discussion of regulatory or legislative steps that are recommended or that may be necessary to address concerns identified in the study.

Title VIII CORPORATE AND CRIMINAL FRAUD ACCOUNTABILITY

[¶ 1051] Section 801—SHORT TITLE.

This title may be cited as the 'Corporate and Criminal Fraud Accountability Act of 2002'.

[¶ 1052] Section 802—CRIMINAL PENALTIES FOR ALTERING DOCUMENTS.

(a) IN GENERAL—Chapter 73 of title 18, United States Code, is amended by adding at the end the following:

'Sec. 1519. Destruction, alteration, or falsification of records in Federal investigations and bankruptcy

'Whoever knowingly alters, destroys, mutilates, conceals, covers up, falsifies, or makes a false entry in any record, document, or tangible object with the intent to impede, obstruct, or influence the investigation or proper administration of any matter within the jurisdiction of any department or agency of the United States or any case filed under title 11, or in relation to or contemplation of any such matter or case, shall be fined under this title, imprisoned not more than 20 years, or both.

'Sec. 1520. Destruction of corporate audit records

'(a)(1) Any accountant who conducts an audit of an issuer of securities to which section 10A(a) of the Securities Exchange Act of 1934 (15 U.S.C. 78j-1(a)) applies, shall maintain all audit or review workpapers for a period of 5 years from the end of the fiscal period in which the audit or review was concluded.

'(2) The Securities and Exchange Commission shall promulgate, within 180 days, after adequate notice and an opportunity for comment, such rules and regulations, as are reasonably necessary, relating to the retention of relevant records such as workpapers, documents that form the basis of an audit or review, memoranda, correspondence, communications, other documents, and records (including electronic records) which are created, sent, or received in connection with an audit or review and contain conclusions, opinions, analyses, or financial data relating to such an audit or review, which is conducted by any accountant who conducts an audit of an issuer of securities to which section 10A(a) of the Securities Exchange Act of 1934 (15 U.S.C. 78j-1(a)) applies. The Commission may, from time to time, amend or supplement the rules and regulations that it is required to promulgate under this section, after adequate notice and an opportunity for comment, in order to ensure that such rules and regulations adequately comport with the purposes of this section.

'(b) Whoever knowingly and willfully violates subsection (a)(1), or any rule or regulation promulgated by the Securities and Exchange Commission under subsection (a)(2), shall be fined under this title, imprisoned not more than 10 years, or both.

'(c) Nothing in this section shall be deemed to diminish or relieve any person of any other duty or obligation imposed by Federal or State law or regulation to maintain, or refrain from destroying, any document.'.

(b) CLERICAL AMENDMENT—The table of sections at the beginning of chapter 73 of title 18, United States Code, is amended by adding at the end the following new items:

'1519. Destruction, alteration, or falsification of records in Federal investigations and bankruptcy.

'1520. Destruction of corporate audit records.'.

[¶ 1053] Section 803—DEBTS NONDISCHARGEABLE IF INCURRED IN VIOLATION OF SECURITIES FRAUD LAWS.

Section 523(a) of title 11, United States Code, is amended—

(1) in paragraph (17), by striking 'or' after the semicolon;

(2) in paragraph (18), by striking the period at the end and inserting '; or'; and

(3) by adding at the end, the following:

'(19) that—

'(A) is for—

'(i) the violation of any of the Federal securities laws (as that term is defined in section 3(a)(47) of the Securities Exchange Act of 1934), any of the State securities laws, or any regulation or order issued under such Federal or State securities laws; or

'(ii) common law fraud, deceit, or manipulation in connection with the purchase or sale of any security; and

'(B) results from—

'(i) any judgment, order, consent order, or decree entered in any Federal or State judicial or administrative proceeding;

'(ii) any settlement agreement entered into by the debtor; or

'(iii) any court or administrative order for any damages, fine, penalty, citation, restitutionary payment, disgorgement payment, attorney fee, cost, or other payment owed by the debtor.'.

[¶ 1054] Section 804—STATUTE OF LIMITATIONS FOR SECURITIES FRAUD.

(a) IN GENERAL—Section 1658 of title 28, United States Code, is amended—

(1) by inserting '(a)' before 'Except'; and

(2) by adding at the end the following:

'(b) Notwithstanding subsection (a), a private right of action that involves a claim of fraud, deceit, manipulation, or contrivance in contravention of a regulatory requirement concerning the securities laws, as defined in section 3(a)(47) of the Securities Exchange Act of 1934 (15 U.S.C. 78c(a)(47)), may be brought not later than the earlier of—

'(1) 2 years after the discovery of the facts constituting the violation; or

'(2) 5 years after such violation.'.

(b) EFFECTIVE DATE—The limitations period provided by section 1658(b) of title 28, United States Code, as added by this section, shall apply to all proceedings addressed by this section that are commenced on or after the date of enactment of this Act.

(c) NO CREATION OF ACTIONS—Nothing in this section shall create a new, private right of action.

[¶ 1055] Section 805—REVIEW OF FEDERAL SENTENCING GUIDELINES FOR OBSTRUCTION OF JUSTICE AND EXTENSIVE CRIMINAL FRAUD.

(a) ENHANCEMENT OF FRAUD AND OBSTRUCTION OF JUSTICE SENTENCES—Pursuant to section 994 of title 28, United States Code, and in accordance with this section, the United States Sentencing Commission shall review and amend, as appropriate, the Federal Sentencing Guidelines and related policy statements to ensure that—

(1) the base offense level and existing enhancements contained in United States Sentencing Guideline 2J1.2 relating to obstruction of justice are sufficient to deter and punish that activity;

(2) the enhancements and specific offense characteristics relating to obstruction of justice are adequate in cases where—

(A) the destruction, alteration, or fabrication of evidence involves—

(i) a large amount of evidence, a large number of participants, or is otherwise extensive;

(ii) the selection of evidence that is particularly probative or essential to the investigation; or

(iii) more than minimal planning; or

(B) the offense involved abuse of a special skill or a position of trust;

(3) the guideline offense levels and enhancements for violations of section 1519 or 1520 of title 18, United States Code, as added by this title, are sufficient to deter and punish that activity;

(4) a specific offense characteristic enhancing sentencing is provided under United States Sentencing Guideline 2B1.1 (as in effect on the date of enactment of this Act) for a fraud offense that endangers the solvency or financial security of a substantial number of victims; and

(5) the guidelines that apply to organizations in United States Sentencing Guidelines, chapter 8, are sufficient to deter and punish organizational criminal misconduct.

(b) EMERGENCY AUTHORITY AND DEADLINE FOR COMMISSION ACTION—The United States Sentencing Commission is requested to promulgate the guidelines or amendments provided for under this section as soon as practicable, and in any event not later than 180 days after the date of enactment of this Act, in accordance with the prcedures set forth in section 219(a) of the Sentencing Reform Act of 1987, as though the authority under that Act had not expired.

[¶ 1056] Section 806—PROTECTION FOR EMPLOYEES OF PUBLICLY TRADED COMPANIES WHO PROVIDE EVIDENCE OF FRAUD.

(a) IN GENERAL—Chapter 73 of title 18, United States Code, is amended by inserting after section 1514 the following:.SEC. 1107. RETALIATION AGAINST INFORMANTS.(a) IN Section 1513 of title 18, United-States Code, is amended by adding at the end the following:

'Sec. 1514A. Civil action to protect against retaliation in fraud cases

'(a) WHISTLEBLOWER PROTECTION FOR EMPLOYEES OF PUBLICLY TRADED COMPANIES—No company with a class of securities registered under section 12 of the Securities Exchange Act of 1934 (15 U.S.C. 78l), or that is required to file reports under section 15(d) of the Securities Exchange Act of 1934 (15 U.S.C. 78o(d)), or any officer, employee, contractor, subcontractor, or agent of such company, may discharge, demote, suspend, threaten, harass, or in any other manner discriminate against an employee in the terms and conditions of employment because of any lawful act done by the employee—

'(1) to provide information, cause information to be provided, or otherwise assist in an investigation regarding any conduct which the employee reasonably believes constitutes a violation of section 1341, 1343, 1344, or 1348, any rule or regulation of the Securities and Exchange Commission, or any provision of Federal law relating to fraud against shareholders, when the information or assistance is provided to or the investigation is conducted by—

'(A) a Federal regulatory or law enforcement agency;

'(B) any Member of Congress or any committee of Congress; or

'(C) a person with supervisory authority over the employee (or such other person working for the employer who has the authority to investigate, discover, or terminate misconduct); or

'(2) to file, cause to be filed, testify, participate in, or otherwise assist in a proceeding filed or about to be filed (with any knowledge of the employer) relating to an alleged violation of section 1341, 1343, 1344, or 1348, any rule or regulation of the Securities and Exchange Commission, or any provision of Federal law relating to fraud against shareholders.

'(b) ENFORCEMENT ACTION—

'(1) IN GENERAL—A person who alleges discharge or other discrimination by any person in violation of subsection (a) may seek relief under subsection (c), by—

'(A) filing a complaint with the Secretary of Labor; or

'(B) if the Secretary has not issued a final decision within 180 days of the filing of the complaint and there is no showing that such delay is due to the bad faith of the claimant, bringing an action at law or equity for de novo review in the appropriate district court of the United States, which shall have jurisdiction over such an action without regard to the amount in controversy.

'(2) PROCEDURE—

'(A) IN GENERAL—An action under paragraph (1)(A) shall be governed under the rules and procedures set forth in section 42121(b) of title 49, United States Code.

'(B) EXCEPTION—Notification made under section 42121(b)(1) of title 49, United States Code, shall be made to the person named in the complaint and to the employer.

'(C) BURDENS OF PROOF—An action brought under paragraph (1)(B) shall be governed by the legal burdens of proof set forth in section 42121(b) of title 49, United States Code.

'(D) STATUTE OF LIMITATIONS—An action under paragraph (1) shall be commenced not later than 90 days after the date on which the violation occurs.

'(c) REMEDIES—

'(1) IN GENERAL—An employee prevailing in any action under subsection (b)(1) shall be entitled to all relief necessary to make the employee whole.

'(2) COMPENSATORY DAMAGES—Relief for any action under paragraph (1) shall include—

'(A) reinstatement with the same seniority status that the employee would have had, but for the discrimination;

'(B) the amount of back pay, with interest; and

'(C) compensation for any special damages sustained as a result of the discrimination, including litigation costs, expert witness fees, and reasonable attorney fees.

'(d) RIGHTS RETAINED BY EMPLOYEE—Nothing in this section shall be deemed to diminish the rights, privileges, or remedies of any employee under any Federal or State law, or under any collective bargaining agreement.'.

(b) CLERICAL AMENDMENT—The table of sections at the beginning of chapter 73 of title 18, United States Code, is amended by inserting after the item relating to section 1514 the following new item:

'1514A. Civil action to protect against retaliation in fraud cases.'.

[¶ 1057] Section 807—CRIMINAL PENALTIES FOR DEFRAUDING SHAREHOLDERS OF PUBLICLY TRADED COMPANIES.

(a) IN GENERAL—Chapter 63 of title 18, United States Code, is amended by adding at the end the following:

'Sec. 1348. Securities fraud

'Whoever knowingly executes, or attempts to execute, a scheme or artifice—

'(1) to defraud any person in connection with any security of an issuer with a class of securities registered under section 12 of the Securities Exchange Act of 1934 (15 U.S.C. 78l) or that is required to file reports under section 15(d) of the Securities Exchange Act of 1934 (15 U.S.C. 78o(d)); or

'(2) to obtain, by means of false or fraudulent pretenses, representations, or promises, any money or property in connection with the purchase or sale of any security of an issuer with a class of securities registered under section 12 of the Securities Exchange Act of 1934 (15 U.S.C. 78l) or that is required to file reports under section 15(d) of the Securities Exchange Act of 1934 (15 U.S.C. 78o(d));

shall be fined under this title, or imprisoned not more than 25 years, or both.'.

(b) CLERICAL AMENDMENT—The table of sections at the beginning of chapter 63 of title 18, United States Code, is amended by adding at the end the following new item:

'1348. Securities fraud.'.

TITLE IX WHITE-COLLAR CRIME PENALTY ENHANCEMENTS

[¶ 1059] Section 901—SHORT TITLE.

This title may be cited as the 'White-Collar Crime Penalty Enhancement Act of 2002'.

[¶ 1060] Section 902—ATTEMPTS AND CONSPIRACIES TO COMMIT CRIMINAL FRAUD OFFENSES.

(a) IN GENERAL—Chapter 63 of title 18, United States Code, is amended by inserting after section 1348 as added by this Act the following:

'Sec. 1349. Attempt and conspiracy

'Any person who attempts or conspires to commit any offense under this chapter shall be subject to the same penalties as those prescribed for the offense, the commission of which was the object of the attempt or conspiracy.

(b) CLERICAL AMENDMENT—The table of sections at the beginning of chapter 63 of title 18, United States Code, is amended by adding at the end the following new item:

'1349. Attempt and conspiracy.'.

[¶ 1061] Section 903—CRIMINAL PENALTIES FOR MAIL AND WIRE FRAUD.

(a) MAIL FRAUD—Section 1341 of title 18, United States Code, is amended by striking 'five' and inserting '20'.

(b) WIRE FRAUD—Section 1343 of title 18, United States Code, is amended by striking 'five' and inserting '20'.

[¶ 1062] Section 904—CRIMINAL PENALTIES FOR VIOLATIONS OF THE EMPLOYEE RETIREMENT INCOME SECURITY ACT OF 1974.

Section 501 of the Employee Retirement Income Security Act of 1974 (29 U.S.C. 1131) is amended—

(1) by striking '$5,000' and inserting '$100,000';

(2) by striking 'one year' and inserting '10 years'; and

(3) by striking '$100,000' and inserting '$500,000'.

[¶ 1063] Section 905—AMENDMENT TO SENTENCING GUIDELINES RELATING TO CERTAIN WHITE-COLLAR OFFENSES.

(a) DIRECTIVE TO THE UNITED STATES SENTENCING COMMISSION—Pursuant to its authority under section 994(p) of title 18, United States Code, and in accordance with this section, the United States Sentencing Commission shall review and, as appropriate, amend the Federal Sentencing Guidelines and related policy statements to implement the provisions of this Act.

(b) REQUIREMENTS—In carrying out this section, the Sentencing Commission shall—

(1) ensure that the sentencing guidelines and policy statements reflect the serious nature of the offenses and the penalties set forth in this Act, the growing incidence of serious fraud offenses which are identified above, and the need to modify the sentencing guidelines and policy statements to deter, prevent, and punish such offenses;

(2) consider the extent to which the guidelines and policy statements adequately address whether the guideline offense levels and enhancements for violations of the sections amended by this Act are sufficient to deter andpunish such offenses, and specifically, are adequate in view of the statutory increases in penalties contained in this Act;

(3) assure reasonable consistency with other relevant directives and sentencing guidelines;

(4) account for any additional aggravating or mitigating circumstances that might justify exceptions to the generally applicable sentencing ranges;

(5) make any necessary conforming changes to the sentencing guidelines; and

(6) assure that the guidelines adequately meet the purposes of sentencing, as set forth in section 3553(a)(2) of title 18, United States Code.

(c) EMERGENCY AUTHORITY AND DEADLINE FOR COMMISSION ACTION—The United States Sentencing Commission is requested to promulgate the guidelines or amendments provided for under this section as soon as practicable, and in any event not later than 180 days after the date of enactment of this Act, in accordance with the procedures set forth in section 219(a) of the Sentencing Reform Act of 1987, as though the authority under that Act had not expired.

[¶ 1064] Section 906—CORPORATE RESPONSIBILITY FOR FINANCIAL REPORTS.

(a) IN GENERAL—Chapter 63 of title 18, United States Code, is amended by inserting after section 1349, as created by this Act, the following:

'Sec. 1350. Failure of corporate officers to certify financial reports

(a) CERTIFICATION OF PERIODIC FINANCIAL REPORTS—Each periodic report containing financial statements filed by an issuer with the Securities Exchange Commission pursuant to section 13(a) or 15(d) of the Securities Exchange Act of 1934 (15 U.S.C. 78m(a) or 78o(d)) shall be accompanied by a written statement by the chief executive officer and chief financial officer (or equivalent thereof) of the issuer.

'(b) CONTENT—The statement required under subsection (a) shall certify that the periodic report containing the financial statements fully complies with the requirements of section 13(a) or 15(d) of the Securities Exchange Act of 1934 (15 U.S.C. 78m or 78o(d)) and that information contained in the periodic report fairly presents, in all material respects, the financial condition and results of operations of the issuer.

'(c) CRIMINAL PENALTIES—Whoever—

'(1) certifies any statement as set forth in subsections (a) and (b) of this section knowing that the periodic report accompanying the statement does not comport with all the requirements set forth in this section shall be fined not more than $1,000,000 or imprisoned not more than 10 years, or both; or

'(2) willfully certifies any statement as set forth in subsections (a) and (b) of this section knowing that the periodic report accompanying the statement does not comport with all the requirements set forth in this section shall be fined not more than $5,000,000, or imprisoned not more than 20 years, or both.'.

(b) CLERICAL AMENDMENT—The table of sections at the beginning of chapter 63 of title 18, United States Code, is amended by adding at the end the following:

'1350. Failure of corporate officers to certify financial reports.'.

TITLE X CORPORATE TAX RETURNS

[¶ 1065] Section 1001—SENSE OF THE SENATE REGARDING THE SIGNING OF CORPORATE TAX RETURNS BY CHIEF EXECUTIVE OFFICERS.

It is the sense of the Senate that the Federal income tax return of a corporation should be signed by the chief executive officer of such corporation.

TITLE XI CORPORATE FRAUD ACCOUNTABILITY

[¶ 1067] Section 1101—SHORT TITLE.

This title may be cited as the 'Corporate Fraud Accountability Act of 2002'.

[¶ 1068] Section 1102—TAMPERING WITH A RECORD OR OTHERWISE IMPEDING AN OFFICIAL PROCEEDING.

Section 1512 of title 18, United States Code, is amended—

(1) by redesignating subsections (c) through (i) as subsections (d) through (j), respectively; and

(2) by inserting after subsection (b) the following new subsection:

'(c) Whoever corruptly—

'(1) alters, destroys, mutilates, or conceals a record, document, or other object, or attempts to do so, with the intent to impair the object's integrity or availability for use in an official proceeding; or

'(2) otherwise obstructs, influences, or impedes any official proceeding, or attempts to do so,

shall be fined under this title or imprisoned not more than 20 years, or both.'.

[¶ 1069] Section 1103—TEMPORARY FREEZE AUTHORITY FOR THE SECURITIES AND EXCHANGE COMMISSION.

(a) IN GENERAL—Section 21C(c) of the Securities Exchange Act of 1934 (15 U.S.C. 78u-3(c)) is amended by adding at the end the following:

'(3) TEMPORARY FREEZE—

'(A) IN GENERAL—

'(i) ISSUANCE OF TEMPORARY ORDER—Whenever, during the course of a lawful investigation involving possible violations of the Federal securities laws by an issuer of publicly traded securities or any of its directors, officers, partners, controlling persons, agents, or employees, it shall appear to the Commission that it is likely that the issuer will make extraordinary payments (whether compensation or otherwise) to any of the foregoing persons, the Commission may petition a Federal district court for a temporary order requiring the issuer to escrow, subject to court supervision, those payments in an interest-bearing account for 45 days.

'(ii) STANDARD—A temporary order shall be entered under clause (i), only after notice and opportunity for a hearing, unless the court determines that notice and hearing prior to entry of the order would be impracticable or contrary to the public interest.

'(iii) EFFECTIVE PERIOD—A temporary order issued under clause (i) shall—

'(I) become effective immediately;

'(II) be served upon the parties subject to it; and

'(III) unless set aside, limited or suspended by a court of competent jurisdiction, shall remain effective and enforceable for 45 days.

'(iv) EXTENSIONS AUTHORIZED—The effective period of an order under this subparagraph may be extended by the court upon good cause shown for not longer than 45 additional days, provided that the combined period of the order shall not exceed 90 days.

'(B) PROCESS ON DETERMINATION OF VIOLATIONS—

'(i) VIOLATIONS CHARGED—If the issuer or other person described in subparagraph (A) is charged with any violation of the Federal securities laws before the expiration of the effective period of a temporary order under subparagraph (A) (including any applicable extension period), the order shall remain in effect, subject to court approval, until the conclusion of any legal proceedings related thereto, and the affected issuer or other person, shall have the right to petition the court for review of the order.

'(ii) VIOLATIONS NOT CHARGED—If the issuer or other person described in subparagraph (A) is not charged with any violation of the Federal securities laws before the expiration of the effective period of a temporary order under subparagraph (A) (including any applicable extension period), the escrow shall terminate at the expiration of the 45-day effective period (or the expiration of any extension period, as applicable), and the disputed payments (with accrued interest) shall be returned to the issuer or other affected person.'.

(b) TECHNICAL AMENDMENT—Section 21C(c)(2) of the Securities Exchange Act of 1934 (15 U.S.C. 78u-3(c)(2)) is amended by striking 'This' and inserting 'paragraph (1)'.

[¶ 1070] Section 1104—AMENDMENT TO THE FEDERAL SENTENCING GUIDELINES.

(a) REQUEST FOR IMMEDIATE CONSIDERATION BY THE UNITED STATES SENTENCING COMMISSION—Pursuant to its authority under section 994(p) of title 28, United States Code, and in accordance with this section, the United States Sentencing Commission is requested to—

(1) promptly review the sentencing guidelines applicable to securities and accounting fraud and related offenses;

(2) expeditiously consider the promulgation of new sentencing guidelines or amendments to existing sentencing guidelines to provide an enhancement for officers or directors of publicly traded corporations who commit fraud and related offenses; and

(3) submit to Congress an explanation of actions taken by the Sentencing Commission pursuant to paragraph (2) and any additional policy recommen-

dations the Sentencing Commission may have for combating offenses described in paragraph (1).

(b) CONSIDERATIONS IN REVIEW—In carrying out this section, the Sentencing Commission is requested to—

(1) ensure that the sentencing guidelines and policy statements reflect the serious nature of securities, pension, and accounting fraud and the need for aggressive and appropriate law enforcement action to prevent such offenses;

(2) assure reasonable consistency with other relevant directives and with other guidelines;

(3) account for any aggravating or mitigating circumstances that might justify exceptions, including circumstances for which the sentencing guidelines currently provide sentencing enhancements;

(4) ensure that guideline offense levels and enhancements for an obstruction of justice offense are adequate in cases where documents or other physical evidence are actually destroyed or fabricated;

(5) ensure that the guideline offense levels and enhancements under United States Sentencing Guideline 2B1.1 (as in effect on the date of enactment of this Act) are sufficient for a fraud offense when the number of victims adversely involved is significantly greater than 50;

(6) make any necessary conforming changes to the sentencing guidelines; and

(7) assure that the guidelines adequately meet the purposes of sentencing as set forth in section 3553(a)(2) of title 18, United States Code.

(c) EMERGENCY AUTHORITY AND DEADLINE FOR COMMISSION ACTION—The United States Sentencing Commission is requested to promulgate the guidelines or amendments provided for under this section as soon as practicable, and in any event not later than the 180 days after the date of enactment of this Act, in accordance with the procedures sent forth in section 21(a) of the Sentencing Reform Act of 1987, as though the authority under that Act had not expired.

[¶ 1071] Section 1105—AUTHORITY OF THE COMMISSION TO PROHIBIT PERSONS FROM SERVING AS OFFICERS OR DIRECTORS.

(a) SECURITIES EXCHANGE ACT OF 1934—Section 21C of the Securities Exchange Act of 1934 (15 U.S.C. 78u-3) is amended by adding at the end the following:

'(f) AUTHORITY OF THE COMMISSION TO PROHIBIT PERSONS FROM SERVING AS OFFICERS OR DIRECTORS—In any cease-and-desist proceeding under subsection (a), the Commission may issue an order to prohibit, conditionally or unconditionally, and permanently or for such period of time as it shall determine, any person who has violated section 10(b) or the rules or regulations thereunder, from acting as an officer or director of any issuer that has a class of securities registered pursuant to section 12, or that is required to file reports pursuant to section 15(d), if the conduct of that person demonstrates unfitness to serve as an officer or director of any such issuer.'.

(b) SECURITIES ACT OF 1933—Section 8A of the Securities Act of 1933 (15 U.S.C. 77h-1) is amended by adding at the end of the following:

'(f) AUTHORITY OF THE COMMISSION TO PROHIBIT PERSONS FROM SERVING AS OFFICERS OR DIRECTORS—In any cease-and-desist proceeding under subsection (a), the Commission may issue an order to prohibit, conditionally or unconditionally, and permanently or for such period of time as it shall determine, any person who has violated section 17(a)(1) or the rules or regulations thereunder, from acting as an officer or director of any issuer that has a class of securities registered pursuant to section 12 of the Securities Exchange Act of 1934, or that is required to file reports pursuant to section 15(d) of that Act, if the conduct of that person demonstrates unfitness to serve as an officer or director of any such issuer.'.

[¶ 1072] Section 1106—INCREASED CRIMINAL PENALTIES UNDER SECURITIESEXCHANGE ACT OF 1934.

Section 32(a) of the Securities Exchange Act of 1934(15 U.S.C. 78ff(a)) is amended

(1) by striking "$1,000,000, or imprisoned not more than 10 years" and inserting "$5,000,000, or imprisoned not more than 20 years"; and

(2) by striking "$2,500,000" and inserting "$25,000,000".

[¶ 1073] Section 1107—RETALIATION AGAINST INFORMANTS

(a)In General—Section 1513 of Title 18, United States Code, is amended by adding at the end the following:

"(e) Whoever knowingly, with the intent to retaliate, takes any action harmful to any person, including interference with the lawful employment or livelihood of any person, for providing to a law enforcement officer any truthful information relating to the commission or possible commission of any Federal offense, shall be fined under thism title or imprisoned not more than 10 years, or both.

Part III Legislative History

The Sarbanes-Oxley Act of 2002 represents a reconcilation of the Public Company Accounting Reform and Investor Protection Act of 2002 (S. 2673), which passed the Senate on July 15, 2002, and the Corporate and Auditing Accountability, Responsibility, and Transparency Act of 2002 (H.R 3763), which passed the House of Representatives on April 24, 2002. It also includes provisions from the Corporate Fraud Accountability Act of 2002 (H.R. 5118), which passed the House on July 16, 2002. The Sarbanes-Oxley Act is largely composed of S. 2673. A House-Senate conference to reconcile the House and Senate bills filed a conference report on July 24, 2002 (107-610). The conference report is essentially the Sarbanes-Oxley Act of 2002. The Senate and House both agreed to the conference report on July 25, 2002.

The following are relevant portions of Senate and House committee reports that accompanied S. 2673 and H.R. 3763, as well as portions of the Senate floor debate on S. 2673.

¶ 2001 SELECTED PORTIONS OF SENATE REPORT NO. 107-205

Report of the Committee on Banking, Housing, and Urban Affairs of the United States Senate to accompany S. 2673. July 3, 2002.

PURPOSE OF THE BILL

The purpose of the bill is to address the systemic and structural weaknesses affecting our capital markets which were revealed by repeated failures of audit effectiveness and corporate financial and broker-dealer responsibility in recent months and years. The bill creates a strong independent board to oversee the conduct of the auditors of public companies, and it strengthens auditor independence from corporate management by limiting the scope of non-audit services that auditors can offer their public company audit clients. However, the bill applies only to the auditing of public companies. The statutory intent is that state regulatory authorities should make independent determinations of the proper standards for small- and medium-sized accounting firms that do not audit public companies; state authorities should not presume that the standards applied under the bill should apply to those companies under state regulatory schemes.

The bill also requires steps to enhance the direct responsibility of senior corporate management for financial reporting and for the quality of financial disclosures made by public companies. The bill establishes clear statutory rules to limit, and expose to public view, possible conflicts of interest affecting securities analysts. Finally, the bill authorizes substantially higher funding for the Securities and Exchange Commission.

TITLE-BY-TITLE SUMMARY OF MAJOR PROVISIONS

TITLE I—PUBLIC COMPANY ACCOUNTING OVERSIGHT BOARD

Title I of the bill creates a Public Company Accounting Oversight Board (the "Board"), to provide for more effective oversight of the part of the nation's accounting industry that audits public companies. Title I reflects significant portions of S. 2004, authored by Senators Dodd and Corzine, as well as the terms of an amendment offered at the Committee's June 18 mark-up by Senator Enzi, which was adopted by voice vote.

The new Board may, subject to review by the Securities and Exchange Commission (the "SEC" or the "Commission"), establish, adopt, or modify auditing, quality control, ethics, and independence standards for public company audits, inspect accounting firms, investigate potential violations of applicable rules relating to audits, and impose sanctions if those violations are established. The Board will have authority only with respect to audits of public companies. It has no jurisdiction over the work of accountants in auditing other companies.

The Board will bring together various issues and responsibilities that have in the past been subject to what one Committee witness characterized as 'a bewildering array of monitoring groups' under the auspices of the accounting profession. (See Testimony of John H. Biggs, Chairman, President and CEO, Teachers' Insurance and Annuity Association—College Retirement Equities Fund (TIAA-CREF), and former member of the Public Oversight Board, before the Committee on February 27, 2002).

As Shaun O'Malley, Chairman of the 2000 Panel on Audit Effectiveness (and former Chairman of Price Waterhouse LLP), explained to the Committee in greater detail:

> The profession's combination of public oversight and voluntary self-regulation is extensive, Byzantine, and insufficient. The Panel found that the current system of governance lacks sufficient public representation, suffers from divergent views among its members as to the profession's priorities, implements a disciplinary system that is slow and ineffective, lacks efficient communication among its various entities and with the SEC, and lacks unified leadership and oversight. (See testimony of Shaun O'Malley, Chairman, 2000 Public Oversight Board Panel on Audit Effectiveness, and former Chairman, Price Waterhouse LLP, before the Committee on March 6, 2002).

Twenty witnesses who appeared before the Committee in its ten days of hearings on accounting reform and investor protection stressed the need for a strong Board to oversee the auditors of public companies. Paul Volcker, the former Chairman of the Federal Reserve Board, told the Committee that:

> over the years, there have also [i.e., in addition to the SEC] been repeated efforts to provide oversight by industry or industry/public member boards. By and large, I think we have to conclude that those efforts at self-regulation have been unsatisfactory. Thus, experience strongly suggests that governmental oversight, with investigation and enforcement powers, is necessary to assure discipline. (See testimony of Paul Volcker, Chairman of the Trustees of the International Accounting Standards Committee, and former Chairman of the Board of Governors of the Federal Reserve System, before the Committee on February 14, 2002).

* * *

The concerns of the Committee extend beyond immediate allegations of wrongdoing, to the fundamental principles on which the functioning of free markets and the protection of investors are based. Each of the country's federal securities laws—the 1933, 1934, 1935, and 1940 Acts—requires comprehensive financial statements that must be prepared, in the words of the Securities Act of 1933, by 'an independent public or certified accountant.' (See Schedule A(25) of the Securities Act of 1933, 15 U.S.C. Sec. 77(aa)(25) (emphasis added); see also section 13(a)(2) of the Securities Exchange Act of 1934, 15 U.S.C. 78m(a)(2), section 14 of the Public Utility Holding Company Act of 1935, at U.S.C. 79n, and section 30(g) of the Investment Company Act of 1940, 15 U.S.C. 80a-29(g)).

* * *

However, the franchise given to public accountants by the securities laws is conditional; it comes in return for the CPA's faithful assumption of a public trust. (The Supreme Court's now-classic statement of that trust, in United States v. Arthur Young, 465 U.S.C. 805 (1984) is discussed below.) The testimony heard by the Committee repeatedly indicated that a number of forces have undermined the fulfillment of this public trust over the years.

A. Appointment and operation of board

The successful operation of the Board depends upon its independence and professionalism. The Board will have five members, each of whom must have a demonstrated commitment to the interests of investors, as well as an understanding of the financial disclosures required of public companies, and the responsibilities for those disclosures, under the federal securities laws. Three members of the Board will have a general background, and two members will have an accountancy background. Senator Enzi suggested that the bill require, not merely permit, that two Board members have an accountancy background. (The Board's Chairperson may have an accountancy background, but if so, he or she may not have been a practicing accountant for at least five years prior to appointment to the Board.)

Board members are to be appointed by the SEC after consultation with the Federal Reserve Board and the Department of the Treasury. They will serve full-time, for five-year (staggered) terms, with a two-term limit. To further assure their independence, Board members may engage in no other business activities of any nature, or receive any payments from any accounting firms (except for standard retirement payments) or other persons. In addition, former Board members will be subject to a one-year 'cooling off' period at the end of their Board service, during which time they may not work for an accounting firm registered with the Board.

It is essential that the Board have a strong, well-trained, and experienced staff, of sufficient size to carry out its responsibilities. A number of witnesses emphasized, for example, that inspections must no longer be left to peer reviews of one accounting firm by another. The bill makes it plain, as the Committee intends, that the Board is to provide for staff salaries that are fully competitive with those for comparable private-sector self-regulatory, accounting, technical, supervisory, or related staff or management positions. The Board itself will be a corporation created under the D.C. Nonprofit Corporation Act. It will be neither an agency nor establishment of the federal government, and its members and employees are not to be deemed to be federal officers or employees by reason of their Board service.

The Committee believes that the new oversight arrangements must come into effect quickly. The SEC is to appoint the initial Board within three months of the bill's enactment, so that the Board can take the steps necessary to begin its operation within six months of its appointment, and the registration of accounting firms (below) can be completed within six months after the Board begins operation.

B. Registration of accounting firms

Accounting firms that audit public companies must register with the Board, no later than six months after the SEC determines that the Board is ready to begin operation. It is unlawful for a firm that has not registered to continue to audit public companies.

Conditioning eligibility to audit public companies on registration with the Board is the linchpin of the Board's authority. Suspension or revocation of registration renders a firm unable to continue its public company audit practice.

As part of its registration process, each accounting firm must execute a consent to comply with any requests, within the Board's authority, for documents or testimony made in the course of the Board's operation. The firm must also agree to obtain (and ultimately, if necessary, to enforce) similar consents from the firm's partners and employees, who are subject to the Board's investigative and disciplinary jurisdiction.

Certain necessary information is to accompany the registration materials (including a list of the firm's accountants who perform public company audits), and the Board will determine within 45 days of receipt whether an application is complete and the applicant can be registered. Basic registration information is to be public, but each accounting firm may protect from public disclosure information that it reasonably identifies as proprietary or that is otherwise protected by law. Each registrant is to file a report annually to update the required information.

The Board is to assess a registration fee, and an annual fee, to recover the costs of processing and reviewing applications and annual reports.

C. Auditing, quality control, ethics, and independence standards and rules

The bill requires the Board to establish or adopt auditing, quality control, and ethics standards for the audit of public companies. The Committee has concluded that the Board's plenary authority in this area is essential for the Board's effective operation, a position taken during the hearings by a number of witnesses, including former SEC Chairman Levitt, former Comptroller General Bowsher, and former FDIC Chairman Seidman (himself once a principal of a substantial accounting firm). (See testimony of Arthur Levitt, former SEC Chairman (1993-2000), before the Committee on February 12, 2002; Bowsher Testimony, March 19, 2002; testimony of L. William Seidman, former Chairman, Federal Deposit Insurance Corporation and Resolution Trust Corporation, and former partner, Seidman & Seidman, before the Committee on March 19, 2002.).

The Board's standard-setting authority, however, is neither intended nor structured to exclude practicing accountants from participation in the standard-setting process. The Board may adopt as part of its rules (and modify as appropriate for that purpose, at the time of adoption or thereafter), any portion of a statement of auditing, quality control, or ethics standards that meets the bill's statutory tests and that is proposed (i) by a professional group of accountants (designated by a rule of the Board for that purpose), or (ii) by one or more advisory groups of practicing accountants or other interested parties convened by the Board. (Pre-existing standards of designated professional groups of accountants may be adopted during the Board's transitional period.) The Board is to cooperate on an ongoing basis with the designated professional groups of accountants noted above, with its own advisory groups, and with other interested groups (and the accounting profession and the investing public at large), in examining the need for changes in any standards subject to Board authority.

It is to recommend issues for inclusion on the agendas of these groups, take other steps to facilitate the standard-setting process, and respond in a timely fashion to requests for changes in the standards. Finally, rules are open to comment by accountants and any other interested persons in a public process before they are approved either by the Board or, ultimately, by the SEC. Many of these provisions were suggested by Senator Enzi.

Although the Board's power to establish or adopt auditing and related standards extends to the full range of those standards, the bill specifies certain provisions that must be part of the standards. These include (i) preparation, and maintenance for at least seven years, by public company auditors of audit work papers and related information in sufficient detail to support each audit's conclusions, (ii) 'second partner' review and approval of each public company audit report and its issuance, and (iii) inclusion in each audit report of a description of the auditor's testing of the public company's systems for compliance with the requirements of section 13(b)(2) of the Securities Exchange Act and of the company's controls over its receipts and expenditures, together with specific notation of any significant defects or material noncompliance of which the auditor should know on the basis of such testing. In addition, the quality control standards adopted by the Board must address an accounting firm's monitoring of ethics and independence; internal and external consulting on audit issues; audit supervision; hiring, development, and advancement of audit personnel; acceptance and continuance of engagements; and internal inspection.

The Board is also authorized to issue rules to implement the provisions of title II of the bill relating to auditor independence.

D. Inspections of registered accounting firms

Virtually every witness who addressed the details of auditor oversight agreed on the critical need for a regular and comprehensive review, by an independent body of inspectors, of each audit firm's compliance with audit standards and procedures. A program of inspections is essential to identify problems in firm procedures, training, and 'culture' before those problems can produce audit failures that trigger large investor losses and threaten confidence in the capital markets. (See e.g., Ruder Testimony, February 12, 2002; Seligman Testimony, March 5, 2002; Seidler Testimony, March 6, 2002.).

The Board is to inspect the operations of each registered accounting firm, in order to assess compliance of that firm, and of its partners and employees, with the new statute, the Board's rules, and professional accounting standards. Initially, firms that audit more than 100 public companies are to be inspected each year, and firms that audit 100 or fewer public companies are to be inspected at least every three years. The Board is given the power to adjust these inspection schedules if it finds different schedules to be consistent with the bill's purposes, the protection of investors, and the public interest.

During an inspection, the Board is to review particular audit engagements (that it selects) of a firm and the firm's general quality control systems and policies, as well as to perform such other testing of the firm's audit, supervisory, and quality control procedures as is necessary or appropriate. The Board is specifically given authority to require firms to retain their records for inspection purposes regardless of whether retention of those records is otherwise required.

After each inspection, the Board will prepare an inspection report, which will be available for comment in draft form by the firm under inspection. Quality control defects found by the Board may be disposed of simply by corrective action, but specific violations identified during inspections may form the basis for a more formal investigation or disciplinary action by the Board and are to be reported, if appropriate, to the SEC and relevant state accountancy boards; final inspection reports are to be sent to the SEC and relevant state accountancy boards in any event. The reports will also be made public, subject to appropriate protection of confidential or proprietary information. However, firms will be given 12 months to correct defects in their quality control systems, to the satisfaction of the Board, before portions of the reports dealing with those defects are added to the public record. The bill creates a right to interim SEC review of certain inspection-related disputes.

E. Investigations and disciplinary proceedings

Committee witnesses stressed that the Board must possess investigative and disciplinary authority. Arthur Levitt, who served as Chairman of the SEC during most of the 1990s, told the Committee that:

> We need a truly independent oversight body that has the power not only to set the standards by which audits are performed, but also to conduct timely investigations that cannot be deferred for any reason and to discipline accountants. (See Levitt Testimony, February 12, 2002.).

Robert Glauber, the Chairman and CEO of the National Association of Securities Dealers, explained that:

> Any form of private-sector regulation must be empowered to effectively enforce the rules: [it must possess] the ability to levy meaningful fines, place conditions on continued participation in the industry, suspend, and where appropriate, banish those who misbehave from the industry. This 'ultimate sanction' is both a powerful deterrent for would-be violators and an important investor protection. (Glauber Testimony, March 5, 2002).

In response, the bill grants the Board broad authority to investigate any act or practice, or omission, by a registered accounting firm, or its associated persons, that may violate the new statute, the Board's rules, professional accounting standards, or the portions of the Federal securities laws (and SEC rules) relating to the preparation and issuance of audit reports and the obligations and liabilities of accountants with respect to those reports.

The Board's rules are to prescribe fair investigative and disciplinary procedures. It may, under those rules, require testimony or the production of audit work papers and other documents from (and may inspect the records of) registered firms or their associated persons, and it may suspend or revoke the registration of a firm, or suspend or bar from further association with a firm an 'associated person,' for non-cooperation with a Board investigation, subject to review of that action by the SEC. The Board may request, but not require, the testimony of, or production of documents, in the possession of any other person (for example, an audit firm's client). Its rules may provide for procedures to seek issuance of a subpoena from the SEC to any person.

Committee witnesses also emphasized that information gathered by Board investigators should be 'privileged from outsiders' during the investigative process. Under the bill, any information gathered in the course of an investigation is to be confidential and privileged for all purposes (including civil discovery), unless and until particular information is presented in connection with a public proceeding. However, the Board may disclose investigative information, if it determines that such disclosure is 'necessary to accomplish the purposes of the Act or to protect investors,' to the SEC, any federal financial supervisor (if the investigation pertains to an institution under the latter's supervision), the Attorney General, and, with the SEC's permission, to state attorneys general, in connection with criminal investigations, or state accountancy boards. (The Board may also refer an investigation to the SEC or other agencies to which disclosure of information is permitted.)

A full range of sanctions is available if the Board finds that a registered firm (or its partners or employees) has violated one or more of the rules within the Board's investigative jurisdiction. Potential sanctions include revocation or suspension of an accounting firm's registration, or of the ability of particular individuals to remain associated with that firm or become associated with any other registered accounting firm (effectively barring the subject of the sanction from participating in audits of public companies), substantial civil money penalties, required professional education or training, and censure; the breadth of these sanctions is intended to encourage flexible and appropriate action, designed to correct if possible. The Board's ability to suspend or bar an associated person from the auditing of public companies, and its ability to impose civil money penalties above a certain amount, is limited to situations involving intentional, knowing, or reckless conduct, or repeated negligent conduct. Fines imposed by the Board are to be used to fund a scholarship program for students in undergraduate or graduate programs in accounting.

An important provision of the bill permits the Board to impose sanctions upon a registered accounting firm for failure reasonably to supervise a partner or employee who is found to have violated applicable rules. The terms for liability for failure to supervise are similar to those that apply to broker-dealers under section 15(b)(4) of the Securities Exchange Act of 1934; they permit an accounting firm to defend itself from supervisory liability by showing that its internal control procedures were reasonable and were operating fully in the situation at issue.

The Board's determination that a violation has occurred and that a sanction should be imposed may be appealed to the Commission (as described below). Disciplinary sanctions must be reported to the Commission, appropriate state or foreign boards of accountancy, and the public (once any stay of enforcement pending appeal has been lifted).

F. Foreign public accounting firms

Companies that sell shares to U.S. investors, and are subject to the federal securities laws, can be organized and operate in any part of the world. Their financial statements are not necessarily audited by U.S. accounting firms, and the Committee believes that there should be no difference in treatment of a public company's auditors under the bill simply because of a particular auditor's place of operation. Otherwise, a significant loophole in the protection offered U.S. investors would be built into the statutory system.

Thus, accounting firms organized under the laws of countries other than the United States that issue audit reports for public companies subject to the U.S. securities laws are covered by the bill in the same manner as domestic accounting firms, subject to the exemptive authority of both the Board and the SEC. (Registration under the bill will not in itself provide a basis for subjecting a foreign accounting firm to U.S. jurisdiction other than with respect to controversies between such a firm and the Board.) The Board is also authorized to determine that other foreign accounting firms play a sufficiently substantial role in the preparation and furnishing of such reports for particular issuers that their coverage under the bill is necessary or appropriate to protect investors and the public interest.

Finally, the bill sets terms for the production in the United States by a foreign public accounting firm of its audit work papers, for any audit in which the foreign accounting firm issues an opinion or otherwise performs material services upon which an accounting firm registered under the bill relies in issuing all or part of a public company audit report. The foreign firm is deemed, by performing such work, to have consented to production, and the domestic accounting firm that relies on the foreign accounting firm's work must have secured, as a condition of its reliance, the foreign firm's agreement to the production.

G. SEC oversight of the Board

The Board is subject to SEC oversight and review to assure that the Board's policies are consistent with the administration of the federal securities laws, and to protect the rights of accounting firms and individuals subject to the Board's jurisdiction. Oversight also allows the public an important forum for commenting on Board rules relating to auditing, quality control, and related standards.

The rules for SEC oversight of the Board are generally the same as those that apply to SEC oversight of the National Association of Securities Dealers, under section 19 of the Securities Exchange Act. Thus, the Board's proposed rules will be filed with the SEC and published by the SEC for public comment; SEC approval is necessary in most cases before rules of the Board take effect, and the SEC may itself abrogate or amend Board rules (as well as disapprove proposed Board rules). (Transitional rules are to be separately approved by the SEC at the time of the SEC's determination that the Board is ready to begin operation.) Disciplinary sanctions imposed by the Board are subject to SEC review and may be canceled or modified (or in some cases enhanced) by the SEC. The SEC can relieve the Board of any responsibility to enforce any provision of the bill, or censure or limit operations of the Board, or remove a Board member, for cause. Finally, the bill makes clear that any violations of its terms will constitute a violation of the Securities Exchange Act itself for purposes of the SEC's enforcement (including injunctive and cease-and-desist) authority under that Act, so that the SEC may proceed under the bill's provisions directly if appropriate.

H. Accounting principles

Since 1973, the SEC has generally required public companies operating in the United States to prepare their financial statements in accordance with 'principles, standards, and practices' promulgated by the Financial Accounting Standards Board (the 'FASB') in the absence of specific SEC pronouncements on particular accounting questions. See Accounting Series Release No. 150, 3 SEC Dock. 275 (1973).

The bill seeks to formalize the SEC's reliance on the FASB and, as discussed below, to strengthen the independence of the FASB by assuring its funding and eliminating any need for it to seek contributions from accounting firms or companies whose financial statements must conform to FASB's rules. Thus, the bill amends the Securities Act of 1933 specifically to allow the SEC to recognize as 'generally accepted' (for securities law purposes) accounting principles established by a private entity that is funded as outlined in the bill (described below) and that has adopted procedures (including acting by majority vote) to ensure prompt consideration of necessary changes to the body of accounting principles.

An important issue presented to the Committee was the potential difference between an accounting regime that contains detailed rules for the treatment of particular items, and a regime that simply outlines general concepts (or 'principles') to be applied to particular items. Witnesses noted the possibility that the overly-detailed approach of U.S. standard-setters may have delayed updating of necessary guidance and at the same time drawn the focus of auditors away from the overriding principle that a set of financial statements, taken as a whole, must fairly and completely reflect the economic results and operations of the company being audited. To allow more careful consideration of the differences between various formulations of accounting standards, the bill requires the Commission to conduct a study, within 12 months, of the adoption by the U.S. financial reporting system of a principles-based accounting system.

I. Funding

The Committee's witnesses overwhelmingly agreed that both the Board and the FASB required guaranteed sources of funding, in order to protect their independence. Several witnesses testified to the problems various attempts at oversight of auditors had encountered when voluntary funding was withheld. With respect to the FASB, Michael Sutton, a former SEC Chief Accountant, testified to the Committee that '[t]o restore confidence in our standards setters, we should take immediate steps to secure independent funding for the FASB—funding that does not depend on contributions from constituents that have a stake in the outcome of the process.' (See testimony of Michael Sutton, former SEC Chief Accountant (1995-98), before the Committee on February 26, 2002.).

Under the bill, public companies are required to pay 'accounting support fees' to support the annual budgets of the Board and the FASB. (The Board's budget will be subject to approval by the SEC.) Amounts payable by public companies to either body will generally be allocated among those companies based on relative average annual monthly market capitalization for the 12 months prior to the year to which the support fee relates; both the Board and the FASB are permitted to differentiate among various classes of public companies in allocating fees.

TITLE II—AUDITOR INDEPENDENCE

The issue of auditor independence is at the center of this legislation. Public confidence in the integrity of financial statements of publicly-traded companies is based on belief in the independence of the auditor from the audit client. As noted above, each of the country's federal securities laws requires comprehensive financial statements that must be prepared, in the words of the Securities Act of 1933, by 'an independent public or certified accountant.'

The statutory independent audit requirement has two sides. It grants a franchise to the nation's public accountants—their services, and only their services, and certification, must be secured before an issuer of securities can go to market, have the securities listed on the nation's stock exchanges, or comply with the reporting requirements of the securities laws. This is a source of significant private benefit to the public accountants.

But the franchise is conditional. It comes in return for the CPA's assumption of a public duty and obligation. As a unanimous Supreme Court noted nearly 20 years ago: 'In certifying the public reports that collectively depict a corporation's financial status, the independent auditor assumes a public responsibility. * * * [That auditor] owes ultimate allegiance to the corporation's creditors and stockholders, as well as to the investing public. This 'public watchdog' function demands that the accountant maintain total independence from the client at all times and requires complete fidelity to the public trust.' United States v. Arthur Young, 465 U.S. 805, 817-18 (1984) (emphasis added).

Richard Breeden, Chairman of the SEC from 1989-93, put it succinctly in testimony before the Committee:

> While companies in the U.S. do not have to employ a law firm, an underwriter, or other types of professionals, federal law requires a publicly-traded company to hire an independent accounting firm to perform an annual audit. In addition to this shared federal monopoly, more than a hundred million investors in the U.S. depend on audited financial statements to make investment decisions. This imbues accounting firms with a high level of public trust, and also explains why there is a strong federal interest in how well the accounting system functions. (See testimony of Richard Breeden, former SEC Chairman (1989-93), before the Committee on February 12, 2002).

There is arguably an inherent conflict in the fact that an auditor is paid by the company for which the audit is being performed. That conflict is implicit in the relationship between the auditor and the audit client. In the last 15 years, however, the rapid growth in management consulting services offered by the major accounting firms has created a second, more substantial conflict that has eroded the independence that the auditor must bring to the audit function.

* * *

A. Services outside the scope of practice of auditors

A number of the witnesses who testified before the Committee during the course of the hearings, as well as other informed observers, argued that the growth in the non-audit consulting business done by the large accounting firms for their audit clients has so compromised the independence of the audits that a complete prohibition is required on the provision of consulting services by accounting firms to their audit clients.

* * *

The Committee considered adopting a complete prohibition on non-audit services by accounting firms for their audit clients, but instead decided on a somewhat more flexible approach. The approach adopted by the Committee is supported by former Comptroller General Bowsher, former SEC Chairman Arthur Levitt, and former Federal Reserve Board Chairman Paul Volcker. (See Bowsher Testimony, March 19, 2002; Levitt Testimony, February 12, 2002; Volcker Testimony, February 14, 2002).

The bill provides that it shall be unlawful for a public accounting firm registered with the Board which performs an audit for a public company to provide, contemporaneously with the audit, the following non-audit services:

(1) bookkeeping or other services related to the accounting records or financial statements of the audit client;

(2) financial information systems design and implementation;

(3) appraisal or valuation services, fairness opinions, or contribution-in-kind reports;

(4) actuarial services;

(5) internal audit outsourcing services;

(6) management functions or human resources;

(7) broker or dealer, investment adviser, or investment banking services;

(8) legal services and expert services unrelated to the audit; and

(9) any other services that the Board determines, by regulation, is impermissible.

The Board may, on a case-by-case basis, exempt any person, issuer, public accounting firm, or transaction from the prohibition on the provision of non-audit services to the extent that such exemption is necessary or appropriate in the public interest and is consistent with the protection of investors. A registered public accounting firm may engage in any non-audit service, including tax services, that is not on the list for an audit client only if the activity is approved in advance by the audit committee of the issuer. No limitations are placed on accounting firms in providing non-audit services to public companies which they do not audit or to any non-public companies.

The need for this provision was clearly stated by David M. Walker, Comptroller General of the United States, in a statement he released on June 18, in which he said:

I believe that legislation that will provide a framework and guidance for the SEC to use in setting independence standards for public company audits is needed. History has shown that the AICPA [American Institute of Certified Public Accountants] and the SEC have failed to update their independence standards in a timely fashion and that past updates have not adequately protected the public's interests. In addition, the accounting profession has placed too much emphasis on growing non-audit fees and not enough emphasis on modernizing the auditing profession for the 21st century environment. Congress is the proper body to promulgate a framework for the SEC to use in connection with independence related regulatory and enforcement actions in order to help ensure confidence in financial reporting and safeguard investors and the public's interests.

The independence provision [of the bill] * * * strikes a reasoned and reasonable balance that will enable auditors to perform a range of non-audit services for their audit clients and an unlimited range of non-audit services for their non-audit clients. Most importantly, the proposed legislation adopts a 'principle based' and 'substance over form' approach that can stand the test of time and, if adopted, will better protect the public's interests. In my opinion, the time to act on independence legislation is now. (Statement of David Walker, Comptroller General of the United States, June 18, 2002.).

Some argue that standards for auditor independence should be left to the SEC and the new Board. The approach adopted by the bill reflects the Committee's belief that the issue of auditor independence is so fundamental to the problems currently being experienced in our financial markets that statutory standards are needed to assure the independence of the auditor from the audit client.

The intention of this provision is to draw a clear line around a limited list of non-audit services that accounting firms may not provide to public company audit clients because their doing so creates a fundamental conflict of interest for the accounting firms. The list is based on simple principles. An accounting firm, in order to be independent of its audit client, should not audit its own work, which would be involved in providing bookkeeping services, financial information systems design, appraisal or valuation services, actuarial services, and internal audit outsourcing services to an audit client.

The accounting firm should not function as part of management or as an employee of the audit client, which would be required if the accounting firm provides human resources services such as recruiting, hiring, and designing compensation packages for the officers, directors, and managers of an audit client. The accounting firm should not act as an advocate of the audit client, which would be involved in providing legal and expert services to an audit client in legal, administrative, or regulatory proceedings, or serving as a broker-dealer, investment adviser, or investment banker to an audit client, which places the auditor in the role of promoting a client's stock or other interests.

The accounting industry itself has announced voluntarily that it will not provide two of these non-audit services—internal audit services and financial information systems design and implementation—to public company audit clients because of the conflicts they present. The other prohibited non-audit services also pose clear conflicts of interest for accounting firms when provided for audit clients. For example, in its oversight hearing earlier this year on the failure of Superior Bank, FSB, in Hinsdale, Illinois, the Committee learned first-hand the risks associated with allowing accounting firms to audit their own work. ('Analysis of the Failure of Superior Bank, FSB, Hinsdale, Illinois,' Hearing before the Senate Committee on Banking, Housing, and Urban Affairs, February 7, 2002). In that case, the accounting firm audited and certified a valuation of risky residual assets calculated according to a methodology it had provided as a consultant. The valuation was excessive and led to the failure of the institution.

The Board is given authority to make case-by-case exemptions in instances where the Board believes an exemption is in the public interest and consistent with the protection of investors. Further, no limitations are placed on accounting firms in providing non-audit services to public companies that they do not audit or to any private companies. The purpose is to assure the independence of the audit, not to put an end to the provision of non-audit services by accounting firms.

In summary, the bill adopts a strong, balanced approach to assure that in return for the significant private benefits conferred on accounting firms by our securities laws, they maintain their independence from the companies they audit and fulfill their 'public trust.'

B. Audit committee pre-approval of audit and non-audit services

The legislation requires that audit services, as well as non-audit services other than those proscribed by the bill, must be pre-approved by the audit committee of the public company's board of directors.

* * *

After studying this issue, the Committee believes the protection of investors warrants a requirement that a public company's audit committee approve in advance the services that the auditor will provide to such company (if those services are not explicitly prohibited under the bill). Accordingly, the bill requires the audit committee of a public company to pre-approve all of the services, both audit and non-audit, provided to that company by a registered public accounting firm. The bill does not require an issuer's audit committee to pre-approve non-audit services provided by an accounting firm that is not auditing the issuer.

The bill does not require the audit committee to make a particular finding in order to pre-approve an activity. The members of the audit committee shall vote consistent with the standards they determine to be appropriate in light of their fiduciary responsibilities and such other considerations they deem to be relevant.

The audit committee must pre-approve a non-audit service before it commences. The audit committee may pre-approve at any time in advance of the activity. For example, an audit committee may grant pre-approval at its March meeting for a non-audit service that would begin in August. However, the Commission or the Board under its general authority may specify a maximum period of time in advance of which the approval may not be granted, such as, for example, requiring the pre-approval to be granted no earlier than one year prior to the commencement of the service.

The bill does not limit the number of non-audit services that the audit committee may pre-approve at one meeting or occasion. The Committee intends, however, that each non-audit service be specifically identified in order to be approved by the audit committee. The Committee does not intend for the statutory requirement to be satisfied by an audit committee voting, for example, to permit 'any service that management determines appropriate for the auditor to perform' or 'all non-audit services permissible under law.'

The Committee has chosen to offer audit committees a delegation option in their administration of the pre-approval requirement. The bill permits the audit committee to delegate to one or more of its members (who are members of the board of directors) the authority to pre-approve non-audit services. After a delegated member has granted a pre-approval, he or she is required to report the decision at the next meeting of the full audit committee. This delegation of authority may be useful where, for example, the audit committee is asked to determine whether or not to permit the issuer's auditor to perform a new non-audit service within a short period of time.

The Committee has taken into account the atypical circumstance where an auditor is providing to the issuer a service that was anticipated to be an audit service within the scope of the engagement, but is later discovered to be a non-audit service. The bill provides that the pre-approval requirement is waived with respect to a non-audit service if: (1) the service was not recognized by the issuer at the time of the audit engagement to be a non-audit service, (2) the aggregate amount paid for all services described in (1) is not more than 5 percent of the total amount of revenues paid by the issuer to the auditor, and (3) the service is promptly brought to the attention of the audit committee, and (4) the audit committee approves the activity prior to the conclusion of the audit. This post-approval may be granted by the entire audit committee or by one or more audit committee members (who are members of the board of directors) to whom authority to grant such approvals has been delegated by the audit committee. This flexibility was suggested by Senator Enzi.

The bill requires that the audit committee approvals be disclosed to investors in periodic reports filed with the Commission.

The bill specifically notes that audit services 'may entail providing comfort letters in connection with securities underwriting' in order to make clear that providing such a comfort letter is an audit service.

C. Audit partner rotation

The Committee heard testimony from numerous witnesses on whether, in order to maintain the objectivity of its audits, an issuer should be required to rotate its audit firm after a number of consecutive years. For example, former SEC Chairman Arthur Levitt proposed 'that serious consideration be given to requiring companies to change their audit firm—not just the partners—every 5-7 years to ensure that fresh and skeptical eyes are always looking at the numbers.'(See Levitt Testimony, on February 12, 2002). Former SEC Chairman Harold Williams recommended a requirement that issuers '[h]ire auditors with a fixed term with no right to terminate for five or seven years.' (See Williams Testimony, February 12, 2002). John Whitehead, former Co-Chairman, Goldman Sachs & Co., recommended requiring '[t]erm limits of 8 to 10 years.' (See Whitehead Testimony, March 19, 2002.). Lynn Turner, former SEC Chief Accountant, recommended requiring 'mandatory rotation (5 to 7 years).' (See Testimony of Lynn Turner, former SEC Chief Accountant (1998-2001), before the Committee on February 26, 2002.).

Other witnesses felt that accounting firm rotation could be disruptive to the issuer and that the costs of mandatory rotation might outweigh the benefits. Former SEC Chairman Rod Hills said that '[f]orcing a change of auditors can only lower the quality of audits and increase their costs.' (See testimony of Roderick M. Hills, former SEC Chairman (1975-77), before the Committee on February 12, 2002). Shaun O'Malley, Chairman, 2000 Public Oversight Board Panel on Audit Effectiveness, said that 'forcing issuers to change auditors every few years * * * would undermine audit effectiveness.' (See O'Malley Testimony, March 6, 2002).

The Committee determined that the possibility of requiring audit firm rotation merits further study. The bill directs the U.S. General Accounting Office ('GAO') to analyze the merits and potential effects of requiring mandatory rotation of auditors, and to report its analysis to Congress within one year.

While the bill does not require issuers to rotate their accounting firms, the Committee recognizes the strong benefits that accrue for the issuer and its shareholders when a new accountant 'with fresh and skeptical eyes' evaluates the issuer periodically. Accordingly, the bill requires a registered public accounting firm to rotate its lead partner and its review partner on audits so that neither role is performed by the same accountant for the same issuer for more than five consecutive years. The 'lead' partner is the partner who is in charge of the audit engagement. The 'review' partner refers to the outside partner brought in to review the work done by the lead partner and the audit team.

D. Disclosures of accounting issues.

The Committee believes that it is important for the audit committee to be aware of key assumptions underlying a company's financial statements and of disagreements that the auditor has with management. The audit committee should be informed in a timely manner of such disagreements, so that it can independently review them and intervene if it chooses to do so in order to assure the integrity of the audit.

Accordingly, the bill requires a registered independent public accounting firm performing an audit for a public company to report in a timely manner to that company's audit committee (1) the critical accounting policies and practices to be used; (2) all alternative treatments of financial information within GAAP (generally accepted accounting principles) that have been discussed with management; (3) any accounting disagreements between the auditor and management; and (4) other material written communications between the auditor and management.

E. Cooling off period

The Committee received extensive testimony on whether to impose a cooling off period between an accountant's employment by an auditor and his or her employment by an issuer.

* * *

The Committee considered various options, including imposing a cooling off period of one, two, or three years, and applying a cooling off period to all employees who worked for the auditor, regardless of whether they worked on the audit of a particular issuer and regardless of the position they would take with that issuer, or applying a cooling off period only to certain groups of employees.

The Committee decided to impose a one-year cooling off period that would apply to an employee of the accounting firm who worked on the issuer's audit and subsequently seeks to be employed by that issuer in a senior management capacity. Thus, the bill provides that an accounting firm may not provide audit services for a public company if that company's chief executive officer, controller, chief financial officer, chief accounting officer, or other individual serving in an equivalent position, was employed by the accounting firm during the one year before the start of the audit services. The cooling off period does not take effect if the CEO or other senior official worked for the auditor but did not work on the issuer's audit or if a member of the audit team is hired by the issuer for a position other than CEO, CFO, controller, chief accounting officer, or an equivalent position. However, if an issuer hires an accountant from the audit team as its CEO, for example, it would be required to change auditors.

F. The bill does not create state regulatory standards

Titles I and II are designed to apply only to accounting firms that audit public companies. They are not designed to apply to audits of private companies. Nonetheless, some have raised the concern that the bill could lead state regulatory authorities to impose similar requirements for audits of private companies.

The bill indicates clearly that Congress does not intend that state regulatory authorities should find this Act controlling in their regulation of non-registered accountants. The bill states that it is the intention of the Act that, in supervising non-registered accounting firms, state regulatory authorities should make an independent determination of the proper standards, and should not presume the standards applied by the Board under this bill to be applicable to small- and medium-sized non-registered accounting firms. Senators Hagel and Enzi proposed this provision.

TITLE III—CORPORATE RESPONSIBILITY

In further response to recent corporate failures, title III of the bill makes a number of changes to improve the responsibility of public companies for their financial disclosures. To that end, the bill incorporates a number of reform proposals made by the President on March 7, 2002. These reforms are supplemented with additional provisions that the Committee believes will improve investor protection in connection with the operation of public companies.

Recent events have highlighted the failure of companies' internal audit committees to properly police their auditors and have raised awareness of the need for strong, competent audit committees with real authority. Several witnesses suggested that the Committee make changes in the role of audit committees in order to enhance the audit process. In response, under the bill, the SEC must draft rules directing national securities exchanges and associations to require listed companies to comply with a number of enumerated provisions regarding audit committees. The Committee believes that the bill's approach to strengthening audit committees will help avoid future auditing breakdowns.

The bill also contains a number of provisions aimed at corporate management. Defects in procedures for monitoring financial results and controls have been blamed for recent corporate failures. The bill therefore requires CEOs and CFOs to certify their companies' financial reports, outlaws fraud and deception by managers in the auditing process, prevents CEOs and CFOs from benefitting from profits they receive as a result of misstatements of their company's financials, amd facilitates the imposition of judicial bars against officers and directors who have violated the securities laws. Finally, title III includes a provision intended to prevent employees from being required to hold company stock in their retirement accounts while officers and directors are free to sell their shares.

A. Issuer audit committees

Witnesses at the Committee's hearings suggested that the auditing process may be compromised when auditors view their main responsibility as serving the company's management rather than its full board of directors or its audit committee. For this reason, the bill requires audit committees to be directly responsible for the appointment, compensation, and oversight of the work of auditors, and requires auditors to report directly to the audit committee.

* * *

Many recent failures have been attributed to close ties between audit committee members and management. In 1998-99, the NYSE and Nasdaq sponsored the Blue Ribbon Committee on Improving the Effectiveness of Corporate Audit Committees. The Blue Ribbon Committee, chaired by Committee witnesses Ira Millstein and John Whitehead, made a number of recommendations to enhance audit procedures and effectiveness, including recommendations to increase the independence of audit committee members. Mr. Millstein and Mr. Whitehead, as well as Blue Ribbon Committee member John Biggs, testified at the hearings in support of adoption of the Blue Ribbon Committee's recommendations. (Testimony of Ira Millstein, Senior Partner, Weil, Gotshal & Manges LLP, before the Committee on February 27, 2002; Whitehead Testimony, March 19, 2002; Biggs Testimony, February 27, 2002.)

Consistent with their recommendations, the bill enhances audit committee independence by barring audit committee members from accepting consulting fees or being affiliated persons of the issuer or the issuer's subsidiaries other than in the member's capacity as a member of the board of directors or any board committee.

* * *

The bill contains several additional provisions regarding audit committees. The bill requires audit committees to have in place procedures to receive and address complaints regarding accounting, internal control, or auditing issues. Further, the bill includes an amendment by Senator Stabenow providing protection for corporate 'whistleblowers' by specifying that audit committees must establish procedures for employees' anonymous submission of concerns regarding accounting or auditing matters.

The bill also requires public companies to provide their audit committees with authority and funding to engage independent counsel and other advisers as they determine necessary in order to carry out their duties. Comptroller General Walker agreed that audit committee members must be 'adequately resourced,' suggesting that audit committee members 'may need their own staff.' (See testimony of David Walker, Comptroller General of the United States, before the Committee on March 5, 2002).

In light of recent events, the Committee believes that these audit committee provisions should be codified in the securities laws in order to help rectify auditing misconduct and to enhance the effectiveness of audit committee oversight of public company audits.

B. Corporate responsibility for financial reports

The Committee believes that management should be held responsible for the financial representations of their companies. The bill therefore clearly establishes that CEOs and CFOs are responsible for the presentation of material in their company's financial reports. Under one of the recommendations put forward by the President on March 7, 'CEOs would personally attest each quarter that the financial statements and company disclosures accurately and fairly disclose the information of which the CEO is aware that a reasonable investor should have to make an informed investment decision.' In effect the bill adopts this proposal, in an approach developed with Senator Miller, by requiring CEOs and CFOs to certify, in periodic reports containing financial statements filed with the Commission pursuant to section 13(a) or 15(d) of the Exchange Act, the appropriateness of financial statements and disclosures contained therein, and that those financials and disclosures fairly present the company's operations and financial condition.

These provisions reflect the Committee's concern regarding the reliability of companies' audited financial statements. In his testimony before the Committee, former SEC Chairman Breeden recognized that there is 'growing doubt about whether audited financial statements are believable.' (See Breeden Testimony, on February 12, 2002). Council of Institutional Investors Executive Director Sarah Teslik echoed this concern in testifying that 'CEOs, audit committee members and outside auditors' should be required to 'sign the financials as true and accurate.' (See Teslik Testimony, March 20, 2002).

C. Prohibited influence

Numerous witnesses testifying before the Committee, including Shaun O'Malley, Chair of the 2000 Public Oversight Board Panel on Audit Effectiveness, and Sarah Teslik, Council of Institutional Investors Executive Director, were concerned with addressing fraud and misconduct in the audit process. (See O'Malley Testimony, March 6, 2002; Teslik Testimony, March 20, 2002).

In response, title III of the bill makes it unlawful for any officer or director of an issuer, or person acting under the direction thereof, to fraudulently influence, coerce, manipulate, or mislead any accountant engaged in preparing an audit of that issuer, for the purpose of rendering the audit report misleading. The Commission is provided with exclusive authority to enforce this section. The bill establishes a 90-day deadline for proposed rules or regulations by the Commission under this section, and a 270-day deadline for final rules or regulations.

D. Forfeiture of bonuses and profits

Recent events have raised concern about management benefitting from unsound financial statements, many of which ultimately result in corporate restatements. The President has recommended that 'CEOs or other officers should not be allowed to profit from erroneous financial statements,' and that 'CEO bonuses and other incentive-based forms of compensation [sh]ould be disgorged in cases of accounting restatement and misconduct.'

Title III includes provisions designed to prevent CEOs or CFOs from making large profits by selling company stock, or receiving company bonuses, while management is misleading the public and regulators about the poor health of the company. The bill requires that in the case of accounting restatements that result from material non-compliance with SEC financial reporting requirements, CEOs and CFOs must disgorge bonuses and other incentive-based compensation and profits on stock sales, if the non-compliance results from misconduct. The required disgorgement applies to amounts received for the 12 months after the first public issuance or filing of a financial document embodying such financial reporting requirement. Under this section, the SEC may exempt any person from this requirement as it deems necessary and appropriate.

E. Officer and director bars and penalties

Title III also includes several measures affecting officers and directors who have violated the securities laws. The staff of the Commission indicated to the Committee staff that when enforcement proceedings are brought under the securities laws, courts in some cases have been reluctant to impose prospective bars against violators serving as officers or directors of companies. The bill would facilitate not only the SEC's prevention of individuals who have violated the securities laws from serving as officers and directors, but also the imposition of penalties on violators of securities laws.

Currently, it must be proved that an officer or director has both violated the securities laws, and has shown 'substantial unfitness' to serve before a bar can be imposed. The Commission has argued that the 'substantial unfitness' standard for imposing bars is inordinately high, causing courts to refrain from imposing bars even in cases of egregious misconduct. The proposed bill rectifies this deficiency by modifying the standard governing imposition of officer and director bars from 'substantial unfitness' to 'unfitness.'

These provisions also reflect the President's recommendation that 'CEOs or other officers who clearly abuse their power should lose their right to serve in any corporate leadership positions.'

The Commission has also suggested that it should be allowed to obtain additional relief in enforcement cases. For a securities law violation, currently an individual may be ordered to disgorge funds that he or she received 'as a result of the violation.' Rather than limiting disgorgement to these gains, the bill will permit courts to impose any equitable relief necessary or appropriate to protect, and mitigate harm to, investors.

F. Prohibition on insider trades during pension fund blackout periods

As former SEC Chairman Breeden observed, 'The spectacle of corporate insiders plundering their own companies or selling their stock quietly in advance of a looming collapse has awakened a sense of revulsion among investors who were left with worthless stock. (See Breeden Testimony, on February 12, 2002).

In some cases, officers and directors have profited by selling off large portions of company stock during a time when employees were prevented from selling company stock in their section 401(k) retirement plans. To address this problem, the bill prohibits key individuals from engaging in transactions involving any equity security of the issuer during a 'blackout' period when at least half of the issuer's individual account plan participants are not permitted to purchase, sell, or otherwise transfer their interest in that equity security. Upon Senator Miller's recommendation, this section applies to directors and executive officers in order to ensure that the prohibition is limited to individuals in policy-making positions.

The bill provides added protection for participants in retirement plans by requiring that they be provided with written notice at least 30 days before a blackout period. Two exceptions to the 30-day notice are provided in response to Senator Enzi's recommendations. First, an exception is allowed in cases where a deferral of the blackout period to comply with the 30-day notice requirement would violate ERISA provisions that require fiduciaries to act exclusively on behalf of participants, and those that require trustees to act prudently, in their decisions regarding plan assets. Second, an exception may be provided where the inability to provide the notice is due to unforeseeable events or circumstances beyond the reasonable control of the plan administrator.

The Committee is concerned that without the provisions of title III, our financial markets will witness numerous corporate restatements in the future. The Committee believes that title III incorporates needed reforms that will enhance corporate responsibility among public companies.

TITLE IV—ENHANCED FINANCIAL DISCLOSURES

The Committee heard testimony about the imperative necessity for investors to have accurate and full financial information available on a timely basis in order to make appropriate investment decisions. The Committee has identified certain key disclosures that require legislative action.

A. Accounting adjustments

The bill requires that financial statements filed with the Commission reflect the material adjustments under GAAP that have been identified by the auditor.

B. Off-balance sheet transactions

Former SEC Chairman Richard Breeden testified, after the problems of Enron Corp. and its special purpose entities, on the need for 'enhance[d] disclosure of 'off-balance sheet' transactions and debt.' (See Breeden Testimony, February 12, 2002).

To address this need, the bill requires annual and quarterly reports filed with the SEC to disclose all material off-balance sheet transactions, arrangements, obligations (including contingent obligations), and other relationships of the issuer with unconsolidated entities or other persons that may have a material current or future effect on financial condition, changes in financial condition, results of operations, liquidity, capital expenditures, capital resources, or significant components of revenues or expenses.

C. Pro-forma financial disclosures

* * *

The Committee seeks to address problems attendant to pro forma financial disclosures by requiring the SEC to promulgate rules requiring that issuers publish pro forma data with a reconciliation to comparable financial data calculated according to GAAP and in a way that is not misleading and does not contain untrue statements. The reconciliation presumes, and would require, the issuer to publish financial data calculated according to GAAP at the same time as it publishes pro forma data. This should enable investors to, at the least, simultaneously compare the pro forma financial data with the same types of financial disclosures (e.g., earnings) calculated according to GAAP for the comparable reporting period.

The Committee recognizes from the recent experience of Enron Corp. and other public companies the need for additional types of disclosures. The Committee supports public and private efforts that result in greater quality, clarity, and completeness in the disclosures made by public companies.

* * *

E. Disclosures of transactions involving management

The Committee received testimony that insiders should be required to report their transactions in the stock of their companies more promptly. Ira Millstein, Senior Partner, Weil, Gotshal & Manges LLP and Co-Chair of the Blue Ribbon Committee on Improving the Effectiveness of Corporate Audit Committees, testified that, 'SEC rules should be amended to mandate prompt disclosure of transactions between the corporation (or its affiliates) and members of senior management, directors or controlling shareholders.' (See Millstein Testimony, February 27, 2002).

Former Comptroller General Bowsher echoed this objective when he testified: 'To discourage conflicts of interest involving public corporations, Congress should amend the Securities Exchange Act of 1934 to require more meaningful and timely disclosure of related party transactions among officers, directors, or other affiliated persons and the public corporation.' (See Bowsher Testimony, March 19, 2002).

At present, Section 16(a) of the Exchange Act requires insiders to report trades by the tenth day of the month following the month in which the transaction was executed. The Committee recognizes that some investors find trades by insiders to be probative of whether investing in a company is desirable and feel that, in today's markets, the current deadline imposed by Section 16(a) allows too long a delay in reporting.

The bill would amend Section 16(a) to require directors, officers and 10 percent equity holders to report their purchases and sales of securities more promptly, that is, by the end of the second day following the transaction or such other time established by the SEC where the two-day period is not feasible. The purpose is to make available to investors information about insider transactions more promptly so they can make better informed investment decisions. F. Management assessment of internal controls

* * *

In order to enhance the quality of reporting and increase investor confidence, the bill requires that annual reports filed with the SEC must be accompanied by a statement by the management of the issuer that management is responsible for creating and maintaining adequate internal controls. Management must also present its assessment of the effectiveness of those controls. A similar requirement was enacted in 1991 and has been imposed on depository institutions through Section 36 of the Federal Deposit Insurance Act.

In addition, the company's auditor must report on and attest to management's assessment of the company's internal controls. In requiring the registered public accounting firm preparing the audit report to attest to and report on management's assessment of internal controls, the Committee does not intend that the auditor's evaluation be the subject of a separate engagement or the basis for increased charges or fees. High quality audits typically incorporate extensive internal control testing. The Committee intends that the auditor's assessment of the issuer's system of internal controls should be considered to be a core responsibility of the auditor and an integral part of the audit report.

G. Exemptions for investment companies

The bill exempts investment companies from certain disclosure requirements. The Committee feels that the objectives of those disclosure sections are adequately addressed by existing Federal securities laws and the rules thereunder affecting investment companies.

For example, Section 17(a) of the Investment Company Act of 1940 and Rule 17j-1 thereunder prohibit affiliated persons of an investment company from borrowing money or other property from, or selling or buying securities or other property to or from the investment company, or any company that the investment company controls. Investment company officials therefore would not have any insider loans to report, as would be required under the bill.

H. Code of ethics for senior financial officers

The problems surrounding Enron Corp. and other public companies raise concerns about the ethical standards of corporations and their senior financial managers. The Committee believes that investors have a legitimate interest in knowing whether a public company holds its financial officers to certain ethical standards in their financial dealings. The bill requires issuers to disclose whether or not they have adopted a code of ethics for senior financial officers and, if not, why not. This section was recommended by Senator Corzine.

I. Disclosure of audit committee financial expert

As discussed above, the Committee received testimony about the important role played by the audit committee in corporate governance. The Committee believes the effectiveness of the audit committee depends in part on its members' knowledge of and experience in auditing and financial matters. Investors may find it relevant in making their investment decisions whether an issuer's audit committee has at least one member who has relevant, sophisticated financial expertise with which to discharge his or her duties.

The bill requires the SEC to adopt rules requiring issuers to disclose whether their audit committees include among their members at least one 'financial expert.' In defining 'financial expert,' the SEC shall consider whether a person understands GAAP and financial statements, has experience preparing or auditing financial statements, has experience with internal accounting controls, and understands audit committee functions.

TITLE V—ANALYST CONFLICTS OF INTEREST

The Committee heard persuasive testimony that a serious problem exists regarding conflicts of interest between Wall Street stock analysts and their employing brokerage firms, on the one hand, and the public companies that the stock analysts cover, on the other hand. Growing knowledge of these conflicts is harming the integrity and credibility to the public of stock analyst recommendations.

* * *

The Committee feels that it is critical to restore investor confidence in this area. The bill is intended to prevent certain pressures on analysts which could compromise their objectivity and to provide disclosure to investors of certain conflicts of interest that can also influence the objectivity of the analyst in preparing a research report.

* * *

The bill creates new Section 15A(n)(1)(C) of the Securities Exchange Act of 1934, which mandates rules 'to establish structural and institutional safeguards within registered brokers or dealers to assure that securities analysts are separated by appropriate informational partitions within the firm from the review, pressure, or oversight of those whose involvement in investment banking activities might potentially bias their judgment or supervision.'

Professor Coffee cited abuses involving the so-called 'Booster Shot' and recommended that research reports not be issued during certain periods. He testified:

> Firms contemplating an IPO increasingly seek to hire as lead underwriter the firm that employs the star analyst in their field. The issuer's motivation is fueled in large part by the fact that the issuer's management almost invariably is restricted from selling its own stock (by contractual agreement with the underwriters) until the expiration of a lock-up period that typically extends six months from the date of the offering. The purpose of the lock-up agreement is to assure investors that management and the controlling shareholders are not 'bailing out' of the firm by means of the IPO. But as a result, the critical date (and market price) for the firm's insiders is not the date of the IPO (or the market value at the conclusion of the IPO), but rather the expiration date of the lock-up agreement six months later (and the market value of the stock on that date). From the perspective of the issuer's management, the role of the analyst is to 'maintain a buzz' about the stock and create a price momentum that peaks just before the lock-up's expiration. To do this, the analyst may issue a favorable research report just before the lock-up's expiration (a so-called 'booster shot' in the vernacular). To the extent that favorable ratings issued at this point seem particularly conflicted and suspect, an NASD rule might forbid analysts associated with underwriters from issuing research reports for a reasonable period (say, thirty days)

both before and after the lock-up expiration date. Proposed Rule 2711 [of the NASD] stops well short of this and only extends the 'quiet period' so that it now would preclude research reports for this first 40 days after an IPO. Such a limited rule in no way interferes with the dubious tactic of 'booster shots.' (See Coffee Testimony, March 5, 2002 (internal citations omitted).

The bill directs that rules be adopted 'to define periods during which brokers or dealers who have participated, or are to participate, in a public offering of securities as underwriters or dealers should not publish or otherwise distribute research reports relating to such securities or to the issuer of such securities.' The 'booster shot' is a type of situation that the SEC and the self-regulatory organizations should consider in framing such rules.

Thomas A. Bowman, President and CEO of the Association for Investment Management and Research, recommended disclosure of 'the nature of the relationship or services provided' by an analyst's firm to the subject company. (See Bowman Testimony, March 20, 2002). The bill requires disclosure of the types of services provided.

Michael Mayo, Managing Director of Prudential Securities, recommended that Congress '[t]ake actions to minimize the interference of investment bankers with the job of research analysts' and '[d]isclose investment banking relationships to investors.' (See testimony of Michael Mayo, Managing Director, Prudential Securities, Inc., before the Committee on March 19, 2002). The bill prohibits the pre-publication clearance of research or recommendations by investment banking or other staff not directly responsible for investment research and requires disclosure of whether the issuer is or has recently been a client of the analyst's firm, and if so, the services provided.

Lynn Turner, former SEC Chief Accountant, testified: 'As long as the investment-banking arm of Wall Street has influence over the work of the research analysts or their compensation, analysts will not be able to provide independent research.' (See Turner Testimony, February 26, 2002). The bill requires the creation of rules that limit the supervision and compensatory evaluation of research personnel to officials who are not engaged in investment banking activities.

Mr. Mayo raised the concern, 'Does the retail investor know that the brokerage firm pitching shares is also earning investment banking fees from the company?' and also recommended that the Congress 'eliminate deal-based incentive pay' for research analysts. (See Mayo Testimony, March 19, 2002.]

The bill requires disclosure of whether any compensation has been received by the broker-dealer from the issuer, subject to such exemptions as the Commission may determine necessary and appropriate to prevent disclosure of material non-public information regarding specific potential future investment banking transactions of such issuer, as is appropriate in the public interest and consistent with the protection of investors. The bill, while not eliminating deal-based pay, requires disclosure of whether the analyst received compensation based on an affiliate's investment banking revenues from the subject of any research report. 740TE0The Committee heard testimony about the serious problem of retaliation against analysts who wrote negative research reports. Professor Coffee testified, 'In self-reporting studies, securities analysts report that they are frequently pressured to make positive buy recommendations or at least to temper negative opinions.' (See Coffee Testimony, March 5, 2002). He added, 'According to one survey, 61% of all analysts **have** experienced retaliation—threats of dismissal, salary reduction, etc- as the result of negative research reports. Clearly, negative research reports (and ratings reductions) are hazardous to an analyst's career. Congress could either adopt, or instruct the NASD to adopt, an anti-retaliation rule: no analyst should be fired, demoted, or economically penalized for issuing a negative report, downgrading a rating, or reducing an earnings, price, or similar target.' (See Coffee Testimony, March 5, 2002 (internal citations omitted).

Eliot Spitzer, Attorney General of the State of New York, concluded that the analyst conflict regulations put forth by the self-regulatory organizations 'fall short of what should be legislated in this area [because], [f]or example, the regulations fail to address the problem of intimidation or retaliation against analysts who publish unfavorable research about a company.' (See Spitzer Letter, June 5, 2002).

The bill requires rules to be promulgated to protect securities analysts from retaliation or intimidation because of negative, or otherwise unfavorable, research reports, subject to the proviso that such rules may not limit a broker-dealer from disciplining a securities analyst in accordance with firm policies and procedures for causes other than writing such a research report.

Professor Coffee recommended that a no-retaliation rule should:

> not bar staff reductions or reduced bonuses based on economic downturns or individualized performance assessments. Thus, given the obvious possibility that the firm could reduce an analyst's compensation in retaliation for a negative report, but describe its action as based on an adverse performance review of the individual, how can this rule be made enforceable? The best answer may be NASD arbitration. That is, an employee who felt that he or she had been wrongfully terminated or that his or her salary had been reduced in retaliation for a negative research report could use the already existing system of NASD employee arbitration to attempt to reverse the decision. Congress could also establish the burden of proof in such litigation and place it on the firm, rather than the employee/analyst. Further, Congress could entitle the employee to some form of treble damages or other punitive award to make this form of litigation viable. Finally, Congress could mandate an NASD penalty if retaliation were found, either by an NASD arbitration panel or in an NASD disciplinary proceeding. (See Coffee Testimony, March 5, 2002).

The exception is intended to make certain that writing a negative research report does not protect an analyst who is, for example, incompetent or otherwise deficient. However, it is not intended to be used to permit a broker-dealer to discipline a good analyst for writing a negative report using a false pretext. In adopting a proposed rule, the SEC or a self-regulatory organization should consider Professor Coffee's recommendations.

The Committee heard testimony about various additional concerns and recommendations to prevent analyst conflicts of interest and otherwise enhance investor protection, some of which are discussed below.

Professor Coffee recommended 'A No-Selling Rule.' He testified:

> If we wish the analyst to be a more neutral and objective umpire, one logical step might be to preclude the analyst from direct involvement in selling activities. For example, it is today standard for the 'star' analyst to participate in 'road shows' managed by the lead underwriters, presenting its highly favorable evaluation of the issuer and even meeting on a

> one-to-one basis with important institutional investors. Such sales activity seems inconsistent with the much-cited 'Chinese Wall' between investment banking and investment research * * *.
>
> Although a 'no-selling' rule would do much to restore the objectivity of the analyst's role, one counter-consideration is that the audience at the road show is today limited to institutions and high net worth individuals. Hence, there is less danger that the analyst will overreach unsophisticated retail investors. For all these reasons, this is an area where a more nuanced rule could be drafted by the NASD at the direction of Congress that would be preferable to a legislative command. (See Coffee Testimony, March 5, 2002).

Dean Joel Seligman also recommended considering 'a new form of adviser liability for recommendations without a reasonable basis.' (See Seligman Testimony, March 5, 2002).

Mr. Bowman recommended disclosure of '[i]nvestment holdings of Wall Street analysts, their immediate families, the Wall Street firm's management and the firms themselves' as well as disclosure of '[m]aterial gifts received by the analyst from either the subject company or the Wall Street firm's investment-banking or corporate finance department.' (See Bowman Testimony, March 20, 2002).

Mr. Bowman explained the need for greater explanatory information about analysts' rating systems. He said that 'rating systems need to be overhauled so that investors can better understand how ratings are determined and compare ratings across firms. Ratings must be concise, clear, and easily understood by the average investor' and he recommended disclosures of 'where and how to obtain information about the firm's rating system.' (See Bowman Testimony, March 20, 2002).

He also said that 'Wall Street analysts and their firms should also be required to update or re-confirm their recommendations on a timely and regular basis, and more frequently in periods of high market volatility. They should be required to issue a 'final' report when coverage is being discontinued and provide a reason for discontinuance. Quietly and unobtrusively discontinuing coverage or moving to a 'not rated' category, i.e., a 'closet' sell, does not serve investors' interests.' (See Bowman Testimony, March 20, 2002).

The Committee also heard testimony about the intimidation of analysts by issuers. Mr. Bowman testified that:

> strong pressure to prepare 'positive' reports and make 'buy' recommendations comes directly from corporate issuers, who retaliate in both subtle, and not so subtle, ways against analysts they perceive as 'negative' or not 'understanding' their company. Issuers complain to Wall Street firms' management about 'negative' or uncooperative analysts. They bring lawsuits against firms and analysts personally for negative coverage. But more insidiously, they 'blackball' analysts by not taking their questions on conference calls or not returning their individual calls to investor relations or other company management. This puts the 'negative' analyst at a distinct competitive disadvantage, increases the amount of uncertainty an analyst must deal with in doing valuation and making a recommendation, and disadvantages the firm's clients, who pay for that research. Such actions create a climate of fear and intimidation that fosters neither independence nor objectivity. Analysts walk a tightrope

when dealing with company managements. A false step may cost them an important source of information and ultimately their jobs. (See Bowman Testimony, March 20, 2002).

Mr. Mayo, a victim of issuer retaliation, gave testimony from first-hand experience of the problem. He said, 'It is still hard for an analyst to be objective and critical. When an analyst says 'Sell,' there can be backlash from investors who own the stock, from the company being scrutinized, and even from individuals inside the analyst's firm. While much attention in Washington is being paid to the pressures related to a firm's investment banking operations, other pressures can be as great or more. The main point: Some companies may intimidate analysts into being bullish. Those who stand up may face less access to company information and perhaps backlashes, too.' (See Mayo Testimony, March 19, 2002).

While the bill does not specifically identify remedies to these situations, it authorizes the Commission, or a registered securities association or exchange at the Commission's direction, to create rules to address such other issues as it determines appropriate and to require such other disclosures of conflicts of interest that are material to investors, research analysts, or the broker or dealer as it deems appropriate. The Commission, and the association and exchanges, should consider the issues noted above as they adopt other rules necessary and appropriate to protect investors in the area of analyst recommendations. The prohibition of specific activities identified in title V is not an exhaustive solution to the analyst conflicts problem, and the Committee expects the Commission and the self-regulatory organizations to use their authority to apply such additional rules as they deem appropriate.

The bill requires that rules be adopted within one year. Existing rules that satisfy the requirements of the bill do not have to be reproposed or readopted. Existing rules that do not contradict the bill or that impose requirements that are not imposed by the bill do not have to be withdrawn or reproposed. For example, self-regulatory organization rules that require disclosure of statistics regarding analyst ratings or of the securities holdings of an analyst's family members in a subject company are not adversely affected by this bill.

It should be noted that title V of the bill creates a new Section 15A(n)(B), (C) and (D) of the Exchange Act, which requires disclosure of simply 'affirmative' or 'negative' in response to 'whether' an event has occurred. Further, Section 15A(n)(C) requires a description of the types of services provided, rather than a list of all specific services. This requirement is to enable the investor to assess whether the relationship is likely to influence the objectivity of the subjective portions of the research report.

The new Section 15A(n)(B) of the Exchange Act created by the bill authorizes the Commission to grant exemptions to prevent disclosure of material non-public information about specific future investment banking revenues. In determining whether to grant an exemption, the Commission should take into account the importance that Congress places on providing investors with this information for making investment decisions and the likelihood that stating an affirmative response would divulge material non-public information that would be understood by investors, particularly in light of the size and complexity of the brokerage firm. For example, a complex brokerage firm which has received money from an issuer may be far less likely to disclose material nonpublic information simply by responding 'yes,' and therefore not merit an exception, than a small firm that only is engaged to find buyers for an issuer and has received compensation.

The Committee heard testimony from authorities which stated that the rules set forth by self-regulatory organizations are inadequate to address the analyst conflicts of interest issue. Former SEC Chairman Arthur Levitt testified, 'we must better expose Wall Street analysts' conflicts of interest * * * the New York Stock Exchange and the National Association of Securities Dealers [rulemaking] * * * is not enough.' (See Levitt Testimony, on February 12, 2002).

Also, Attorney General Spitzer stated 'the proposed regulations by the National Association of Securities Dealers and the New York Stock Exchange fall short of what should be legislated in this area.' (See Spitzer Letter, June 5, 2002).

The Committee feels that while the NYSE and NASD rules will improve the quality of analysts' stock recommendations, title V is needed to address analyst conflicts and to strengthen investor protection.

TITLE VI—COMMISSION RESOURCES AND AUTHORITY

The Committee determined that it is necessary to increase the resources available to the SEC and to increase the authority of the SEC to enable it more effectively to accomplish its mission of assuring the integrity of the markets and protecting investors.

* * *

The bill authorizes an appropriation of $776,000,000 for the SEC for fiscal year 2003. This includes:

$102,700,000 to fund pay on a par with the federal bank regulators for SEC employees' salaries as well as their fringe benefits, as authorized by the Investor and Capital Markets Fee Relief Act (P.L. 107-123);

$108,400,000 to fund enhanced information technology, security enhancements, and recovery and mitigation activities; and

$98,000,000 to fund at least 200 more professionals to oversee auditors and auditing services, and additional staff to improve SEC investigative and disciplinary efforts and strengthen the SEC's oversight and regulation of market participants and of issuer disclosure, securities markets, and investment companies.

Codifying Rule of Procedure.

In its Rules of Procedure, the SEC has a procedure to discipline professionals, including accountants, who lack the requisite qualifications to practice before the Commission. Professor Coffee testified before the Committee that '[t]he SEC's authority under Rule 102(e) was clouded by the D.C. Circuit's decision in Checkosky v. SEC, 139 F.3d 221 (D.C. Cir. 1998) (dismissing Rule 102(e) proceeding against two accountants of a 'Big Five' firm). The SEC revised Rule 102 in late 1998 in response to this decision (see Securities Act Rel. No. 7593 (Oct. 18, 1998)), but its authority in this area is still subject to some doubt that Congress may wish to remove or clarify.' (See Coffee Testimony, March 5, 2002). Lynn E. Turner, former SEC Chief Accountant, said, '[t]he statutory authority of the SEC also needs to be examined and beefed up as it relates to Rule 102(e) proceedings.' (See Turner Testimony, February 26, 2002).

The bill codifies the authority of the SEC in 17 CFR 210.102(e) to censure or deny, temporarily or permanently, the privilege of appearing or practicing before it to any person found by the SEC after notice and opportunity for hearing: (i) not to possess the requisite qualifications to represent others, (ii) to be lacking in character or integrity or to have engaged in unethical or improper professional conduct, or (iii) to have willfully violated, or willfully aided and abetted the violation of, any provision of the federal securities laws or the rules and regulations thereunder.

Penny Stock Bar.

Under current law, the penny stock bar is available only in administrative proceedings. However, the Commission frequently brings cases involving serious microcap or penny stock fraud in federal district court in order to obtain injunctive relief. In such a case, if the Commission also wishes to obtain a penny stock bar, it must bring a separate administrative proceeding, typically after the district court case is concluded. The Commission would be able to obtain all necessary relief more efficiently if the district courts had the authority to order penny stock bars.

The bill authorizes federal courts to impose penny stock bars, or conditionally or unconditionally and temporarily or permanently prohibit a person from participating in a penny stock offering. The Commission has requested this authority in order to deal more swiftly with penny stock fraud.

Qualifications of Associated Persons of Brokers and Dealers.

The SEC staff has advised the Committee that in recent years, there has been a growing perception that fraud artists are able to exploit gaps in federal and state regulatory systems and to move from one sector of the financial services industry to another without sufficient impediment. The SEC lacks the enforcement authority to bar individuals from coming into the securities industry who have been found by other financial regulators to have engaged in fraudulent, deceptive, or dishonest conduct in other financial industries. The bill gives the SEC this power. In order to reduce the migration of fraud perpetrators into the securities industry, the bill authorizes the Commission to bar from the securities industry persons who have been suspended or barred by a state securities, banking, or insurance regulator because of fraudulent, manipulative, or deceptive conduct. The Commission requested this authority.

TITLE VII—STUDIES AND REPORTS

The Committee identified two subjects of concern for additional study: the ongoing consolidation of the accounting industry and the performance of credit rating agencies.

Historically, the accounting industry has been consolidating into fewer large accounting firms. James E. Copeland, CPA and Chief Executive Officer, Deloitte & Touche, testified, 'I've been on record since the last spate of proposed mergers saying that I thought the further consolidation of our industry would not be in the public's interest.' (See Copeland Testimony, March 14, 2002).

The bill, in a section authored by Senator Akaka, directs the Comptroller General, in consultation with the SEC, similar regulatory agencies of the other G-7 nations, and the Department of Justice, to conduct a study identifying the factors that have led to the consolidation of public accounting firms since 1989, the impact of such consolidation, and solutions to any problems caused by such consolidation. The study shall also examine the problems faced by businesses as a result of limited competition among public accounting firms, and consider whether federal or state regulations impede competition among public accounting firms. A report is to be submitted to the Senate Banking Committee and the House Financial Services Committee within one year of enactment of this legislation.

The Federal regulation of credit-rating bureaus was raised at the hearing of March 21, 2002. The bill, in a section authored by Senator Bunning, directs the SEC to conduct a study of the role of credit rating agencies in the operation of the securities market, including an examination of the role of credit rating agencies in the evaluation of issuers, the importance of that role to investors, any impediments to the rating agencies' accurate appraisal of issuers, any barriers to entry into the business of acting as a credit rating agency, measures to improve the dissemination of information about issuers when credit rating agencies announce credit ratings, and any conflicts of interest in the operation of credit rating agencies. A report is to be submitted to the President, the Senate Banking Committee, and the House Financial Services Committee within 180 days of enactment.

SECTION-BY-SECTION ANALYSIS

Section 1. Short title and table of contents

Section 2. Definitions

Section 2 contains a set of definitions of terms that are used in the bill.

1. An 'appropriate state regulatory authority' is a state authority responsible for licensing or other regulation of the practice of accounting in a state that has jurisdiction over an accounting firm or its personnel in connection with a particular matter.

2. An 'audit' is an examination of the financial statements of an issuer by an independent public accounting firm, in accordance with rules of the new accounting oversight board or the SEC, for the purpose of expressing an opinion on those statements. This definition should be read in connection with the definitions of 'issuer' and 'audit report,' below.

3. An 'audit committee' is a committee of an issuer's board of directors created to oversee the accounting and financial reporting processes and audits of the financial statements of the issuer.

4. An 'audit report' is a document, prepared following an audit performed for purposes of an issuer's compliance with the federal securities laws, in which a public accounting firm sets forth its opinion regarding a financial statement, report, or other document, or asserts that no such opinion can be expressed.

5. The 'Board' is the Public Company Accounting Oversight Board established by section 101 of the bill.

6. The 'Commission' is the U.S. Securities and Exchange Commission.

7. An 'issuer' is a company that issues or proposes to issue securities, if the securities are registered under section 12 of the Securities Exchange Act of

1934, or if the company is required to file reports with the SEC under section 15(d) of the Securities Exchange Act (or will be required to file those reports at the end of the fiscal year in which a registration statement for the issuer's securities has become effective under the Securities Act of 1933).

8. 'Non-audit services' are professional services provided to an issuer by an accounting firm registered with the Board, other than those required to be provided in connection with an audit or other review of the issuer's financial statements.

9. A 'person associated with a public accounting firm' is a proprietor, partner, shareholder, principal, or an accountant or other professional employee of a public accounting firm, or any independent contractor or entity that shares in compensation or profits, or that participates on behalf of the firm in an activity, in connection with preparation or issuance of an audit report.

10. 'Professional standards' include (i) accounting principles established by the standard-setting body recognized under the bill or prescribed or recognized by the SEC that are relevant to particular audit reports or accounting firm quality control systems, and (ii) auditing standards, standards for attestation engagements, quality control policy, ethical and competency standards, and independence standards that relate to the preparation of audit reports and are established or adopted by the Board or SEC.

11. A 'public accounting firm' includes a proprietorship or entity engaged in the practice of public accounting or preparing or issuing audit reports. To the extent the new oversight board designates in its rules, the term can also include an associated person of an accounting firm.

12. A 'registered public accounting firm' is a firm that registers with the new oversight board, as required by section 102 of the bill.

13. The 'rules of the Board' include both the formal bylaws and rules adopted by the new oversight board (subject to action of the SEC under section 107 of the bill) and stated policies, practices, and interpretations of the board that the SEC deems to be rules of the board.

14. The term 'security' has the same meaning as in section 3(a) of the Securities Exchange Act.

15. The term 'securities laws' has the meaning given that term in section 3(a)(47) of the Securities Exchange Act, and includes the SEC's rules, regulations and orders. (Section 2(b), in a conforming amendment, makes the bill a part of the section 3(a)(47) definition.)

16. A 'State' includes any state of the United States, the District of Columbia, Puerto Rico, the Virgin Islands, and any other U.S. territory or possession.

Section 3. Commission rules and enforcement

Section 3 generally gives the Securities and Exchange Commission (the 'Commission' or the 'SEC') authority to promulgate rules consistent with the Act and provides that a violation of the Act, or of any rule of the Commission or of the new Public Company Accounting Oversight Board created by title I of the Act, will be treated for all purposes as a violation of the Securities Exchange Act of 1934 and the rules thereunder; similarly, the new Board will be treated as if it were a self-regulatory organization under the 1934 Act for purposes of the Commission's investigative and enforcement authority. It should be emphasized that the new Board's own authority is limited to the work of accountants in auditing public companies; the Board has no jurisdiction with respect to the work of accountants in performing audits of other companies.

Section 3 thus confirms that the Commission will have the authority to enforce the Act directly. Section 3 also makes clear that nothing in the Act or the rules of the new Board limits the Commission's own authority over accounting firms and their personnel, or accounting, auditing, independence, or other standards relating to auditors' reports.

TITLE I—PUBLIC COMPANY ACCOUNTING OVERSIGHT BOARD

Section 101. Establishment.

Section 101 creates a new Public Company Accounting Oversight Board (the 'Board'). The Board will oversee the auditing of companies that are subject to the federal securities laws (i.e., companies ('public companies' or 'issuers') that have chosen to sell stock or debt instruments to public investors). Accounting firms that perform audits of public companies must register with the Board, and the Board will possess authority, subject to action by the Commission, to (i) set auditing, quality control, ethics, and independence standards (the latter supplementing statutory provisions on that subject), with respect to audits of the financial statements of public companies, (ii) inspect accounting firms' audit operations with respect to public companies, (iii) investigate potential violations by the firms or their partners or employees of the Act, the Board's rules, related provisions of the securities laws (and the Commission's rules), and professional accounting and conduct standards, and (iv) impose sanctions for violations.

Again, the Board's authority in these areas is focused on, and limited to, the audit of public companies; it has no jurisdiction over accountants performing other audits. The Board is to submit an annual report of its activities to the Commission, which in turn is to send a copy to the House Committee on Financial Services and the Senate Committee on Banking, Housing, and Urban Affairs within 30 days of receipt.

Legally, the Board will be a private nonprofit corporation subject to the District of Columbia Nonprofit Corporation Act. The Board will not be an agency or establishment of the United States. It is explicitly given authority to set compensation for its employees at levels comparable to similar positions in the private sector.

Membership. Section 101(e) provides that the Board will have five members. The initial Board will be appointed by the Commission, after consultation with the Federal Reserve Board and the Department of the Treasury, within 90 days of the date of enactment; vacancies will be filled by the Commission after similar consultations. Board members will serve full-time, for five-year (staggered) terms, with a two-term limit. All Board members must have an understanding of the responsibilities for and the nature of the financial disclosures and accountants' responsibilities required by the securities laws. Three members of the Board will have a general background, and two members will have an accountancy background; the Board's Chairperson may be one of the two Board members with an accountancy background, but if so, he or she may not have been a practicing accountant for at least five years prior to appointment to the Board. Internal Board standard of conduct rules must include a one-year ban on practice before the Board (or before the Commission, with respect to Board-related matters) for former Board members and appropriate 'cooling off' periods (not to exceed one year) for former Board staff.

The initial Board's first task will be to hire staff, propose or adopt its first sets of rules and generally bring the organization into operational existence, so that the Commission can make a determination, required under section 101(d) within 270 days of enactment, that the Board possesses the capacity to carry out its responsibilities and enforce compliance with title I of the Act.

Section 102. Registration with the Board

The Commission's determination that the Board can begin to exercise its authority starts the running of a 180-day period within which each public accounting firm that prepares or issues audit reports for public companies must register with the Board. At the end of the 180-day period it will become unlawful for an unregistered accounting firm to audit a public company. (Again, lack of registration will have no effect on an accounting firm's ability to perform any other sort of work.) An application for registration must include information about the identity of the public companies for which an accounting firm currently or during the previous year performs or has performed audit work, certain current financial information about the accounting firm itself, a statement of the firm's quality control policies for its accounting and auditing practice, a list of the firm's accountants who participate in public company audits, and information about pending civil, criminal, or disciplinary actions, and client-auditor disputes, relating to the firm's audits of public companies.

The application must also include a consent to compliance with any requests for documents or testimony, within the Board's authority, made to the registrant in the course of the Board's operation and an agreement to obtain and if necessary to enforce similar consents from the firm's partners and employees who participate in public company audits. Registered accounting firms will be required to report changes in this information to the Board annually (or more frequently if the Board so requires).

Information submitted to the Board as part of each application will be made available to the public, subject to limitations to protect the confidentiality of proprietary, personal, and other information for which such protection is necessary or required by law. In particular, information 'reasonably identified by [the registrant] as proprietary information' will be withheld from disclosure.

The Board is authorized by section 102(f) to impose a registration fee and an annual fee on each registrant, to cover the cost of processing and reviewing applications and annual reports.

Section 103. Auditing, quality control, and independence standards and rules

Section 103 requires the Board to establish auditing, quality control, and ethical standards, as required by the Act or the rules of the Commission or necessary or appropriate in the public interest or for the protection of investors, to be used by registered accounting firms in the preparation of audit reports for public companies. The Board is also to adopt rules to implement the provisions on the independence of public company auditors contained in title II of the Act.

The Board's rules specifically must require (i) preparation and maintenance for 7 years by public company auditors of audit work papers and related information in sufficient detail to support each audit's conclusions, (ii) 'second partner' review and approval of each public company audit report and its issuance, and (iii) inclusion in each audit report of a description of the auditor's testing of the public company's systems for compliance with the requirements of section 13(b)(2) of the Securities Exchange Act and of the company's controls over its receipts and expenditures, together with specific notation of any significant defects or material noncompliance of which the auditor should know on the basis of such testing.

Section 103 also specifies the subjects that the quality control standards adopted by the Board must address. These are: monitoring of ethics and independence; internal and external consulting on audit issues; audit supervision; hiring, development, and advancement of audit personnel; acceptance and continuance of engagements; and internal inspection.

The Board may adopt as part of its rules (and modify as appropriate for that purpose, at the time of adoption or thereafter), any portion of a statement of auditing, quality control, or ethics standards that meet the statutory test prepared (i) by a professional group of accountants designated by a rule of the Board for that purpose, or (ii) by one or more advisory groups convened by the Board. (Pre-existing standards of designated professional groups of accountants that may be adopted during the Board's nine-month transitional period are to be separately approved by the Commission at the time of the Commission's determination (pursuant to section 101(d), noted above) that the Board is ready to begin operation.)

The Board will convene advisory groups of practicing accountants and other experts, as well as representatives of other interested groups (subject to appropriate conflict of interest rules), to make recommendations concerning, or propose drafts of, the content of any required standards for public company auditors.

The Board is to cooperate on an ongoing basis with both the designated professional groups of accountants noted above, and with its own advisory groups, in examining the need for changes in any standards subject to Board authority. The Board is to recommend issues for inclusion on the agendas of these groups, and take other steps to facilitate the standard-setting process, and it is to respond in a timely fashion to requests for changes in the standards over which the Board has authority.

Finally, the Board is to include a summary of the results of its standard-setting responsibilities in each of its annual reports. Each summary must include a discussion of the Board's work with any designated professional group of accountants or advisory group, as well as the Board's pending agenda for future standard-setting projects.

Section 104. Inspections of registered public accounting firms

Section 104 outlines the duty of the staff of the Board to undertake annual inspections of registered public accounting firms that prepare audit reports for more than 100 public companies, and triennial inspections of firms that prepare audit reports for 100 or fewer public companies, to assess the degree of compliance by those firms with the Act, the rules of the Board, and professional standards relating to audits of public companies. (The inspection cycles for different-sized accounting firms may be subsequently changed by the Board.) The Board is to (i) identify in the course of each inspection any act, practice, or omission by the firm or its partners or employees revealed by the inspection that may violate the Act, the Board's or related Commission rules, the firm's own quality control policies, or professional standards, (ii) report any such finding, if appropriate, to the Commission and each state accountancy board with jurisdiction over the matter, and (iii) commence a formal investigation or take any appropriate disciplinary action with respect to the violation.

The scope of each inspection will include both particular audit and review engagements (which may include engagements that are otherwise the subject of ongoing controversy between the accounting firm under inspection and third parties), selected solely by the Board, as well as a review of each firm's quality control system and its compliance with professional standards relating to audit reports for public companies. The term 'professional standards' means, for purposes of title I and the Board's authorization, (i) generally accepted accounting principles, (ii) auditing standards, standards for attestation engagements and quality control policies, and ethical and competency standards that the Board adopts, and (iii) independence standards that the Board adopts to implement title II of the Act.

The rules of the Board are to provide a procedure for review and comment on a draft inspection report by the firm inspected; the text of any comment by the firm on a draft inspection report is to be attached, with appropriate redactions to protect confidential information, to the final report. That report is to be sent to the Commission and the appropriate state board of accountancy and made available to the public (subject, again, to protection of confidential and proprietary information). Portions of an inspection report which deal with criticisms of or potential defects in the quality control systems of a firm will not be made public if the defects are addressed to the satisfaction of the Board within 12 months of the date of the report. In certain cases interim Commission review of certain inspection-related disputes is available.

Section 105. Investigations and disciplinary proceedings

Section 105 outlines the investigative and disciplinary authority of the Board over firms that audit public companies and partners and employees of these firms.

Investigations. Section 105(a) authorizes the Board to investigate any act or practice by a registered accounting firm, or its partners or employees, that may violate the Act, the Board's rules, professional standards, and the portion of the securities laws and SEC rules that relate to the preparation and issuance of audit reports and the obligations and liabilities of accountants with respect thereto. The Board may require testimony or production of documents or information, or inspect documents or information, in the possession of any registered public accounting firm or its partners or employees. The Board's investigative activities and any information gathered in the course of an investigation are to be confidential and privileged for all purposes (including civil discovery), unless and until particular information is presented in connection with a public proceeding.

The Board may refer investigations to the Commission, any other federal functional regulator (in the case of an investigation relating to the audit of an institution subject to the jurisdiction of such functional regulator), and, at the direction of the Commission, to the Attorney General, state attorneys general in connection with any criminal investigation, or appropriate state boards of accountancy, and may share information derived from investigations with the same parties, but only if the Board determines that such disclosure is 'necessary to accomplish the purposes of the Act or to protect investors.' The Board's investigators are granted civil immunity for their activities during an investigation to the same extent that a federal investigator would enjoy such immunity.

Disciplinary proceedings. Section 105(b) authorizes the Board to impose a full range of sanctions if it finds that a registered firm, or its partners or employees, have engaged in any act or practice that violates the Act, the Board's rules, professional standards, or the portion of the securities laws (and SEC rules) relating to audits of public companies. Potential sanctions include revocation or suspension of the registration of an accounting firm, or of the ability of particular individuals to remain associated with that firm or become associated with any other registered accounting firm (effectively barring the subject of the sanction from participating in audits of public companies), substantial civil money penalties, required professional education or training, or censure; the Board's ability to suspend or bar an associated person from the auditing of public companies, and the Board's ability to impose civil money penalties above a certain amount, is limited to situations involving intentional, knowing, or reckless conduct, or repeated negligent conduct. The Board may also impose sanctions upon a registered accounting firm for failure reasonably to supervise a partner or employee (in terms similar to those that apply to broker-dealers under section 15(b)(4) of the Securities Exchange Act of 1934, which permit the firm to defend by showing that its internal control procedures were reasonable and were operating fully in the case at issue).

The Board's rules must set out fully the procedural requirements for disciplinary proceedings. Disciplinary sanctions finally imposed must be reported to the Commission, appropriate state or foreign boards of accountancy, and the public (once any stay of enforcement pending appeal has been lifted). Any sanction may be appealed to the Commission under the provisions of section 107(c) (described below).

Fines imposed by the Board are to be used to fund a scholarship program for students in undergraduate or graduate programs in accounting.

Section 106. Foreign public accounting firms

Section 106 provides that accounting firms organized under the laws of countries other than the United States that issue audit reports for public companies subject to the U.S. securities laws are covered by the Act in the same manner as domestic accounting firms, subject to the exemptive authority of both the Board and the Commission. (Registration under the Act will not in itself provide a basis for subjecting a foreign accounting firm to U.S. jurisdiction other than with respect to controversies between such a firm and the Board.) The Board is authorized to determine that other foreign accounting firms play a sufficiently substantial role in the preparation and furnishing of such reports for particular issuers that their coverage under the Act is necessary or appropriate, in light of the purposes of the Act and in the public interest or for the protection of investors.

Section 106 also sets terms for the production in the United States by a foreign public accounting firm of its audit work papers, for any audit in which the foreign accounting firm issues an opinion or otherwise performs material services upon which an accounting firm registered under the Act relies in issuing all or part of an audit report for a public company.

Section 107. Commission oversight of the Board

Section 107 makes the Board generally subject to the same degree of control by the Commission as the National Association of Securities Dealers or the New York Stock Exchange. Section 107(b) provides that the Board's proposed rules must be filed with the Commission and published by the Commission for public comment. No Board rule may take effect without Commission approval (except in limited situations), and the Commission retains the power not only to disapprove, but to abrogate or amend, any rules of the Board. Section 107(c) incorporates the provisions of section 19(d)(2) and (e)(1) of the Securities Exchange Act of 1934 to give the Commission full authority to review, modify, or cancel any disciplinary sanction imposed by the Board (including any sanction imposed for failure to comply with a demand for testimony or documents in the course of a Board investigation), either upon the Commission's own motion or on the motion of an aggrieved party. (The Commission may, in some cases, also review registration- or inspection-related disputes.)

Finally, the Commission possesses authority to limit the authority and activities, or to censure, or even to remove members, of the Board itself, if the Commission finds that the Board, or a particular member, has violated, is unable to comply with, or has failed to enforce compliance with the Act, the Board's or the Commission's rules, or the securities laws, has failed to enforce compliance with professional standards, or, in the case of a particular Board member, has willfully abused his or her authority.

Section 108. Accounting standards

Section 108 amends section 19 of the Securities Act of 1933 specifically to allow the Commission to recognize as 'generally accepted' (for securities law purposes) accounting principles established by a standard-setting body that meets certain criteria. First, the body must be a private entity and be funded by public companies in the same manner as the Board (provided in section 109 of the Act), and it must have adopted procedures, including acting by majority vote, to ensure prompt consideration of necessary changes to the body of accounting principles. Second, the Commission must determine that the standard-setting body has the ability to assist the Commission, because the standard-setting body has proved able to improve the accuracy and effectiveness of financial reporting and the protection of investors. Any such standard-setting body must report annually to the Commission. Finally, section 108 requires the Commission to conduct a study of the adoption by the U.S. financial reporting system of a principles-based accounting system.

Section 109. Funding

Section 109 provides that the Board and the accounting principles standard-setting body recognized under section 108 of title I are to be funded by an 'accounting support fee.' (The Board's budget, but not the budget of the standard-setting body, is to be subject to approval by the Commission.) In the case of both the Board and the standard-setting body, the annual support fee is to be assessed against each public company. Amounts payable by public companies to either body will generally be allocated among those companies based on relative average annual monthly market capitalization for the 12 months prior to the year to which the support fee relates; both the Board and the standard-setting body are permitted to differentiate among various classes of public companies, as necessary or appropriate, in allocating fees. Fees are to be collected in such manner as is deemed appropriate in each case.

TITLE II—AUDITOR INDEPENDENCE

Section 201. Services outside the auditor scope of practice

The Act restricts a registered public accounting firm in the non-audit services it may provide to its audit clients that are public companies in order to preserve the firm's independence. The Act specifies eight categories of activities that an auditor may not provide to a public company that is its audit client. These include: (1) bookkeeping or other services related to the accounting records or financial statements of the issuer; (2) financial information systems design and implementation consulting services; (3) appraisal or valuation services, fairness opinions, or contribution-in-kind reports; (4) actuarial services; (5) internal audit services; (6) any management or human resources function; (7) broker, dealer, investment adviser, or investment banking services; and (8) legal services and expert services unrelated to the auditing service. In addition, the Public Company Accounting Oversight Board may determine that any other non-audit service is prohibited.

The Board has the authority to grant exemptions on a case-by-case basis to the extent necessary or appropriate in the public interest and consistent with the protection of investors, subject to SEC review. A registered public accounting firm would be permitted to perform for a public company audit client any other non-audit service, including tax services, that the public company's Audit Committee pre-approves in accordance with the requirements adopted in Section 202.

The Act would not affect the services that a registered public accounting firm provides to non-public companies or to public companies that are not its audit clients. Thus, a firm could provide any consulting service to any public company for which it does not provide audit services as well as to any non-public company.

Section 202. Pre-approval requirements

The Audit Committee of a public company must pre-approve all the services, both audit and non-audit, provided to that company by a registered public accounting firm. The public company is required to disclose the Audit Committee's approvals of non-audit services to shareholders in SEC filings. The pre-approval requirement is waived if an auditor provides a service that was not recognized to be a non-audit service at the time of the engagement and if the aggregate amount of all such non-audit services is 5% or less of total auditor fees and such services are promptly brought to the attention of the Audit Committee and approved by the Audit Committee prior to the completion of the audit. Approval may be made by one or more members of the Audit Committee, to whom such authority has been delegated. The decisions of any delegated member to pre-approve an activity shall be presented to the full Audit Committee at each of its meetings.

Section 203. Audit partner rotation

A registered public accounting firm must rotate its lead partner and review partner on its audits of a public company so that no partner performs an audit on the same issuer as a lead partner or review partner for more than five consecutive years.

Section 204. Auditor report to Audit Committees

A registered independent public accounting firm performing an audit for a public company will timely report to that company's Audit Committee the critical accounting policies and practices to be used and all alternative treatments of financial information within GAAP that have been discussed with management, any accounting disagreements between the auditor and management and other material written communications between the auditor and management.

Section 205. Conforming amendments

Section 206. Conflicts of interest

An accounting firm may not provide audit services for a public company if that company's chief executive officer, controller, chief financial officer, chief accounting officer, or other individual serving in an equivalent position, was employed by the accounting firm and worked on the audit of the public company during the one year before the start of the audit services.

Section 207. Study of mandatory rotation of registered public accounting firms

The GAO will study the potential effects of requiring the mandatory rotation of registered public accounting firms and report to Congress within one year.

Section 208. Commission authority

A registered independent public accounting firm must comply with the restrictions in sections 201-204 and 206 in order to perform an audit for a public company.

Section 209. Considerations by appropriate state regulatory authorities

It is the intent of this Act that in supervising non-registered accounting firms, state regulatory authorities should make an independent determination of the proper standards, and should not presume the standards applied by the Board under this Act to be applicable to small- and medium-sized non-registered accounting firms.

TITLE III—CORPORATE RESPONSIBILITY

Section 301. Issuer Audit Committees

The Exchange Act is amended to require the SEC to draft rules directing national securities exchanges and national securities associations to require listed companies to make Audit Committees responsible for the appointment, compensation, and oversight of the work of auditors and to require auditors to report directly to the Audit Committee. The amendments also: bar Audit Committee members from accepting consulting fees or being affiliated persons of the issuer or the issuer's subsidiaries other than in the member's capacity as a member of the board of directors or any board committee; require Audit Committees to have in place procedures to receive and address complaints regarding accounting, internal control or auditing issues; require Audit Committees to establish procedures for employees' anonymous submission of concerns regarding accounting or auditing matters; and require public companies to provide their Audit Committees with authority and funding to engage independent counsel and other advisers as they determine necessary.

Section 302. Corporate responsibility for financial reports

CEOs and CFOs must certify, in periodic reports containing financial statements filed with the Commission pursuant to section 13(a) or 15(d) of the Exchange Act, the appropriateness of financial statements and disclosures contained therein, and that those financials and disclosures fairly present the company's operations and financial condition.

Section 303. Prohibited influence

It is unlawful for any officer, director, or person acting under their direction to fraudulently influence, coerce, manipulate, or mislead any accountant engaged in preparing an audit report, for the purpose of rendering the audit report misleading.

Section 304. Forfeiture of certain bonuses and profits

In the case of accounting restatements that result from material non-compliance with SEC financial reporting requirements, CEOs and CFOs must disgorge bonuses and other incentive-based compensation and profits on stock sales, if the non-compliance results from misconduct. The required disgorgement applies to the 12 months after the first public issuance or filing of a financial document embodying such financial reporting requirement. The SEC may exempt any person from this requirement as it deems necessary and appropriate.

Section 305. Officer and director bars and penalties

The sanction of barring securities law violators from serving as officers or directors of public companies is strengthened by modifying the standard that governs judicial imposition of officer and director bars. In addition, courts may impose any equitable relief necessary or appropriate to protect, and mitigate harm to, investors.

Section 306. Insider trades during pension fund blackout periods prohibited

Directors and executive officers are prohibited from engaging in transactions involving any equity security of the issuer during a 'blackout' period when at least half of the issuer's individual account plan participants are not permitted to purchase, sell or otherwise transfer their interest in that equity security. No blackout period may take effect until at least 30 days after written notice of the blackout is provided by the plan administrator to the participants or beneficiaries. Exceptions to the 30-day notice are allowed in cases: (1) where a deferral of the blackout period would violate ERISA fiduciary provisions; or (2) where the inability to provide the notice is due to unforeseeable events or circumstances beyond the reasonable control of the plan administrator.

TITLE IV—ENHANCED FINANCIAL DISCLOSURES

Section 401. Disclosures in periodic reports

A public company in periodic reports filed with the SEC will present: (1) disclosures of financial information that reflect all material correcting adjustments that have been identified by the auditor in accordance with GAAP and (2) the material off-balance sheet transactions, arrangements, obligations, and other relationships of the issuer with unconsolidated entities or other persons that may have a material current or future effect on financial condition, changes in financial condition, results of operations, liquidity, capital expenditures, capital resources or significant components of revenues or expenses.

Issuers that disseminate 'pro forma' financial information in their filings with the SEC, press releases or other public disclosures must present pro forma data in a manner that does not contain an untrue statement or omit to state a material fact necessary in order to make the information, in light of the circumstances under which it is presented, not misleading, and that reconciles it with the issuer's financial condition under GAAP.

Section 402. Enhanced disclosures of loans

An issuer in its current reports must disclose within 7 days, or such other time period determined to be appropriate by the SEC: (A) all loans, except credit card loans, made by the issuer and its affiliates to any executive officer or director, specifying amounts paid and balances owed on such obligations and (B) any conflicts of interest, as defined by the SEC.

Section 403. Disclosures of transactions involving management

Section 16(a) of the Exchange Act is amended to require directors, officers and 10% equity holders to report their purchases and sales of securities more promptly, by the end of the second day following the transaction or such other time established by the SEC in any case in which the two-day period is not feasible.

Section 404. Management assessment of internal controls

Annual reports filed with the SEC must be accompanied by a statement by the management of its responsibility for creating and maintaining adequate internal controls. Management must also present its assessment of the effectiveness of those controls. In addition, the company's auditor must report on and attest to management's assessment of the company's internal controls. Such attestation shall not be the subject of a separate engagement.

Section 405. Exemption

Investment companies are exempted from the disclosure requirements of sections 401, 402 and 404.

Section 406. Code of ethics for senior financial officers

Issuers are required to disclose whether or not they have adopted a code of ethics for senior financial officers, and if not, the reason therefor.

Section 407. Audit Committee financial expert

The SEC is required to adopt rules to require issuers to disclose whether their Audit Committees include among their members at least one 'financial expert.' In defining 'financial expert,' the SEC shall consider whether a person understands GAAP and financial statements, has experience preparing or auditing financials, has experience with internal accounting controls, and understands Audit Committee functions.

TITLE V—CONFLICTS OF INTEREST

Section 501. Treatment of securities analysts by registered securities associations

The Act requires the Commission, or upon the authorization and direction of the Commission, a registered securities association or national securities exchange, within one year to adopt rules designed to address conflicts of interest facing securities analysts.

The rules will (A) foster greater public confidence in securities research and protect the objectivity and independence of stock analysts who publish research intended for the public by (i) prohibiting the pre-publication clearance of such research or recommendations by investment banking or other staff not directly responsible for investment research, (ii) limiting the supervision and compensatory evaluation of such research personnel to officials who are not engaged in investment banking activities, and (iii) protecting securities analysts from retaliation or threats of retaliation by investment banking staff because of negative or otherwise unfavorable research reports that might adversely affect investment banking relations with the issuer described in the report, provided that the rules shall not limit the authority of a broker or dealer to discipline a securities analyst for causes other than such report in accordance with the firm's policies and procedures, (B) define periods during which broker-dealers who participate in a public offering of securities as underwriters or dealers shall not publish research or recommendations about the securities of the issuer, (C) establish structural and institutional safeguards within broker-dealers to assure that securities analysts preparing research reports are separated by appropriate informational partitions from the review, pressure, or oversight of those whose involvement in investment banking activities might potentially bias their judgment or supervision, and (D) address such other issues as the SEC or the SROs deem appropriate.

The Act also requires the Commission, or upon the direction of the Commission, a registered securities association or national securities exchange, to adopt rules requiring disclosures about conflicts of interest in reports and public appearances. These disclosures include (A) the extent to which the analyst holds securities in the issuer, (B) whether compensation has been received from the issuer, subject to such exemptions as the Commission may determine appropriate and necessary to prevent disclosure of material non-public information regarding specific potential future investment banking transactions as is appropriate in the public interest and consistent with investor protection, (C) whether the issuer is or has recently been a client of the analyst's firm, and if so, the types of services provided, (D) whether the analyst received compensation based on an affiliate's investment banking revenues, and (E) such other disclosures as the SEC or the SROs deem appropriate. The regulator would have the authority to amend its rules.

TITLE VI—COMMISSION RESOURCES AND AUTHORITY

Section 601. Authorization of appropriations

There is authorized an appropriation of $776,000,000 for the SEC for fiscal year 2003, of which: $102,700,000 would fund the pay parity of salary and benefits for SEC employees, as authorized in the Investor and Capital Markets Fee Relief Act (P.L. 107-123); $108,400,000 would fund information technology, security enhancements, and recovery and mitigation activities in light of the terrorist attacks of September 11, 2001; and $98,000,000 would fund at least 200 more professionals to oversee auditors and auditing services, and additional staff to improve SEC investigative and disciplinary efforts and strengthen the SEC's oversight and regulation of market participants and of issuer disclosure, securities markets and investment companies.

Section 602. Appearance and practice before the SEC

The SEC is authorized to censure or deny, temporarily or permanently, the privilege of appearing or practicing before it to any person found by the SEC after notice and opportunity for hearing: (i) not to possess the requisite qualifications to represent others, (ii) to be lacking in character or integrity or to have engaged in unethical or improper professional conduct, or (iii) to have willfully violated, or willfully aided and abetted the violation of any provision of the federal securities laws or the rules and regulations thereunder. This codifies Section 102(e) of the SEC's Rules of Practice.

Section 603. Federal court authority to impose penny stock bars

Federal courts are authorized to conditionally or unconditionally and temporarily or permanently prohibit a person from participating in a penny stock offering.

Section 604. Qualifications of associated persons of brokers and dealers

The SEC is authorized to bar from the securities industry persons who have been suspended or barred by a state securities, banking or insurance regulator because of fraudulent, manipulative or deceptive conduct.

TITLE VII—STUDIES AND REPORTS

Section 701. GAO study and report regarding consolidation of public accounting firms

The Comptroller General, in consultation with the SEC, similar regulatory agencies of the other G-7 nations, and the Department of Justice, is to conduct a study identifying the factors that have led to the consolidation of public accounting firms since 1989, the impact of such consolidation, and solutions to any problems caused by such consolidation. The study shall also examine the problems faced by businesses as a result of limited competition among public accounting firms, and consider whether federal or state regulations impede competition among public accounting firms. A report is to be submitted to the Senate Banking Committee and the House Financial Services Committee within one year of enactment.

Section 702. Commission study and report regarding credit rating agencies

The SEC is to conduct a study of the role of credit rating agencies in the operation of the securities market, including an examination of the role of credit rating agencies in the evaluation of issuers, the importance of that role to investors, any impediments to the rating agencies' accurate appraisal of issuers, any barriers to entry into the business of acting as a credit rating agency, measures to improve the dissemination of information about issuers when credit rating agencies announce credit ratings, and any conflicts of interest in the operation of credit rating agencies. A report is to be submitted to the President, the Senate Banking Committee, and the House Financial Services Committee within 180 days of enactment.

ADDITIONAL VIEWS OF SENATOR GRAMM

President Bush's Ten Point program for regulatory reform in corporate accounting and governance is an excellent plan, and he and his administration are to be commended for wasting no time in implementing it. The actions already being taken by the Securities and Exchange Commission, together with their published regulatory proposals, as well as the actions taken by our nation's stock markets, are firm, clear, and directed to the real problems. They represent substantial reform. It is also undeniable that changes are occurring in every board room, on every corporate audit committee, and with every accounting firm in America. But a legislative response is also called for.

First of all though, it would be hard to overestimate the importance of maintaining our system of private setting of accounting standards through the Financial Accounting Standards Board (FASB). Neither Congress nor any other agency of the government should be in the business of setting accounting standards. A bad accounting standard set by an independent board is better than a good standard set by Congress. But we do need to establish a stable, reliable funding mechanism for FASB.

With regard to legislation, the reported bill is better today than the bill as first proposed, yet the fundamental problems of the original bill remain. We should pass a bill that sets up an independent ethics supervisory board that will oversee and enforce the highest standards of ethics in public accounting. This board should be given power to determine what are conflicts of interest and to make determinations on questions of auditor independence. It should also be independently funded by a source that is committed to the purpose of funding that activity, and the funding source should be reliable.

Yet, even though some flexibility has been added, the structure of the bill is still troubling. If we are going to create this independent panel, we should create one in which we can place our confidence, allowing the panel, for example, to set the standards as to what represents a conflict of interest. While it is tempting to vote on these things and to set out in government writ for all time what we mean and what we want, if we are trying to make this board powerful, why would we want to prejudge what the panel is going to decide? There is a fundamental difference between having the board make decisions or having Congress make them.

When Congress prejudges the board's activities, we eliminate the flexibility that the board will need to apply statutory principles to the variety of circumstances that appear in the real world. The one-size-fits-all approach of the bill cripples the ability of the board to adjust to differences in situations among companies—particularly to distinguish between large and small companies—as well as to stay up to date with changes that occur over time.

This will be particularly hard on smaller companies. While the legislation allows for exceptions to its ban on auditors providing companies with additional services, these exceptions can only be obtained on a case-by-case basis. It is the smaller companies who routinely obtain a number of services from their auditor and who can least afford to pay for a second or third auditing firm to provide these additional services. These smaller business will be most likely to need the exemptions. But the smaller the company, the less likely it will be able to afford the legal services to get its needed exemptions from the new board. This is not a small problem, as the bill would impose its new regulatory requirements on 17,000 companies—the vast majority of which are small businesses—all across the country.

It may be easy to envision requiring that General Motors have six different accounting firms to comply with the conflict of interest rules. But it stretches reason and good judgment to legislate those same standards for Joe Green and Son Motor Repair of Texarkana. We should trust the board that we create and let them look at the feasibility for large and small companies, ask them to look at the benefits to shareholders, the integrity of the financial system and long term growth prospects. It is easy to envision that they might end up with standards that would be differentiated based on the size of accounting firms and the size of the businesses that are affected. We would preserve flexibility in doing this. One-size-fits-all will hurt a lot of shareholders and the businesses in which they have invested. And heaping unnecessary costs on struggling small enterprises, it will hurt the economy.

The point is, when you start setting out in law what auditing standards are, what the conflict of interest standard is, and the many other specific mandates in the bill, you eliminate flexibility, you eliminate the ability of the board to learn what works and what does not work, and you eliminate the ability of the board to differentiate between General Motors and Joe Green and Son, Incorporated. In the process of setting up a strong, independent board we have largely done our work. We ought not to be doing the board's work after that.

In addition, before this legislation becomes law, the concerns of constitutional experts with regard to the appointment, regulatory powers, and taxing authority of this new supervisory board will need to be resolved.

ADDITIONAL VIEWS OF SENATOR ENZI

The collapse in the faith of corporate financial statements is alarming. Corporate executive abuses have shattered the savings and dreams of countless Americans. Broad and strong changes need to be implemented to restore that confidence and ensure these abuses do not take place in the future.

A wave of new regulations and legislative proposals have been introduced to protect America's investors against corporate abuses. The securities' self-regulatory organizations (SROs), the Securities and Exchange Commission (SEC), the White House, and Congress are all working on different approaches with the same goal—to ensure executives are providing accurate and reliable information to the public.

However, any approach must also be sensitive to the fact that auditors are a critical element in assuring the quality of a financial statement. Legislation that does not provide adequate liability protections for auditing firms will decrease the already minimal number of companies which can audit and evaluate complex and fast-growing companies. Without a competitive auditing industry, consumers may, at the end of the day, experience less reliable financial statements.

I believe this legislation, as reported by the Senate Banking Committee, will provide a disincentive for small accounting firms to continue to audit publicly traded companies. These small accounting firms may only audit a relatively few public companies, and my fear is that this legislation would increase their liability exponentially, thus the firms would decide to cease offering services to public companies. With current litigation downsizing an already limited number of accounting firms, we cannot allow additional regulations to drive more firms from offering auditing services to public companies.

The legislation also places a negative presumption on any approval of non-prohibited consulting services. Legislation should not mandate to audit committees that all consulting services are inherently conflicted. Audit committees should be left to make their own determination as to what services provided by their auditing companies is in the best interest of their shareholders.

I also have concerns that the setting of auditing standards will be taken out of the hands of accountants. Auditing standards are complicated and detailed and the setting of them requires the knowledge and expertise of individuals who understand and work in the field of accounting. I am hesitant to allow a Board, of which the majority must be non-accountants, to establish the standards under which accountants operate.

I continue to support reform of the accounting industry and will continue to work toward that goal with this legislation. I, however, will work to change aspects of the bill which I believe will impose severe unintended and unnecessary consequences on the accounting industry and their clients.

¶ 3001 SELECTED PORTIONS OF HOUSE REPORT NO. 107-414

Report of the Committee on Financial Services to accompany H.R. 3763, April 22, 2002.

PURPOSE AND SUMMARY

H.R. 3763, the Corporate and Auditing Accountability, Responsibility, and Transparency Act of 2002, will protect investors by improving the accuracy and reliability of corporate disclosures made pursuant to the securities laws. The bill achieves this goal through increased supervision of accountants that audit public companies, strengthened corporate responsibility, increased transparency of corporate financial statements, and protections for employee access to retirement accounts.

With regard to increasing the supervision of accountants, the purpose of the legislation is to allow for the creation of a public regulatory organization or organizations, comprised of persons skilled and knowledgeable in issues related to the audit of public companies, to perform quality or other reviews of the activities of certified public accountants who report on financial statements that are required to be filed with the Securities and Exchange Commission (SEC). The legislation envisions that such an organization will enforce compliance by accountants with professional ethics and competency standards applicable to audits of such financial statements and establish such rules as are deemed necessary to provide for their review and enforcement, and provides for the oversight of such organizations by the Commission.

The legislation also requires that the SEC promulgate rules that would bar the provision by auditors of certain nonaudit services to their audit clients. The Committee heard testimony that two nonaudit services—financial systems design and implementation and internal audit outsourcing—were perceived to raise issues about auditor independence. Because of the importance of public perceptions in this area, the Committee believes these services should be prohibited. The SEC had proposed to prohibit them during a rulemaking in 2000, but ultimately decided to allow them, subject to certain conditions.

Although financial systems and internal audit work are the two nonaudit services that have raised significant investor concerns, the SEC is also authorized to modify its rules if auditing firms begin to offer other services that raise similarly significant independence concerns. Indeed, it is appropriate that these issues be considered carefully by an entity with the Commission's resources and expertise, and that whatever standards are established apply uniformly to public companies throughout the markets. A non-federal approach would lead to uncertainty in our capital markets, particularly if the standards applicable to public companies and audit firms varied by jurisdiction.

The Committee believes that it is appropriate to continue dealing with nonaudit services by having the Commission proscribe specific services rather than casting doubt on a broad range of nonaudit services. In this regard, the Committee heard testimony that a broader ban on nonaudit services could undermine rather than improve audit quality, since certain such services can improve the auditor's understanding of the audit client's business activities. Likewise, a broader ban could reduce corporate efficiencies and impair auditing firms' ability to attract and retain tax and other nonaudit personnel who are essential to the audit process.

The legislation will also ensure that the SEC has sufficient authority to bar individuals from serving as officers or directors of public companies if they demonstrate they are substantially unfit to serve and that company officials disgorge any profits they receive from selling their own shares of their company's stock prior to a restatement of the company's financial statements. The bill also prohibits any company official from fraudulently misleading an auditor and requires the SEC to conduct studies of several areas related to corporate responsibility in order to evaluate other areas of corporate conduct and disclosure which may need reform.

The legislation requires the SEC to issue rules increasing the accuracy and transparency of company disclosures and will strengthen the SEC's procedures for reviewing the financial statements of issuers that play a significant role in the economy. Further, the bill will require that the SEC explore the effectiveness of SRO rules relating to analysts, and report on the role and function of credit rating agencies.

Finally, the legislation will protect employee access to their retirement accounts by preventing company insiders from trading their own shares in a company when their employees cannot do so because of a 'blackout' in a company sponsored employee retirement account.

The legislation is also designed to strengthen the SEC's procedures for reviewing the financial statements of issuers that play a significant role in the economy, explore the effectiveness of SRO rules relating to analysts, and report on the role and function of credit rating agencies.

BACKGROUND AND NEED FOR LEGISLATION

The Federal securities laws are designed to ensure that public companies provide investors with full and accurate disclosure of the true financial condition of the company. Following the bankruptcies of Enron Corporation and Global Crossing LLC, and restatements of earnings by several prominent market participants, regulators, investors and others expressed concern about the adequacy of the current disclosure regime for public companies.

Additionally, they expressed concerns about the role of auditors in approving corporate financial statements. Questions regarding the independence of auditors of public companies led to calls for greater supervision of the profession. The SEC raised the need for the creation of a new oversight body to review compliance of public auditors with the profession's standards of ethics and competency; this suggestion received widespread support.

The bankruptcy of Enron Corporation also raised issues relating to the security of employee retirement accounts. When allegations arose that some

Enron insiders were able to sell their company stock even as Enron employees were prohibited from doing so because of an administrative lockdown in the company's retirement plan, new calls arose for protecting the access of employees to their accounts to the same degree as insiders.

The securities laws, and in particular the Securities Exchange Act of 1934, provide a host of protections for investors with regard to their access to company information. Reflecting the technology available to public companies and investors at that time, the securities laws largely reflect the paper-based system of reporting information that was prevalent up until the advent of the electronic age. With the creation of the internet and continuous televised coverage of the capital markets, the regulatory regime for speeding the availability of company information has been unable to keep pace with the nearly instantaneous demand for investor access to that information. On-line trading of securities broadly expanded both the number of participants in the securities markets and the volume of trading in those markets. This development also heightened the need for more rapid disclosure of company news.

The increased public participation in the securities markets and the broader coverage of those markets also raised the profile of securities analysts that provide recommendations regarding equity securities. Responding to the concerns of some that analysts for companies that also underwrite and trade in the securities markets, the Subcommittee on Capital Markets, Insurance and Government Sponsored Enterprises held a series of hearings on the role of analysts in reporting on equity securities. Following these hearings, the securities industry developed a statement of best practices guiding analysts and their employers in avoiding conflicts of interest. This statement was later followed by a proposed rule by the self regulatory organizations (SROs) establishing guidelines for analysts and their employers to ensure that analyst recommendations are fair and unbiased. This proposal is currently under review by the SEC.

The Committee's hearings on the Enron matter, the collapse of Global Crossing LLC, and the operations of the Nation's capital markets all indicated that reforms were necessary both for the regulators and the regulated. Further, the President's Plan to Improve Corporate Responsibility and Protect America's Investors, announced on March 7, 2002, outlined a path by which corporations and their investors can continue their partnership in growing the Nation's economy, and do so on fair and equal footing. This legislation responds to the problems of the marketplace through a fair and balanced approach that ensures that the Nation's capital markets continue to be the strongest in the world.

Section 3. Improper Influence on Conduct of Audits

Section 3 makes it unlawful for any officer, director, or affiliated person of an issuer to take any action, in contravention of a rule adopted by the Commission, to fraudulently influence, coerce, manipulate, or mislead any independent public or certified accountant engaged in auditing that issuer's financial statements, for the purpose of rendering such financial statements materially misleading. The Commission has exclusive civil authority to enforce section 3 and any rule or regulation thereunder. The authority conferred by this section is in addition to, and does not preempt, any other authority of the Commission with respect to this area, such as the Commission's current authority under Exchange Act Rule 13b2-2, which prohibits making materially false or misleading statements to auditors, and the Commission's cease-and-desist authority under Section 21C of the Exchange Act or its injunctive powers under Section 21 of the Act with respect to third parties who cause others to violate, or aid and abet violations of, the securities laws and rules and regulations thereunder.

Section 4. Real-Time Disclosure of Financial Information

Section 4 amends section 13 of the Securities Exchange Act of 1934 (15 U.S.C. 78m), to require the Commission to adopt rules requiring issuers of securities registered under section 12 of that Act to make public disclosure, on a rapid and essentially contemporaneous basis, of information concerning the issuer's financial condition and operations. The Commission has exclusive civil authority to enforce this provision and any rule or regulation thereunder.

Section 4 also provides that the Commission must adopt rules providing that any disclosure required by the Federal securities laws, or rules or regulations thereunder, concerning any sale of securities by an officer, director, or other affiliated person of the issuer of the securities must be made electronically to the Commission before the end of the business day following the day of the transaction, and must be made available electronically by the Commission before the end of the business day following the day received by the Commission. Any issuer that maintains a corporate web site is also required to publish the disclosure, by any of its officers, directors, or affiliated persons, on its web site by the end of the day following the day the disclosure is received by the Commission. The Commission must also revise its forms and schedules as necessary to facilitate compliance with these requirements.

Section 16. Study of Enforcement Actions

Section 16 requires the Commission to review and analyze all of its enforcement actions involving violations of securities law reporting requirements and all restatements of financial statements over the past five years. The purpose of the review is to identify the areas of reporting most susceptible to fraud, inappropriate manipulation or inappropriate earnings management, such as revenue recognition and the accounting treatment of off-balance sheet special purpose entities. The Commission must report its findings to Congress within 180 days of enactment, and use its findings to revise rules and regulations as necessary.

Section 18. Study of Investment Banks

Section 18 directs the General Accounting Office (GAO) to conduct a study on the role of investment banks and financial advisors in assisting public companies in manipulating their earnings and obfuscating their true financial condition. The section directs the GAO to address the role of investment banks in the bankruptcy of Enron Corporation, the failure of Global Crossing, and in the creation and marketing of transactions designed to obfuscate a company's financial picture. The GAO is directed to report to Congress within 180 days of enactment of the bill.

Section 21. Exclusion for Investment Companies

Section 21 clarifies that certain provisions of the bill are not meant to apply to investment companies registered with the Commission under the

Investment Company Act of 1940. Because those companies are already subject to a thorough regulatory regime, the application of these provisions would be inappropriate.

¶ 4001 SELECTED PORTIONS OF CONGRESSIONAL RECORD STATEMENTS

Statements Made on the Senate and House Floors.

The following are remarks made on the Senate and House floors during the debate over the passage of S. 2673 and H.R. 3763.

Remarks of Sen. Paul Sarbanes, Banking Committee Chairman, on July 8, 2002, Cong. Rec. pages S6330-6333.

Mr. Sarbanes: Title I creates a public company accounting oversight board. This board is subject to SEC review and will establish auditing, quality control, ethics, and independence standards for public company auditors and will inspect accounting firms that conduct those audits. It will investigate potential violations of applicable rules and impose sanctions if those violations are established.

Heretofore we have relied on self-policing of the audit process, private auditing and accounting standards setting, and, for the most part, private disciplinary measures. But questionable accounting practices and corporate failures have raised serious questions, obviously, about this private oversight system. Paul Volcker stated:

> Over the years there have also been repeated efforts to provide oversight by industry or industry/public member boards. By and large, I think we have to conclude that those efforts at self-regulation have been unsatisfactory.

That is obviously one of the reasons we are moving, in this legislation, to an independent public company accounting oversight board. We heard extensive testimony in favor of such a board.

The board would have five full-time members. Two of the members will have an accounting background. All will have to have a demonstrated commitment to the interests of investors, as well as an understanding of the financial disclosures required by our securities law. The board members would be appointed by the SEC after consultation with the Federal Reserve and the Department of the Treasury and would serve staggered 5-year terms. They could not engage in other business while they were doing this work.

Of course, the board will have a staff. We would expect staff salaries to be fully competitive with comparable private-sector positions in order to ensure a high-quality staff.

The bill requires that accounting firms that audit public companies must register with the board. Failure to register or loss of registration would render a firm unable to continue its public company audit practice. Upon registering, a company would consent to comply with requests by the board for documents or testimony made in the course of the board's operations.

The board would possess plenary authority to establish or adopt auditing, quality control, ethics, and independence standards for the auditing of public companies. But this grant of authority is not intended to exclude accountants or other interested parties from participating in the standard-setting process. So the board may adopt rules that are proposed by professional groups of accountants or by one or more advisory groups created by the board.

These provisions reflect an effort to respond to the argument that you need the experts to either set the standards or help to set the standards. The experts in the industry can make these proposals, but the board will have the authority to adopt or to modify such proposals or to act of its own volition.

We provide for the inspection of registered accounting firms by the board. Firms that audit more than 100 public companies are to be inspected by staff of the board each year. Firms that audit less than that are inspected every 3 years, although the board has the power to adjust these inspection schedules.

The board also has investigative and disciplinary authority. Former SEC Chairman Arthur Levitt told the committee:

> We need a truly independent oversight body that has the power not only to set the standards by which audits are performed but also to conduct timely investigations that cannot be deferred for any reason and to discipline accountants.

If the board finds that a registered firm, or one or more of its associated persons, has violated the rules or standards, it will have the full range of sanctions available.

The board also has the power to sanction a registered accounting firm for failure reasonably to supervise a partner or employee, but we allow an accounting firm to defend itself from any supervisory liability by showing that its quality control and related internal procedures were reasonable and were operating fully in the situation at issue. I am mentioning this item, even though it may not seem that important in the context of a bill this complex, to point again to the effort that was made in the committee to balance competing concerns.

In effect, we say the firms have this supervisory responsibility. They should not duck this responsibility. Otherwise, how are we going to assure the people working for accounting firms are meeting high standards? On the other hand, we realize it is extremely difficult in large organizations to control right down to the last person. So we provided that if accounting firms have quality control and related internal procedures in place that are reasonable and that are operating fully, the operation of those procedures can serve as a defense.

The bill applies to foreign public accounting firms that audit financial statements of companies that come under the U.S. securities laws. The board is subject to SEC oversight, which is important. Finally, we formalize the role of the Financial Accounting Standards Board in setting accounting standards accounting standards are different than auditing standards, which the new oversight board will set. The bill provides for guaranteed funding of the new oversight board and the FASB by public companies, something I think we all agree is extremely important.

Some have asked, why do we need a statutory board? Why not let the SEC do something of this sort by regulation? But others have raised questions about the adequacy of the authority the SEC has to accomplish all of this by regulation alone. Clearly, a firmer base would be established, a stronger reference point, if the board were established by statute, and the potential of litigation that might arise with respect to some of these disciplinary and fee-imposing powers if they were created solely by the SEC by regulation would be avoided by a clear statutory underpinning.

Furthermore, I believe, frankly, that we need to establish this oversight board in statute in order to provide an extra guarantee of its independence and its plenary authority to deal with this important situation.

Let me turn to title II on auditor independence. This is a very important issue. Each of the country's Federal securities laws requires comprehensive financial statements. That is what is now required under the securities laws for public companies. They have to have comprehensive financial statements that must be prepared—and I now quote from the statute—"by an independent public or certified accountant."

The statutory requirement of an independent audit has two sides to it. It is a private franchise, and it is also a public trust.

The franchise given to the Nation's public accountants is clear. Their services must be secured before an issuer of securities can go to market, have its securities listed on the Nation's stock exchanges, or comply with the reporting requirements of the securities law. In other words, the accountants have been handed by mandate a major piece of business because the statute says to these public companies that they must have comprehensive financial statements prepared by an independent public or certified accountant.

So in effect we have directed to them a significant amount of business. But the franchise, in a way, is conditional. It comes in return for the certified public accountant's assumption of a public duty and obligation.

The Supreme Court stated this well in a decision almost 20 years ago:

> In certifying the public reports that collectively depict a corporation's financial status, the independent auditor assumes a public responsibility. ..... [That auditor] owes ultimate allegiance to the corporation's creditors and stockholders, as well as to the investing public. This public watchdog function demands that the accountant maintain total independence from the client at all times and requires complete fidelity to the public trust.

Richard Breeden, former chairman of the SEC from 1989 to 1993, under the previous President Bush, said in his testimony before the committee:

> While companies in the U.S. do not have to employ a law firm, an underwriter, or other types of professionals, Federal law requires a publicly-traded company to hire an independent accounting firm to perform an annual audit. In addition to this shared Federal monopoly, more than 100 million investors in the U.S. depend on audited financial statements to make investment decisions. That imbues accounting firms with a high level of public trust, and also explains why there is a strong Federal interest in how well the accounting system functions.

What has happened in recent years is that a rapid growth in management consulting services offered by the major accounting firms has created a conflict in the independence that an auditor must bring to the audit function.

According to the SEC, in 1988, 55 percent of the average revenue of the big five accounting firms came from accounting and auditing services; 22 percent came from management consulting services.

By 1999, 10 years later, these figures had fallen to 31 percent for accounting and auditing services, and 50 percent for management consulting services.

In fact, a number of experts argue that the growth in the non-audit consulting business done by the large accounting firms for their audit clients has so compromised the independence of audits that a complete prohibition on the provision of consulting services by accounting firms to their public audit clients is required—a complete prohibition.

* * *

We looked at this carefully. We had testimony on the other side. In the end, we took the approach that is outlined in the bill. The bill contains a short list, nine items, of non-audit services that an accounting firm doing the audit of a public company cannot provide to that company. These include, for example, bookkeeping or other services related to the accounting records or financial statements of the audit client, financial information systems design, appraisal or valuation services, actuarial services, management functions or human resources, broker or dealer or investment adviser services, and legal services.

The thinking behind drawing this line around a limited list of non-audit services, is that provision of those services to a public company audit client creates a fundamental conflict of interest for the accounting firm in carrying out its audit responsibility. If the accounting firm is not the auditor for the company, it can do any of these consulting services—it can do any consulting service it wants. But if it is the auditor—so there is a conflict of interest problem—then we take certain services and say: those services you can't do. And the reason is, first of all, in order to be independent, the auditor should not audit its own work, as it would do if it did financial information system design or appraisal evaluation services or actuarial services. It should not function as part of the management or as an employee of the audit company, as it would if it were doing human resources services, and it should not act as an advocate of the audit client, as it would do if it were providing legal and expert services. Nor should it be the promoter of the audit client's stock or other financial interest, as it would be if it were the broker-dealer or the investment adviser.

They are the public company's auditors. They have a very defined responsibility as the auditors. The bill doesn't bar accounting firms from offering consulting services. It simply says that if a firm wants to audit the company, there are certain services it cannot perform. And even in that case, the bill provides the board authority to grant case-by-case exceptions, so if a case could be made why an auditor's performing a consulting service ought to be permitted, there is some flexibility to permit it.

David Walker, the Comptroller General of the United States, in a statement on June 18 said:

> I believe that legislation that will provide a framework and guidance for the SEC to use in setting independence standards for public company audits is needed. History has shown that the AICPA and the SEC have failed to update their independence standards in a timely fashion and

that past updates have not adequately protected the public's interests. In addition, the accounting profession has placed too much emphasis on growing non-audit fees and not enough emphasis on modernizing the auditing profession for the 21st century environment. Congress is the proper body to promulgate a framework [on this important issue].

There are a lot of other auditing services, other than the nine I mentioned, that an auditor may want to provide and whose provision we did not preclude. In other words, the statutory system that we are establishing lists certain consulting services that, if you are the auditor, you cannot perform for the public company that is your audit client, unless you can get one of these case-by-case exemptions from the board. And those consulting services were the ones which, upon examination, seemed clearly to raise the most difficult conflict of interest questions that could result in undermining the auditor's fulfillment of his auditing responsibility.

The public company auditor can provide other non-audit services; that is, any but those on the proscribed list, if it clears them with the audit committee of the public company's board of directors. We seek to strengthen the audit committee in very substantial ways, including, as I will mention later, that they should be the ones to hire and fire the auditors—that the auditors really work through the audit committee for the board of directors and that the auditors do not work for the management. I think it is very clear, to some extent, and in some instances, it is management working with the auditors that have done these clever schemes for which we are now paying the price.

We had the issue of auditor rotation before us. Many witnesses thought the audit firm itself should have to rotate every 5 years, periodically. We did not go that far. We recommend here that the lead partner and the review partner on audits must rotate every 5 years—not the audit firm itself. But we do provide that audit firm rotation should be further studied and direct the General Accounting Office to undertake such a study with respect to the mandatory rotation of the audit firm.

* * *

We were concerned about the movement of personnel from audit firms to the public company audit clients. There we put a 1-year cooling off period with respect to the top positions in the company, so that you can't hold out to the audit team the immediate prospect of an important position in the company. Again, we are trying to protect the independence of the audit.

The next two titles, III and IV, deal with corporate responsibility and enhanced financial disclosure. As I said, we provide for a strong public company audit committee that would be directly responsible for the appointment, compensation, and oversight of the work of the public company auditors, which makes it clear that the primary duty of the auditors is to the public company's board of directors and the investing public, and not to the managers. We provide that the audit committee members must be independent from company management.

We require that the audit committee develop procedures for addressing complaints concerning auditing issues and also that they put in place procedures for employee whistleblowers to submit their concerns regarding accounting.

Where does an employee go when he sees a problem and is fearful of taking it up with management because his perception is that management is involved with the problem? We specifically provide that they should be protected in going to the audit committee.

We have a provision prohibiting the coercion of auditors. Some have asserted that officers and directors have sought to coerce their auditors or to fraudulently influence them to provide misleading information. Obviously, the auditors ought to be protected from that as well.

We have a provision that the CEO and the CFO who make large profits by selling company stock or receiving company bonuses while management is misleading the public about the financial health of the company would have to forfeit their profits and bonuses realized after the publication of a misleading report.

We also address the question of remedies against officers and directors who violate securities laws, something in which the SEC is very interested.

We have a provision on insider trades during pension fund blackout periods. We prohibit the insider trades. So you can't have officers and directors free to sell their shares while the majority of the employees of the company are required to hold theirs—as, of course, has happened in some instances.

On enhanced financial disclosures, we require that public companies must disclose all off-balance-sheet transactions and conflicts. We require that pro forma disclosures be done in a way that is not misleading and be reconciled with a presentation based on generally accepted accounting principles. More companies are doing these pro forma disclosures. They really are not accurately reflecting the financial conditions of the company.

We require very prompt disclosure of insider trades—actually, to be reported by the second day following any transactions.

* * *

This is a small item, but it may have a good benefit. We require public companies to disclose to the investors whether they have adopted a code of ethics for senior financial officers and whether their audit committee has among it a member who is a financial expert. We don't require them to have a code of ethics, although we think they should. We just require that they disclose whether they have one or not.

Title V deals with analyst conflicts of interest. We have had this incredible situation that was brought to the public attention by the efforts of the Attorney General of the State of New York, Eliot Spitzer, in which research reports and stock trades of companies that were potential banking clients of a major broker-dealer were often distorted to assist the firm in obtaining investment banking business. There was one document that actually acknowledged the conflict and, as a result, stated:

> We are off base on how we rate stocks and how much we bend over backwards to accommodate banking.

These analysts would recommend a buy rating on the stock essentially to help out the investment banking firm which was trying to get the company's investment banking business. So they get the analysts to say good things about the company, which will then lead the company to be far more favorably inclined and take on that firm in order to do their investment banking business.

In some instances, they were actually recommending buys and then they were saying to one another what a turkey the company was, but the poor investor was being taken at the time.

We set out a number of provisions in this regard. I will not go through all of them.

We prevent investment banking staff from supervising research analysts or clearing their reports.

We prohibit analysts from distributing research reports about a company they are underwriting.

We have a provision to protect analysts from retaliation for making unfavorable stock recommendations.

We heard moving testimony from someone who said: If you make an unfavorable recommendation, who knows what is going to happen to you?

We also provide—the bill here focuses on disclosure instead of prohibition—that an analyst would have to disclose if he owned the company stock. If you are doing an analysis and if you are doing a report and a recommendation, you ought to disclose whether you own the company stocks or bonds, whether you have received compensation from the company, whether your firm has a client relationship with the company, and whether you are receiving compensation based on investment banking revenues from the company. These are not prohibitions, they are just disclosures.

The thought behind this is, if you are an investor and an analyst is making a recommendation and he puts up front in his analysis that he owns the company stock, or that he is receiving compensation from the company, or that his firm has a client relationship with the company, or that he is receiving compensation based on investment banking revenues received from the company, someone is going to look at this and say: wait a second. I have to take his recommendation in the context of his involvement.

Finally, of major importance is the increase we have provided for the budget of the SEC to, No. 1, provide pay parity for SEC employees; No. 2, enhance information technology and security enhancement; and, No. 3, fund more professionals to help carry out the important investigative and disciplinary efforts of the SEC.

We provide for two studies. One concerns the consolidation of public accounting firms. Senator Akaka was very interested in this. There has been a constant consolidation trend. We have asked the Comptroller General to do the study. And the other is by Senator Bunning directing the SEC to conduct a study of the role of credit rating agencies in the operation of the securities markets.

In closing, there has been broad support for this legislation. Just a few days ago, the Business Roundtable came out in favor of it. The Financial Executives International early on in the process was supportive, as well as the Council of Institutional Investors.

We have tried hard to listen to the concerns people raised.

The procedure here was that before the Memorial Day recess—in fact, in early May, we put out a committee print. As we approached markup shortly before the Memorial Day recess, a number of amendments were proposed. It was urged that we put the markup over. We agreed to do that. We took all the amendments that had been put forward, and other suggestions that were being received with respect to the committee print, and went back and reworked it.

I have to say to you that, in all candor, many of those suggestions were meritorious and in fact are now reflected in the legislation that is before the Senate.

So we tried very hard to listen to people at every step of the way. We then reworked the print. We came back with another committee print. We went to markup on June 18. We made a limited number of amendments in markup and brought the bill out to the floor of the Senate by a 17-to-4 vote.

I simply close by saying how strongly I believe that financial irresponsibility and deception of the sort that we have seen in all of the instances that keep appearing on the front pages of our newspapers are a real threat to our economic recovery. We cannot afford to wait for the next corporate deception, followed by the next round of layoffs, followed by the next collapse of a company's pension fund.

We need to take action to restore public trust in our financial markets, and that really begins with restoring public confidence in the accuracy of financial information. That is what this legislation seeks to accomplish. I urge my colleagues to support this critical legislation.

Remarks of Sen. Tom Daschle, Majority Leader, on July 9, 2002, Cong. Rec. p. S6437 on the Leahy-McCain amendment to S. 2673, which was adopted.

Mr. Daschle: I view the Leahy amendment as a necessary complement to the Sarbanes bill. In fact, I think of them as two parts of a vital whole—one element guarantees the truth and honesty of corporate accounting. The other is a deterrent. It says that corporate misrepresentation will be forcefully punished—with jail time.

We need both. We need to improve oversight and independence of the accounting profession and hold corporate wrongdoers accountable for their actions.

We need to act comprehensively to fulfill our promise to the American people that integrity, honesty, and accountability will be restored to our markets.

* * *

The amendment has three aims: punishing criminals; preserving evidence; and protecting victims.

The Leahy amendment punishes criminals by creating a tough new 10-year felony for securities fraud. It provides prosecutors with a new tool that is flexible enough to keep up with the most complex new fraud schemes and tough enough to deter violations on the front end. It also provides a mechanism to raise the fraud sentences that are already on the books.

The amendment also preserves evidence of fraud. It creates two new criminal anti-shredding provisions in federal law. As we say in the Arthur Andersen case, even the most straight-forward obstruction of justice cases can be difficult to prove under current law.

Senator LEAHY's bill closes the loopholes and makes document destruction in fraud cases an unambiguous crime.

The amendment does not just protect "paper evidence," it also protects valuable testimony from people. For the first time, the Leahy bill creates federal protection for whistleblowers. People like Sherron Watkins of Enron will be protected from reprisal for the first time under federal law. This bill is going to help prosecutors gain important insider testimony on fraud and put a permanent dent in the "corporate code of silence."

Finally, the amendment will protect victims of fraud. By extending the time period during which victims can bring cases to recoup their losses, the Leahy bill removes the reward for those fraud artists who are especially gifted at concealing what they've done for lengthy periods of time.

The Leahy bill also prevents fraud artists from declaring bankruptcy to shut out their victims. The amendment would accomplish this by making security fraud debts nondischargeable in bankruptcy.

Remarks of Sen. Patrick Leahy, Judiciary Committee Chairman,, on July 9, 2002, Cong. Rec. pages S6437,6439, and 6440 on the Leahy-McCain amendment to S. 2673, which was adopted.

Mr. Leahy: Our amendment is identical to S. 2010, the Corporate and Criminal Fraud Accountability Act that was reported unanimously by both Republicans and Democrats in the Judiciary Committee on April 25.

* * *

Let me summarize some of the provisions. This bipartisan amendment has three prongs to restore accountability: punishing and preventing fraud, preserving the evidence of fraud, and protecting victims of fraud.

S. 2010, as unanimously reported, accomplishes these goals in a number of ways. It is going to create a tough new Federal felony for securities fraud for a 10-year maximum penalty. The idea of 10 years in the slammer is going to focus the attention of those who are more interested in taking their money and hiding it in offshore bank accounts.

As one who was a prosecutor, I was surprised to learn that unlike bank fraud, health care fraud, and even bankruptcy fraud, there is no specific Federal crime of securities fraud to protect victims of fraud related to publicly traded companies.

Can you imagine, Madam President, while all this talk has been going on, it turns out there is no specific crime of securities fraud. This bill would create such a felony with a tough 10-year jail sentence.

The amendment provides for a review of the existing sentencing guidelines for fraud cases and for organizational misconduct to make them tougher as well.

The new crimes and enhanced criminal penalties in this bill were worked out among Senators HATCH, SCHUMER, and me, and unanimously supported by the Judiciary Committee, and I thank Senators Hatch and Schumer for their support.

The Leahy-McCain amendment also creates two new anti-shredding penalties which set clear requirements for preserving financial audit guides and close loopholes in current anti-shredding laws.

These provisions close loopholes in current laws and set a clear requirement that corporate audit documents must be saved for 5 years. We, incidentally, picked that time period because that is the statute of limitation for most Federal crimes.

These provisions are crucial in preventing recurrences of what happened at Arthur Andersen.

These provisions will preserve evidence that helps law enforcement officers and prosecutors focus immediately on the evidence. It takes a few minutes to warm up the shredder, but it can take years for prosecutors and victims to put together a case without key documents.

The amendment protects corporate whistleblowers. Senator Grassley and I worked out these bipartisan measures in the Judiciary Committee. I thank the Senator from Iowa for his assistance and his constant leadership over the years on whistleblower rights.

When sophisticated corporations set up complex fraud schemes, corporate insiders are often the only ones who can disclose what happened and why.

* * *

The measure lengthens the statute of limitation by extending it from the earlier of 1 year from discovery or 3 years from the fraud to 2 years from discovery or 5 years from the fraud.

Senators Feinstein and Cantwell worked hard to craft a fair compromise on this provision in the Judiciary Committee.

Indeed, the last two SEC Chairmen from both parties, Arthur Levitt and Richard Breeden, both agreed that the current short statute of limitations is unfair to fraud victims.

Attorney General Christine Gregoire testified before the Judiciary Committee in the Enron State pension fund litigation that the current short statute has forced some States to forego claims against Enron.

* * *

We make the debt from security law violations nondischargeable in bankruptcy. We protect fraud victims by amending the bankruptcy code to make judgments and settlements based upon security law violations nondischargeable. Corporate leaders should not be allowed to take the money, run, file bankruptcy, and keep from ever paying any securities fraud judgment. The State security regulators strongly support this change. You cannot have one set of rules which say if you steal $500 from a store, you can go to jail. But if you steal $50 million from the corporate boardroom, keep the money. That makes no sense. Everywhere I went in the State of Vermont last week, people were saying: If I committed an act, if I stole something, if I cash a bad check for $100, I run the risk of going to jail.

But what do you do if you get $50 million or $100 million? You are home free.

Remarks of Sen. John McCain on July 10, 2002, Cong. Rec. pages S6528-6529 on the Leahy-McCain amendment to S. 2673, which was adopted.

Mr. McCain: I rise in strong support of the underlying Leahy amendment, and I hope we can dispose of that amendment within a reasonable length of time and move on to other changes that need to be made to this very important legislation.

Our publicly owned companies are an essential component to the economic health of our country. As we have seen over the past few months, the continued lapses of our corporate leaders, whether they are ethical, criminal or just plain ignorant, have a significant, sometimes crippling, effect on the welfare of our nation. We must make some fundamental changes in the current system of corporate oversight to protect Americans from avarice, greed, ignorance and criminal behavior. Now is the time for Congress to restore investor confidence and take the necessary action to protect the interests of the public shareholders and place those interests above the personal interests of those entrusted with managing and advising those companies. The deterioration of the checks and balances that safeguard the public against corporate abuses must be reversed.

We have to address the shortcomings in Federal law and send the message that prosecutors now have the tools to incarcerate persons who defraud investors or alter or destroy evidence in certain Federal investigations. This amendment is a step in the right direction. It creates two new criminal states that would clarify current criminal laws relating to the destruction or fabrication of evidence and the preservation of financial and audit records. The Enron debacle clearly indicated that there were gaping holes in the current framework. There will be a 10 year criminal penalty for the destruction or creation of evidence with the intent to obstruct a federal investigation. There will be a new 5 year criminal penalty for the willful failure to preserve, for a minimum of five years, audit papers of companies that issue securities.

The amendment also provides for the review and enhancement of criminal penalties in cases involving obstruction of justice and serious fraud cases. All of these actions are necessary to deter future criminal action. Until somebody responsible goes to jail for a significant amount of time, I am not sure that these people are going to get the message. Defrauding the shareholder has to carry a meaningful penalty. Corporate decision-makers can make millions, tens of millions, even hundreds of millions of dollars by cheating investors. A relatively small fine or short prison term is not a deterrent; it's a slap on the wrist. The threat of real time in jail is a deterrent that will make people pay attention.

This amendment also creates a new securities fraud offense. The provision makes it easier, in a limited class of cases, to prove securities fraud. Currently prosecutors are forced to resort to a patchwork of technical offenses and regulations that criminalize particular violations of securities law, or to treat the cases as generic mail or wire fraud that results in a five-year maximum penalty. This new provision would criminalize any scheme or artifice to defraud persons in connection with securities of publicly traded companies or to obtain their money or property. This new ten-year felony is comparable to existing bank and health care fraud statutes. To those who would say that it's hard to define a scheme or artifice to defraud, I would say that full and honest disclosure of material dealings and accounting treatments is the best way for the officers who run America's corporations to protect themselves and those who invest in their companies. There are plenty of felony laws on the books that provide long prison terms for crimes that cause less damage than the losses to shareholders in Enron or WorldCom.

It is important to emphasize that when criminal charges are pursued, it is not necessarily the firm that should be charged but the individuals at the helm of the corporate ship who should be prosecuted. If they are the ones making the decisions out of self-interest, they are the ones that should be held accountable. I also believe that we must protect the "corporate whistleblower" from being punished for having the moral courage to break the corporate code of silence. This amendment does that.

This amendment also extends the current statute of limitations for matters concerning securities fraud, deceit or manipulation. The current statute of limitations for securities fraud cases is short given the complexity of many of these matters, and defrauded investors may be wrongly stopped short in their attempts to recoup their losses under current law. The existing statute of limitations for most securities fraud cases is one year after he fraud was discovered but no more than three years from the date of the fraud regardless of when it was discovered. Because this statute of limitations is so short, the worst offenders may avoid accountability and be rewarded if they can successfully cover up their misconduct for merely three years. The more complex the case, the easier it will be for these wrongdoers to get away with fraud. According to at least one state Attorney General, the current short statute of limitations has forced some states to forgo claims against Enron based on alleged securities fraud in 1997 and 1998.

This situation essentially encourages offenders to attempt to cover up their misdeeds however they can, including by using questionable accounting procedures and financial shell games. Furthermore, in some cases, the facts of a case simply do not come to light until years after the fraud. If a person does not and cannot know they have been defrauded, it is unfair to bar them from the courthouse. We need to recognize the sophistication and complexity of modern-day schemes designed to defraud investors. The Leahy amendment does this.

Finally, this provision amends the federal bankruptcy code to prevent the corporate wrongdoer, the CEO or CFO, from sheltering their assets under the umbrella of bankruptcy and protecting them from judgments and settlements arising from federal and state securities law violations. Too many of these highly paid corporate officers are using bankruptcy laws to protect their assets while maintaining their high-rise penthouses and ski chalets. It is time to force accountability and punish the person, not the institution, who is not willing to abide by the moral and legal codes that accompany leadership and public trust.

I hope we will have an early and overwhelming vote in favor of the Leahy amendment.

Remarks of Sen. Trent Lott, Minority Leader, on July 10, 2002, Cong. Rec. p. S6545 on the Lott amendment to S. 2673, which was adopted.

Mr. Lott: Section 3 freezes payments of potential wrongdoers. This section would allow the SEC, during an investigation, to seek an order in Federal court imposing a 45-day freeze on extraordinary payments to corporate executives.

Again, this year we have seen just that sort of thing happening. While an investigation is underway, basically rewards were given to these corporate executives. While it would require a court order, there would be this 45-day freeze.

The targeted payments would be placed in escrow, ensuring that corporate assets are not improperly taken from an executive's personal benefit.

If an executive is charged with violations of Federal securities laws prior to the expiration of the court order, the escrow would continue until the conclusion of legal proceedings, again, with court approval.

Section 4 involves sentencing guideline enhancements for crimes committed by corporate officers and directors. This section would implement President Bush's call on the Sentencing Commission to quickly adopt the new "aggravating factor" to provide stronger penalties for fraud when the crime is committed by a corporate officer or director. This "aggravating factor" is a term of art used in the law. It would provide, under this section, stronger penalties for such fraud.

Section 5 would bar corporate officers and directors who engage in serious misconduct. Under current law, only a Federal court can issue an order prohibiting a person from acting as an officer or director of a public company.

The SEC cannot order this remedy in its own administrative cease-and-desist proceedings, even in a case of securities fraud where the person's conduct would otherwise meet the standards for imposing such a bar. This section would grant the SEC the authority to issue such orders if a person had committed securities law violation and his or her conduct demonstrated unfitness to serve as an officer or a director.

Remarks of Sen. John Edwards on July 10, 2002, Cong. Rec. p. S6545 on the Edwards amendment to S. 2673, which was adopted and essentially codified by the conference as Sec. 307 of the Sarbanes-Oxley Act.

Mr. Edwards: Let me be a little more specific about what this amendment does and what the responsibility of a lawyer is and should be. If you are a lawyer for a corporation, your client is the corporation and you work for the corporation and you work for the shareholders, the investors in that corporation; that is to whom you owe your responsibility and loyalty. And you have a responsibility to zealously advocate for the shareholders and investors in that corporation.

What we have seen some lawyers do, unfortunately, is different. We have seen corporate lawyers sometimes forget who their client is. What happens is their day-to-day conduct is with the CEO or the chief financial officer because those are the individuals responsible for hiring them. So as a result, that is with whom they have a relationship. When they go to lunch with their client, the corporation, they are usually going to lunch with the CEO or the chief financial officer. When they get phone calls, they are usually returning calls to the CEO or the chief financial officer. The problem is that the CEO and the chief financial officer are not the client. Their responsibility and the client they have to advocate for—and which they have an ethical responsibility to advocate for—is, in fact, the corporation, not the CEO or the chief financial officer.

One of the most critical responsibilities that those lawyers have is, when they see something occurring or about to occur that violates the law, breaks the law, they must act as an advocate for the shareholders, for the company itself, for the investors. They are there and they can see what is happening. They know the law and their responsibility is to do something about it if they see the law being broken or about to be broken.

This amendment is about making sure those lawyers, in addition to the accountants and executives in the company, don't violate the law and, in fact, more importantly, ensure that the law is being followed.

* * *

This is what the amendment says specifically: First, the SEC shall establish rules to protect investors from unprofessional conduct by lawyers, conduct that violates the legal standards of the profession.

Second, the SEC shall make one rule in particular, and it is a simple rule with two parts. No. 1, a lawyer with evidence of a material violation of the law has to report that evidence either to the chief legal counsel or the chief executive officer of the company. No. 2, if the person to whom that lawyer reports doesn't respond appropriately by remedying the violation, by doing something that makes sure it is cured, that lawyer has an obligation to go to the audit committee or to the board. It is that simple. You report the violation. If the violation isn't addressed properly, then you go to the board.

Three important details about this amendment address some of the concerns that I have heard voiced. First, the way we have drafted the bill, the duty to report applies only to evidence of a material violation of the law. That means no reporting is required for piddling violations or violations that don't amount to anything. The obligation to report is triggered only by violations that are material—violations that a reasonable investor would want to know about. So we have been very careful there.

Second, when the evidence is reported within the company, we have not specified how a CEO or a general counsel should act to rectify the violation. That is because the truth is that the appropriate response to cure the problem will vary dramatically, depending on the circumstances. If the CEO can do a short investigation, for example, and figure out that no violation occurred, then the obligation stops there. But if there is a serious violation of the law, the appropriate response is clear: The CEO has to act promptly to remedy the violation. If he doesn't, the lawyer has to go to the board. It is that simple.

One final point. Nothing in this bill gives anybody a right to file a private lawsuit against anybody. The only people who can enforce this amendment are the people at the SEC.

Remarks of Sen. Carl Levin on July 10, 2002, Cong. Rec. p. S6565.

Mr. Levin: The Sarbanes bill takes on another great issue of importance that I've been working on for years, strengthening the independence of the Financial Accounting Standards Board or FASB, which has the task of issuing generally accepted accounting principles, or GAAP.

Among other important measures, the bill grants statutory recognition to FASB and sets outs its obligation to act in the public interest to ensure the accuracy and effectiveness of financial reporting; states that the trustees who elect FASB's members must represent investors and the public, not just the accounting industry or corporate interests; and streamlines FASB's operations by requiring it to act by majority vote instead of through a supermajority.

Most important of all, the bill sets up a system that provides FASB with an independent stable source of funding through fees assessed on publicly traded companies. Once this new system is set up, it will no longer be the case, as it has been for years, that FASB will have to go hat in hand for funds from the very companies and accounting firms that want to affect its decisionmaking. I have no doubt that this conflict of interest has contributed to some of the distortions and weaknesses in current accounting standards. I proposed a similar change in FASB's funding status in my Shareholder Bill of Rights Act, and I appreciate the committee's including the provision from my bill making it clear that FASB's funding cannot be affected by the congressional appropriations process and the political pressures that can be exerted through it. The point of the bill is to set up an independent, stable source of funding that is insulated from political pressure and funding threats so that FASB can do its work free of such pressures and threats.

Once the new funding system is in place, I urge FASB to begin to reassess U.S. accounting standards and to begin to clear up some of the problems that have allowed so many companies to engage in dishonest accounting while claiming to be in compliance with GAAP.

Remarks of Sen. Jean Carnahan on July 12, 2002, Cong. Rec. p. S6687 on the Carnahan amendment to S. 2673, which was adopted.

Mrs. Carnahan: * * * I am pleased the Senate has acted quickly to take up this important reform legislation. I believe that this bill makes tremendous progress in improving the quality of information available to the markets. In the interest of further improvement, I am offering an amendment to modernize the method of disclosure required when insiders trade in their own companies' stock.

One warning sign that a company may be in trouble is when its executives are selling large amounts of company stock, as occurred at Enron. I have learned, however, that information about insider selling is not easily accessible.

Under our current system a company's officers are required to file a disclosure form with the Securities and Exchange Commission, SEC, any time they sell securities of their company. Tens of thousands of these forms are filed annually. These are not complicated forms. I have a copy here. It is a simple 2-page form.

The Office of Management and Budget estimates that the form should not take more than 30 minutes to fill out. With capital markets as sophisticated as they are in the U.S., information must be available quickly to be useful. However, insiders currently have up to six weeks to file their disclosure forms. And the overwhelming majority of these forms—95 percent—are filed on paper, rather than electronically.

The Banking Committee has already addressed the issue of timely disclosure. This legislation would require disclosure of sales within 2 days, a vast improvement over the current deadlines. However, this legislation is silent on the issue of modernizing this arcane paper filing system.

Right now, there is no way for an investor in Missouri to quickly learn that a company executive is selling off company stock. The only ways to get the information are to go to a reading room at the SEC in Washington, or to write a letter to the SEC. These written requests may take weeks to process. This is unacceptable in the electronic age.

My amendment requires that information about insider sales of publicly traded companies be filed electronically. The SEC would then be required to make the forms available to the public over the Internet. Any company that maintains a corporate Web site would be required to post these disclosure forms on the Web site. The SEC, itself, has acknowledged the value of having these forms filed electronically.

Remarks of Rep. Michael Oxley, Chairman of the Financial Services Committee, on April 24, 2002, Cong. Rec. p. H1545.

Mr. Oxley: CARTA recognizes the need for corporate leaders to act responsibly and holds them accountable if they fail to do so.

CARTA ensures the highest standards of auditor independence, ethics and confidence and establishes a public regulatory organization for accountants of publicly traded companies, something that has never been done before.

CARTA improves corporate disclosures by requiring companies to provide the public with more information about their financial condition.

CARTA makes important improvements in the area of corporate transparency, requiring that companies disclose to investors important company news on a real-time basis.

CARTA also directs the SEC to require greater disclosure for off-balance sheet transactions.

I am confident that we are striking the right balance, particularly when it comes to the role of the Securities and Exchange Commission. CARTA gives the SEC the flexibility to deal with problems without legislating every time. Congress created the SEC precisely to deal with situations like this. We need to empower the SEC to act without tying its hands and within flexible statutory changes.

Let us remember that a strong regulator is not one that is completely dictated to by Congress. A strong regulator has some say over his jurisdiction, some power and discretion to shape the capital markets; and I trust the SEC with this authority and so does our bill.

CARTA makes it a crime for anybody to interfere with a corporate audit. It requires CEOs and other corporate insiders to disclose within 48 hours when they sell company stock so that investors and employees and retirees know if a corporate officer is getting out. It prohibits insider sales of company stock while the employee retirement plan is locked down.

Strengthening these areas of corporate responsibility, accounting oversight, and investor information is an important priority as our economy recovers. Let us show the American people that we can respond in a meaningful way to their very real economic concerns. Pass CARTA today.

Remarks of Rep. Marge Roukema, April 24, 2002, Cong. Rec. p. H1548-1549.

Mrs. Roukema: The current structure for regulation and oversight of the accounting industry consists of Federal and State regulators and a complex system of self-regulation by the industry itself. Although the SEC has broad authority to regulate all aspects of corporate accounting and the auditing of publicly-traded companies, the SEC historically has not directly regulated the industry because of a lack of resources. Instead, they have investigated and taken enforcement action in only the most egregious cases. Consequently, the most comprehensive supervision of accountants and auditors has been exercised by the industry's trade association, the American Institute of Certified Public Accountants, a voluntary organization funded entirely by the industry.

H.R. 3763 includes numerous provisions to strengthen supervision and oversight of the accounting industry, increase standards of corporate responsibility, and improve the quality of corporate disclosure and the auditing of publicly-traded companies. The specifics of these provisions have been properly outlined by the Chairman.

First, this legislation establishes a public regulatory organization (PRO) to oversee and review accounts that certify financial statements required under the securities law. This new board would be subject to direct SEC authority and supervision. In addition it makes it illegal—subject to SEC civil penalties—for any corporate official to interfere, mislead, or coerce an accountant performing an audit of the company.

Second, this legislation requires increased and meaningful disclosures, such as information about special purpose entities and other off-balance sheet transactions. It requires real-time disclosure of financial information and immediate disclosures by corporate insiders when they sell securities they own in their company.

This legislation also includes important safeguards and protections for individuals who invest in 401(k) plans. The bill prohibits corporate executives from buying and selling company stock during "blackout" periods when rank-and-file company employees are barred from doing so in their pension 401(k) plans and allows companies, and other shareholders to go to court to recover any profits made from such illegal transactions. The measure also establishes procedures under which the SEC may recover any profits gained, or losses avoided, by executives through stock trades in the six months prior to a company's restatement of earnings, if the executive had knowledge that the company's accounting was misleading.

Finally, H.R. 3763 authorizes new resources and responsibilities for the SEC, requires the SEC to review the audited corporate financial reports of all publicly-traded companies at least every three years, and allows the SEC to ban corporate officers and directors whom the SEC finds guilty of violating securities law from serving in similar positions in other publicly-traded companies.

There are some that may argue today that this bill does not go far enough—I would say to those critics that we must take care not to overreact to this situation—this bill represents a significant and proper first step. We need to enact this legislation—and let the regulatory process go forth. Clearly, we may have to revisit this issue in the months and years ahead, but this bill includes sound, strong and unprecedented measures that I believe will go a long way in addressing this current crisis.

Remarks of Rep. F. James Sensenbrenner, Jr., Chairman of the Judiciary Committee, on July 16, 2002, Cong. Rec. p. H4684-4685, urging passage of, H.R. 5118, the Corporate Fraud Accountability Act of 2002.

Mr. Sensenbrenner: We must return this country to personal accountability and responsibility, and help rebuild America and the world's confidence in our markets. We must crack down on the corporate crooks, and reestablish the honor of the vast majority of men and women in corporate America who are hardworking and honest.

The best way to do that is to punish the corporate wrongdoers, and punish them harshly. The American public needs to know that under this bill, H.R. 5118 , the Corporate Fraud Accountability Act of 2002, corporate criminals will do real time, real long time.

If they commit mail or wire fraud in the furtherance of their corporate crimes, which is often how prosecutors nail these criminals, they will face 20 years in jail, not the current 5 years, nor the 10 years called for in the other body's legislation.

In addition, a distinct securities fraud crime is established with a maximum penalty of 25 years in jail. Again, the other body only calls for a 10-year penalty.

Importantly, H.R. 5118 strengthens laws that criminalize document shredding and other forms of obstruction of justice, and provides a maximum penalty of 20 years. The other body calls for just 10 years.

H.R. 5118 also requires top corporate executives to certify that the financial statements of the company fairly and accurately represent the financial condition of the company. Violating this section can subject corporate executives to fines of up to $5 million and up to 20 years in prison. Under the version passed by the other body, the maximum penalty a corporate officer would face is only a $1 million fine and 10 years in prison.

The Corporate Fraud Accountability Act also increases the criminal penalties for those who file false statements with the Securities and Exchange Commission to a maximum penalty of $5 million and 20 years in prison. If a corporation files a false statement, those fines can increase up to a maximum of $25 million. The bill passed by the other body does not change the current penalties of a maximum fine of $1 million and 10 years in prison, and corporations would still only face maximum fines of $2.5 million.

By passing this bill today, the House is telling the American people that the law will make CEOs directly responsible for the integrity of their company's financial statements, and face severe financial and criminal penalties for falsifying such statements.

Under this legislation, top executives will not be allowed to pilfer the assets of the company by giving themselves huge bonuses and other extraordinary payments if the company is subject to an SEC investigation. Their pay and benefits are frozen when the investigation starts. Americans will know that corporate officers will no longer be able to misuse the bankruptcy laws to discharge liabilities based upon securities fraud, and the honest brokers of corporate America will know that those who abuse the law and tarnish corporate America's reputation will go to jail for a long, long time.

Finally, Mr. Speaker, this bill creates criminal sanctions against those who retaliate against corporate whistleblowers, similar to witness tampering in another context. The only thing the other body's bill does is provide for more lawsuits, a civil cause of action for the whistleblowers against the retaliators. Under the current bankruptcy law, if the whistleblower wins the civil lawsuit, the retaliator will be able to discharge that judgment in bankruptcy.

Table of Statutes Added or Amended

The list below notes all sections of the federal securities laws that were added or amended by the Sarbanes-Oxley Act of 2002. The list reflects the subject matter of each change and shows the paragraph number where the law text is located.

SECURITIES ACT

Sec. 8A(f) (added)	Officer and director bars	¶ 1071
Sec. 19(b) (amended)	Accounting standards	¶ 1108
Sec. 20(d)(3)(A) (amended)	Conforming amendment	1028
Sec. 20(e) (amended)	Office and director bars	¶ 1025
Sec. 20(g) (added)	Penny stock bar	¶ 1043

SECURITIES EXCHANGE ACT

Sec. 3(a)(39)(F) (amended)	Conforming amendment	¶ 1044
Sec. 3(a)(47) (amended)	Conforming amendment	¶ 1000A
Sec. 3(a)(58) (added)	Audit committee	¶ 1015
Sec. 3(a)(59) (added)	Registered public accounting firm	¶ 1015
Sec. 4C (added)	Practice before the SEC	¶ 1042
Sec. 10A (amended)	Conforming amendments	¶ 1015
Sec. 10A(f) (amended)	Conforming amendment	¶ 1015
Sec. 10A(g) (added)	Prohibition on non-audit services	¶ 1011
Sec. 10A(h) (added)	Pre-approval of non-audit services	¶ 1011
Sec. 10A(i) (added)	Pre-approval requirements	¶ 1012
Sec. 10A(j) (added)	Audit partner rotation	¶ 1013

INVESTMENT COMPANY ACT

INVESTMENT ADVISERS ACT

Topical Index

References are to paragraph numbers.

A

B

C